Bad Language,

Naked Ladies,

and Other Threats

to the Nation

Bad Language,

Naked Ladies,

and Other Threats

to the Nation

A Political History of

Comic Books in Mexico

ANNE RUBENSTEIN

Duke University Press   Durham and London   1998

© 1998 Duke University Press
All rights reserved. Printed in the United
States of America on acid-free paper ∞
Designed by Amy Ruth Buchanan
Typeset in Scala by Tseng Information Systems, Inc.
Library of Congress Cataloging-in-Publication Data
appear on the last printed page of this book.

To Sara, Heather, and Liz,
from one Mr. Earbrass
to another.

. . .

And to my grandmothers,
Dina Rubenstein and
Lillian Rabinowitz, with
love and gratitude.

Contents

Acknowledgments

Reading history can make anyone doubt the essential goodness of human nature; writing history restored my faith. This book exists because family, friends, colleagues, and strangers gave me more than I can ever repay. I'm glad to be able to acknowledge their kindnesses, at last.

Thinking is impossible without friends with whom one can argue, so I must first thank the following people for their patience and impatience over the years that we have been disagreeing about art, politics, and Latin America: Sara Rubenstein Kenney, Liz Hollander, Matthew Ostrowski, Christian Huygen, John C. Russell, Heather Levi, Dennis Hanrahan, Greg Bylinsky, Elisabeth Vincentelli, Blanca de Lizaur, Eric Zolov, Jeff Pilcher, Wendy Waters, Pam Ezell, and Yolanda Flores. And thanks, too, to everyone at Brooklyn Women's Martial Arts and Inyo Dojo for what they have taught me about the difference between physical and symbolic forms of coercion.

I gratefully acknowledge the institutions that supported my research: the Graduate School of Rutgers University, the Schlatter Fund of the Rutgers History Department, the Center for Critical Analysis of Contemporary Culture at Rutgers University, and Allegheny College. My grandfather and father offered material support without even making me write a grant application, and I thank them for that. My brother, Nick Rubenstein, graphics wizard, digitized the pictures—which, though it seemed like magic to me, cost him a great deal of time and trouble. Nick, I couldn't have done it without you.

Thanks are equally due to all the librarians and archivists who aided this project; two collections, however, were exceptionally important. The Hemeroteca Nacional de la Ciudad Universitaria allowed me an unusual degree of access to its fabulous collection of comic books and offered the benefit of its staff's knowledgeable enthusiasm. The papers of la Comisión Calificadora de Publicaciones y Revistas Ilustradas are not housed in an archive; with the gracious permission of the Secretario Técnico of the commission, Lic. Heriberto Arriaga Garza, I occupied a desk in its small office for months while going through all their old files. I am deeply grateful for their cooperation, trust, and tolerance. Thanks, too, to Pam Scheinman, John Sherman, Harold Hinds, and Charles Tatum for suggesting sources and helping me locate them.

My dissertation committee—Samuel Baily, William Beezley, Virginia Yans, and Mark Wasserman—gave excellent advice as the thesis gradually evolved into a book manuscript. At one point or another, the manuscript also was read in whole or in part by Glen Kuecker, Blanca de Lizaur, Claudio Lomnitz-Adler, Steve Niblo, Heather Levi, Cami Townsend, David Holtby, and Eric Zolov, all of whom helped enormously. Glen Kuecker and Mark Wasserman both read multiple drafts, and responded with remarkable tact and rigor every time. The anonymous readers were models of scholarly solidarity: sympathetic, careful, and thorough. And everyone at Duke University Press has been more than kind; in particular, this project owes a great deal to Valerie Millholland's good nature and determination. Thank you all.

This book still contains errors of omission and commission, of fact and interpretation: they are my fault and nobody else's.

Introduction

I have sometimes indulged in the fantasy that I am at the gates of Heaven. St. Peter questions me about what good I have done on earth. I reply proudly that I have read and analyzed thousands of comic books—a horrible task and really a labor of love. "That counts for nothing," says St. Peter. "Millions of children read these comic books." "Well," I reply, "I have also read all the articles and speeches and press releases by the experts for the defense [of comic books]." "Okay," says St. Peter. "Come in! You deserve it."

— Fredric Wertham, *Seduction of the Innocent*

 The giant media conglomerate Televisa—which began as a publisher of newspapers and comic books, and then expanded into radio, television, and related industries—has manufactured careers for many pop stars, including singer Gloria Trevi. Trevi distinguished herself from other starlets with a pose of calculated outrageousness; unlike the others, she controls her own products and image, or so her publicity insists. She writes some of the songs she sings, gives lengthy newspaper interviews discussing current politics (more or less in the manner of a literate, left-wing naïf), and even wrote and drew her own comic book, starring herself.

In 1992, Trevi produced a calendar that featured twelve glossy color photos of herself in lascivious poses, all but naked. Sold (along with the usual range of comic books, magazines, and newspapers) at newsstands across Mexico, the calendar quickly became a best-seller. It was much more appealing than any other soft-core smut available in the country: less expensive, less tawdry, wittier, more widely distributed, and with much higher production values. But many Mexicans found Gloria Trevi's calendar distressing, including—as the newspapers gleefully reported—her own family. The calendar seemed more objectionable than similar mild pornography, in part because of its popularity, but also because Trevi had already made herself a symbol of female sexual license and youthful rebellion.[1]

Socially conservative citizens could not prevent Trevi from filling the airwaves with her music and the news programs with her provocative comments. But they did have a legal recourse against her calendar, and at least a few of them took it: they sent complaints to la Comisión Calificadora de Publicaciones y Revistas Ilustradas (the classifying commission for illustrated periodicals and magazines), a small government body charged with "protecting the populace . . . from the influence of morbid contents in frankly anti-educational publications."[2] Since 1944, it has monitored Mexican periodicals for slang, depictions of crime, and images of nudity and sex. It has also responded to numerous complaints from Mexican citizens against particularly visible offenders in the media, such as romance comics and true-crime tabloids. Any Mexicans who wanted the government to do something about Gloria Trevi's pinup calendar would eventually find their complaints routed to the commission. When they did, commissioners took the first step in the complex legal process that can lead to the confiscation of copies, small fines for publishers and distributors, and even the threat of jail for recidivist pornographers: the commissioners asked Trevi to visit their office to explain herself.[3]

Trevi arrived at the commission's grubby office in the basement of a large, modern government building in central Mexico City on a February afternoon in 1992. Sporting tight jeans and a men's shirt unbuttoned to her navel, she exchanged pleasantries with the men who run the commission and signed autographs for awestruck clerical workers from every office in the building, while her lawyer agreed that she would never again publish erotic photographs of herself. Hands were shaken all around.[4] Ten months later, Trevi produced a 1993 calendar that was no less naughty than the previous year, and announced that her 1994 calendar would go even further.[5] The commission would face new complaints, and might have initiated the same process against Trevi, but with doubtful success. Trevi might even have sold a few more copies by generating publicity on the government's halfhearted attempt to censor her.

This should not be read as an account of the commission's failure. Rather, the story shows the commission performing an important job for the Mexican state by giving it the appearance of control over popular culture industries. This illusion strengthens the allegiance of the most socially conservative citizens to the state, without threatening the connection between the government and the highly integrated systems of media that characterize contemporary Mexico.[6] The commission also protects local mass media by deflecting anger from pop stars and magazines to the government, where it can—if necessary—be further diffused by co-opting particularly irate citizens through government efforts at censorship—however futile.

The story of Gloria Trevi and her censors exemplifies a long-standing phenomenon: the debate over the production, distribution, and interpretation of mass media. Such arguments have characterized the spread of new forms—from photography in the mid–nineteenth century to the Internet in the late twentieth—around the world. No medium can remain popular without continuing to inspire an interpretive community, even if that community expresses nothing but disdain for the form in question. These debates provide a cultural and political context for the mass media that enables producers, consumers, and critics to explain themselves, and to shape their relations with each other and the world. Without these debates, mass media would mean nothing.

Mexican History in the Comic Mode

This book examines one exceptionally popular medium, comic books and their related forms, in the cultural and political context of Mexico in the postrevolutionary decades of the mid-1930s through the mid-1970s. In this time and place, the communities and discourses that formed around mass media were, even more than usual in twentieth-century history, central to ordinary people's political practice. Mexicans in the postrevolutionary era used mass media, as the story about Gloria Trevi suggests, as the best available space for dissent, negotiation, and accommodation. As surprising as students of Antonio Gramsci may find it, the interpretive communities gathered around popular culture *were* Mexican civil society in this era.[7] By producing, distributing, and interpreting words and pictures, citizens could and did consent to the general structure of the relationships that formed the state, while also, at times, commenting on and even changing specific government policies.

Compared to other Latin American nations in the twentieth century, Mexico has been an anomaly, notable for a relatively healthy economy and a reasonably broad middle class; a long-lasting, single-party regime that utilized the forms of democracy (including the existence of a thriving and sometimes oppositional intellectual establishment), if not their substance; and generally low levels of state violence. Mexico has also been free from widespread civil war or military rule since the end of the Cristero War in 1929. At the same time, a vast amount of scholarly and popular literature blames the ruling Partido Revolucionario Nacional (PRI) for the poverty, inequality, underdevelopment, limits on freedom of expression, ecological catastrophes, ethnic discrimination, and political corruption that character-ize Mexican postrevolutionary history. Certainly, the PRI has earned all this criticism and more.

And yet, at least when considering the comparatively prosperous de-cades between the late 1940s and the early 1970s, it is impossible not to wonder at how much worse things might have been. How was it that there was so little violence in those years? How did Mexican society withstand the increasing strains of rapid-fire urbanization, industrialization, and emi-gration? How did the state remain so stable under the stress of huge, unpredictable economic expansion and contraction? Why was it that on the few occasions that the government violently suppressed mass political dissent, it was a shocking break from the ordinary course of events, rather than their logical culmination?

Obviously, comic books alone cannot hold the answer to the historical riddle of Mexico's relative peace and prosperity. Political processes cannot entirely explain this condition; some of this social peace was a side effect of an expanding economy, at least from 1950 through 1975. Still, the story of *las historietas* (comic books) does show us how the process worked.[8] The state and its opponents entered into subtle negotiations that began with the ques-tion of what issues could come up for discussion and ended with the government, having accepted a definition of the problem, finding a solution that kept all parties talking. The government has allowed many of its ideo-logical positions to come up for debate in order to draw all dissenters into its own ranks and keep them there. Indeed, episodes such as the 1968 student massacre in Mexico City or the 1994 Zapatista rebellion in Chiapas are im-portant precisely because they are exceptional. The comparative calm that has prevailed is not an artifact of a completely repressive police state, but the achievement of a government that has more or less controlled the course of events in Mexico, while still allowing an adequate space for dissent and maintaining enough flexibility to respond, at times, to those voices. In large part, the success of the Mexican state is attributable to its cultural politics.

Almost all of the subjects that seemed both compelling enough to inspire dissent and safe enough to allow for negotiation were, broadly speaking, cultural; many had to do with the mass media. Beginning about 1920 and continuing into the present (albeit in somewhat attenuated form), arguments flourished over recorded music and popular song, burlesque theater, tabloid journalism, film, television, and imported Broadway musicals. Public space and public behavior became matters for contestation in the booming cities, with battles waged over the naming and renaming of streets after revolutionary heroes or Catholic saints, the imagery on posters and billboards, the conduct of certain categories of tourists, the location of bars and dance halls, and overly suggestive forms of dance. Another burning question was which holidays to celebrate, and how; in the mid-1930s, for example, conservatives attempted to institute Mother's Day as a rejoinder to government-led celebrations of women workers, athletes, and revolutionaries. "Revolutionary" high culture was the focus of political struggle, too: the anticlericalism of murals painted on government buildings (particularly in Diego Rivera's works) led to mass demonstrations in Mexico City. Protests, as well as silent resistance, greeted government efforts to modernize food distribution and preparation. Above all, Mexicans contested the curriculum—indeed, the very existence—of the new public schools.

Each of these struggles, in its way, touched on the same set of issues: postrevolutionary transformations of the household and workplace, masculinity and femininity, and religion. Sometimes they implied resistance to revolutionary nationalism through recourse to local (or "traditional") standards or practices, or through adherence to some international (sometimes Catholic) set of ideas or objects. And all such arguments were, on one level, a means for the participants to negotiate the terms of their entry into that ill-defined condition, modernity.

Economic expansion created, as well as soothed, social tensions. In Mexico after 1940, deep-rooted family structures, strongly attached to moral values and religious beliefs, were challenged by the new widespread patterns of urbanization, industrialization, and migration—above all, by the increasing number of women who worked both outside their homes and (unlike agricultural laborers) away from their families. This transformation of ordinary family life, and of its associated patterns of belief and behavior, was mapped in radio dramas, state-supported films, and comic books. The fetishization of the *soldadera*, the female revolutionary soldier, was only the most visible part of this cultural project.[9] Meanwhile, a new set of female celebrities—writers, artists, singers, models, dancers, and movie

ars—by their mere existence, affronted conservative standards for feminine decorum, while a relatively unfettered press made the most of their
shock value.[10] Conservatives complained in vague terms about the changes
wrought by industrialization and urbanization; but they spoke much more
directly and specifically against the *representations* of those changes as mani-
fested in textbooks, films, songs, soap operas, and periodicals.

Mexican history after 1930 has been produced by the conflicts and
transactions among a revolutionary culture with strong ties to nineteenth-
century liberalism, a conservative culture rooted in one form or another
of Catholicism, and an international capitalist culture created and transmitted by mass media. Some historians have argued that the expansion of
state power in the postrevolutionary era required the imposition of a new,
"revolutionary" national culture.[11] Others see the post-1940 period as one
in which Mexico's national and regional cultures drowned under a wave of
transnational media.[12] This book contends that the postrevolutionary period
did, in fact, see cultures in conflict. But it disagrees with the idea that one
or another of these cultures won. Mexico's cultures all continued to exist in
opposition to each other, while individual Mexicans moved among them as
their situations (and imaginations) warranted. The state kept the peace by
keeping all of Mexico's cultures in constant conflict with each other and,
simultaneously, acting as the mediator among them.

The story of comic books, their readers, their producers, their critics,
and their relationship to the Mexican state offers an excellent window into
such cultural processes. It provides evidence of the continuing power of liberal rhetoric (particularly in relation to questions of education and national
identity) in the "revolutionary" state, even in the face of marketplace pressures. At the same time, it suggests that conservative Catholic culture had
more strength and lasted far longer than anyone would have guessed, that
it could, and did, respond and grow with the changing times. Finally, it
proves that the culture of market capitalism did not simply pour itself over
conservative and revolutionary Mexican ideologies like a layer of cement,
but instead, was molded by them into a shape it would not otherwise
have had. Looking at *historietas* and the controversies that surrounded them
makes this plain.

Debates over comic books, like other cultural arguments, displaced
moral disagreements that had already led to violence and destruction. These
debates over mass media moved tensions between Catholic conservatives

and the central government into the realm of the imaginary. In 1944, for example, it allowed the government to form a symbolic alliance with these organized Catholic protesters against the media conglomerates that were already almost part of the state itself. In the decades that followed, similar debates gave the Mexican government a chance to solidify its alliance with social conservatives while reminding the producers of popular culture of just who was in charge. The intervention of the government into both the production process of comic books and the protests against them had a strong effect on their style.

Meanwhile, the government set the terms by which mass media could be attacked, from either the left or the right; it refused to hear arguments that were not couched in the rhetoric of patriotism and progress, the same imagery and words manipulated by the comic books themselves. Nobody could expect a response to arguments with underlying assumptions that were nostalgic (even if such nostalgia lurked in a reference to the 1917 constitution) or internationalist (even if the standard referred to was that of Catholic universality). Rather than the invisible hand that Gramscian hegemony so often seems to represent, here we can see how the interactions of individual bureaucrats, entrepreneurs, activists, and artists reinforced a political, social, and economic hierarchy.

"Little Stories," Big Audiences

The very phrase comic books, in English, asks us to laugh at them, and the Spanish word *historietas* (literally, "little stories") almost apologizes for the genre. But across the world, hundreds of thousands of people have fought over their content.[13] Why take comic books as a battlefield?

It is not the business of this study to defend comic books on aesthetic grounds.[14] Their power to provoke has other sources: their popularity, their accessibility, the ease with which they can be read, and the plasticity of their content. Anything that can be imagined can be drawn, and anything that can be drawn can be understood far more easily than anything in print. But comic books are not a global medium; they have very different niches in the cultural ecologies of every region where they are found, and they rarely translate well.[15] In Western Europe, they are a relatively expensive form of art book. In Japan, they are commuter entertainments, frequently pornographic (but respectable reading for an adult in a public place). Only in the

United States, however, is the comic book audience essentially confined to boys and young men; and only in the United States do comic books compete for consumer dollars with cinema and video games, rather than other forms of print media.

A caution to U.S. readers is in order here: Mexican *historietas* are not what you may expect. Their audience is neither young nor male. Their stories are usually set in an entirely familiar world, rather than some alternate universe, and it is a world without superheroes. *Historietas* are not sold in specialty stores but, instead, share newsstand space (and readers, as well as a whole set of consumer expectations and criticisms) with similar periodicals that include photonovels, sports papers, women's magazines, and soft-core pornography. Indeed, the lines between these genres have not been clearly drawn, either by their producers or their consumers. What, then, are *historietas*?

In Mexico, comic books are ubiquitous and vulgar, in every sense of the word. *Historietas* are tremendously popular (even in 1990, after two decades of declining circulation, eight of the ten best-selling periodicals were comic books), and their popularity cuts across lines of region, age, gender, and even class.[16] They can be purchased cheaply and quickly on the street corners of any good-sized town all over the country. There are a daunting number of comics available at these corner newsstands: dozens by 1940, more than 100 by 1960. While many produce new editions every week, the most popular appeared daily in the 1940s. Because of their small size and light weight, comic books are easily portable, making them an everyday sight in public spaces like bus stops and barbershops. Their covers, which grew gaudier as printing technology improved, are luridly colored.

And their stories! Melodramatic or comic distortions of the quotidian (and sometimes both at once), local *historietas* alarm Mexican conservatives far more than the escapist North American superhero fantasies could. But such lurid tales have, historically, helped Mexicans cope with the effects of change in their own lives. They showed Mexicans who moved to the cities how to behave at the workplace and in their new neighborhoods, warning them of what to expect while consoling them with the possibilities of middle-class comfort and family happiness.

An Episodic Narrative That Ends Happily

This book does not pretend to provide a complete history of comic books or the comic book industry.[17] Rather, it examines—in more or less chronological order—aspects of the relationships between the comic books' producers, audiences, and critics, and the Mexican state. The first section deals with the comics themselves, the second with public protests against comic books and related forms of print media, and the third with the workings of la Comisión Calificadora.

Chapters one and two analyze the contents of the *historietas*. Chapter one offers a snapshot of a single issue of the most popular comic book of all, *Pepín*. It also looks at how the comics, in their first decade of publication, deployed a range of techniques to develop an audience, including cliff-hanging narratives, contests and other forms of audience participation, and the creation of celebrity cartoonists and writers. Chapter two examines the comics' role in the construction of a discourse of revolutionary modernity and nationalist progress, through both a close reading of a single, long-running episodic melodrama, and a statistical analysis of personal ads in which readers describe ideal versions of themselves and their potential mates. It concludes that the most important gesture in the repertoire of comic book modernism was the depiction of a stock figure, the revolutionary girl, who was new to commercial storytelling but closely related to the heroic women of national myth as reconstructed between 1920 and 1940. Yet this chapter also finds that the audiences who eagerly consumed stories about this *chica moderna* ("modern girl") rarely demonstrated any intention of imitating or marrying her.

Chapter three turns to the comics' critics, their rhetoric and actions. It traces three waves of moral panic over comic books and related print media (such as *fotonovelas*, muscle magazines, or sports tabloids) between the early 1940s and the early 1970s. Concentrating on protesters' language as a means of locating this opposition in the broader context of Mexican cultural history, this chapter suggests that a gendered counterdiscourse of nationalist tradition and conservatism evolved in dialogue with the modernist discourse described in the previous chapter. This traditionalist discourse, too, required the invention of a stock figure, an alternate version of feminine virtue, honor, and *mexicanidad:* the "traditional woman," who exists in relation to her family (unlike the "modern girl," who is shaped by her connections to the state, nation, and workplace) and for whom self-abnegation is the only possible route to power. This imaginary woman, the chapter concludes, was a persuasive fiction often mistaken by outside observers for fact; but like her sister, the *chica moderna*, she began as a counter in a political game and has ended as a campy stereotype. She must, therefore, be studied on her own terms, as a rhetorical trope of substantial and long-lasting political importance.

Chapters four and five describe the workings of the classifying commission, using the censors' own records and related government documents. Chapter four looks at how the commission's members—in a bureaucracy with few powers of enforcement and little institutional support—nonetheless managed to exert a degree of control over comic book producers and satisfy the demands of anti-comic-book protesters. It argues that the commission, without any conscious intention on the part of the commissioners, ended up as a vehicle for the incorporation of conservatives into the Mexican state. Chapter five analyzes the range of comic book producers' responses to government pressure, from acquiescence to financially motivated defiance to, in one unusual case, defiance out of left-wing principle. It finds that, in general, the commission acted to protect Mexican businesses—even Mexican pornographers—from foreign competition (again, not entirely on purpose). Once more, we see the actions of a few frustrated and not particularly powerful bureaucrats adding up to a significant force in the mediating project of the postrevolutionary state: mediating, in this case, between national and transnational consumer cultures.

Between the chapters, portfolios of comic book and photonovel panels offer the iconographic evidence for some of the points argued here: the *historietas'* insistence on local imagery, their endless reiterations of modernity's material aspects, their self-promotion, their attempts to encourage readers to identify with the comics' characters and creators, and the blurred line between *historietas* and other forms of print media narrative. These sections reproduce neither the best nor the worst of comic book art; rather, they represent a sampling of the tens of millions of pictures that have appeared in the tens of thousands of weekly and daily comics and photonovels over the four decades discussed here.

A final note on the nature of this history: comic books and related genres of periodicals, and even the documents of the censorship campaigns and the censors' office, have considerably more charm than most of the materials from which historians reconstruct the past. They can be funny, and not always on purpose. Moreover, this is a story with a happy ending: Mexicans collaborated in building a national culture and negotiating their collective entry into modernity with a surprising degree of success. But if the language and pictures are sometimes goofy, and the conclusions sunny, do not be fooled. The participants in these events, on all sides of the arguments, did not take them lightly. They understood themselves to be engaged in a conflict over the fate of their families and their nation—and they were right.

Chapter One

The Creation of Mexican Comic Books, 1934–1952

 Mexico's first comic book appeared in 1934. By 1940, comic books were part of most Mexicans' experience, as ubiquitous as radio and more common than cinema. A huge audience had been called into being practically overnight. How did comic books find, and keep, these readers?

There are two possible approaches to this question. First, we can see that the Mexican publishing industry took advantage of demographic luck. In the mid-1930s, a vast number of newly literate working people began to visit newsstands; the conditions were right not just for comic books but also for such related forms as tabloids, women's magazines, and collections of song lyrics.

Second, we can examine the contents of the comic books from this era. Comic book publishers used the freedom inherent in a brand-new form to experiment with narrative, imagery, and format until they hit on generic formulas—strategies for making up stories, characters, advertisements, and contests—that promised to build and maintain an audience. These strategies worked by persuading consumers that there was little or no distinction among the readers, creators, and characters of the comic books.

Literacy as a Political Question

The decades between 1930 and 1950 were, for the most part, a healthy time for Mexican industry in general and the newspaper business in particular. An expanding economy as well as a growing population created potential comic book buyers: the number of people with money to spend on cheap entertainment ballooned. For instance, although wages in the manufacturing sector (adjusted for inflation) lost about a third of their value between 1942 and 1947, they climbed steeply between the mid-1930s and mid-1970s. A factory worker in 1975 could expect to earn more than twice the real salary she or he made in 1950, and three times what his or her parents might have earned in 1930. In the same period, the percentage of workers employed outside the ill-paid agricultural sector became a substantial majority. But it was the booming population, increasing from roughly sixteen million in 1930 to some forty million in 1970, that enlarged the pool of potential readers the most.[1]

Comic books and related periodicals were one of the cheapest forms of entertainment available to this growing, relatively prosperous pool of working people and their children. Cover prices stayed at ten centavos per copy from the comics' first appearance through the early 1940s, when prices drifted gradually upward until they reached a peso per magazine around 1950. By comparison, while a Mexico City daily newspaper usually sold for about as much as a comic book, or slightly higher, a first-class movie ticket or a ticket to a bullfight cost five to ten times as much in this era. A comic book cost approximately one-third to one-quarter of what an average worker made in an hour. This ratio held even in times of inflation or scarcity: publishers preferred to cut back on the number of pages per issue or the size of their periodicals rather than raise prices.

The government's commitment to education also helped comic book publishers by producing a startling rise in literacy. In 1930, the census recorded a literacy rate of about 33 percent among Mexicans older than six. That number had climbed to 42 percent by 1940; by 1950, it reached 56 percent.[2] The 1970 census, at the end of the period under consideration here, found a literacy rate of 76 percent among Mexicans over ten. By these measures, the postrevolutionary program of free, universal, mandatory education had worked extremely well.

But literacy, like everything to do with education, was a vexed political issue, which renders government statistics somewhat suspect. Among other problems, literacy was defined generously: for example, while the 1930 and 1940 censuses distinguished between literate people who could read and those who could also write, as late as 1970, less than 10 percent of the total population had studied at the high school level or beyond.[3] Thus, all these numbers should be viewed only as indicators of a broader transformation that created an audience for mass media in general and comic books in particular.

This transformation—what people at the time called modernity, but what could equally well be described as industrial capitalism—can be seen at work in the battles over education that were still occupying public attention in the years that comic books first appeared on Mexican newsstands. In 1917, Article Three of the new revolutionary constitution proposed universal public education. The schools were regarded by all concerned—teachers, parents, government officials, and opponents of public education—as a means for the new government to establish itself and inculcate children with revolutionary ideology. In addition, the government sponsored three well-publicized adult literacy campaigns between 1922 and 1943, which, like the public schools, used highly politicized textbooks and exercises. These campaigns probably were not very effective at teaching reading or writing. Rising literacy rates were caused largely by the increased availability of public schools. But the literacy campaigns did involve hundreds of thousands of citizens as students and volunteer teachers, and suggested to all Mexicans that reading could be a revolutionary, patriotic, or modern act.

"Socialist" education became a site for struggle between local and centralized powers. It also became an arena for conflict over gender ideology. The most sustained and visible project of Mexican conservatism after 1930 was collective opposition to public education.[4] Article Three, because of its anticlerical bent, had been hotly contested even within the 1917 constitutional convention. After the article's enactment, state efforts to bring secular education to remote rural areas were met with powerful resistance, ranging from mild satire—as in the popular 1935 musical revue, *Socialist Education,* in Mexico City[5]—to the burning of rural schoolhouses and the murder of teachers. Indeed, opposition to educational reform was one cause of the 1926–29 Cristero War. Yet in some ways, the schools were successful. Besides improving literacy, as mentioned earlier, they sometimes served to mediate conflict. Mary Kay Vaughan reports that women

schoolteachers (who often found their work experience personally em-
powering) helped temper parents' and children's perception of schools as
"an ideological apparatus of [state] domination" through negotiation over
such questions as sex education, which they joined parents in resisting.[6]

This, then, was the political context of literacy in mid-1930s' Mexico.
Modernity and reading were so connected in the public imagination, and
together provoked so much anxiety, that some advertisements for elec-
trification suggested that parents needed light in their homes to protect
their children' health from the strain occasioned by reading too many
schoolbooks.[7] Reading was a gateway to modern life, although nobody had
unmixed feelings about modernity. And reading was also patriotic, thanks
to the legacy of the literacy campaigns, the canonization of certain revolutionary texts, the public identification of the state with education, and the
state's material support of the publishing industry.

So, in the 1930s, consumers of "trashy" printed materials such as comic
books did not necessarily feel as though they were practicing a slightly
shameful escape from their daily responsibilities, as present-day readers
might. Instead, reading anything at all was an act that reaffirmed a consumer's connection to the nation, as it asserted his or her participation in
an activity that the government had carefully and extensively marked as
revolutionary. Even browsing at a newsstand was evidence of the reader's
participation in modernity. Examining the content of the comics reveals
that their creators understood and exploited these powerful associations
between patriotism, modernity, and reading.

The content of the comics reflected the industry's intense engagement
with economic and political ideologies. This is not to suggest that Mexican
comic books spoke with one voice or that they were deliberate agents of
propaganda. Rather, the historical conditions in which the comics found
themselves shaped both their material form and their ideological meanings, without forcing any goal on the publishing industry other than the
obvious—maximum sales, maximum profits.

The Comic Book Business

The single largest fixed expense in producing comic books was newsprint. Not only was it expensive, but the supply was unreliable as well.
This situation changed after 1940, however, when the government founded

its own wholesale paper monopoly, Productora e Importadora de Papel, S.A. (PIPSA). Originally designed to support book publishers, PIPSA soon shifted to supplying Mexico City newspapers almost exclusively, a reflection of newspaper publishers' vastly greater political clout.[8] (Their printers, much to the disgust of book publishers and regional newspapers, eventually passed some of this bounty on to comic book publishers who rented their rotographic presses, in preference to sharing it with "outsiders."[9]) As a consequence, the newspaper business grew, becoming more competitive. This competition, in turn, resulted in the formation of media conglomerates that were better placed to vie for government favor than individual newspapers, especially those outside the capital. Yet beyond their contests over state affiliation, newspapers also competed for readers.

Particularly in Mexico City, one means by which papers tried to build consumer loyalty was in having the most exciting Sunday funnies. Mexico City newspapers, like their European and North American counterparts, began publishing Sunday comic supplements as soon as rotographic newspaper presses arrived in the mid-1920s. These supplements, called *dominicales,* offered readers translations of American comic strips. For example, one of the biggest papers, *El Universal,* printed "Tarzan" every Sunday on the front page of its *dominical* section for more than forty-five years, from 1932 through 1978. At the same time, *dominicales* presented locally produced comic strips. Cartoonists sometimes drew on Mexico's long tradition of popular graphic art as well as on more recent postrevolution social-realist conventions. More often, they adapted or imitated North American strips. Running the best local comic strips seemed to boost newspaper circulation figures, no matter where the cartoonists were turning for inspiration. From 1923 to 1927, *El Universal* ran a yearly contest for amateur cartoonists that helped them find new talent and also publicized the *mexicanidad* of their Sunday funnies: they announced a preference for "comics about the national project."[10] By 1930, however, the space that Sunday supplements dedicated to local cartoonists was dwindling.

Evolving out of the *dominicales,* and supported by improved conditions in the publishing industry, comic books not only rented newspaper presses, but also shared the PIPSA newsprint allotment of some large dailies. (Eventually, this process would be reversed, with successful comic books providing the start-up capital for other publishing ventures, including newspapers.[11]) In fact, the cartoonists who founded the comic books had worked for the Sunday supplements until they were supplanted by the cheaper products of U.S. cartoon syndicates.[12] The first Mexican comic book, *Adelaido el Conquistador*, featured an eponymous cartoon character who also appeared in a strip running in *El Universal*. *Adelaido* included other comics as well, some by Mexican cartoonists and some translated North American strips. Little or nothing in the new magazine was unavailable in the regular *dominicales*, and so *Adelaido* survived for only 100 weekly issues (1932–33.)[13] Still, it set a pattern that three other new comic books soon followed, with greater success.

Paquín, founded in 1934, was the first Mexican comic book to find a wide audience. It was quickly joined by *Paquito* (1935) and *Chamaco* (1936). The most popular of all, however, was *Pepín*, also founded in 1936. Its influence was such that some Mexicans still refer to comic books as *pepines*, although *Pepín* ceased publication almost four decades ago.[14] Like *Adelaido el Conquistador*, the new comic books mixed syndicated North American newspaper cartoons with local strips and serials.[15] Unlike *Adelaido*, the new comics thrived. *Pepín* appeared three times a week after 1938 and daily after 1940; its competitors followed suit. In 1943 a journalist estimated that Mexicans purchased half a million comic books a day.[16] *Pepín* alone, at its peak in the late 1940s, probably printed as many as 300,000 copies a day, eight times a week—there were two completely distinct editions on Sundays—of sixty-four pages each.[17]

As high as these figures were, they did not represent even a majority of the comic book audience. Trade in used comics sprang up, so that public marketplaces usually had at least one stall where recent *historietas* could be purchased for half price or less. Even less formal mechanisms of passing magazines along helped to ensure that the total readership was far higher than these circulation figures might indicate. As a government official admonished the officers of the Barbers' Social Center of Mexico City in 1955, "barbershops are the most important places where obscene publications are advertised and circulated"; he asked that barbers remove the racy periodicals, including *Pepín* and *Chamaco*, from their shops.[18]

The comic book industry underwent a significant shift by the end of the period under discussion. At first, four publishers printed one comic book each, competing with each other for all potential readers. *Pepín* and *Chamaco* lasted until 1955; *Paquín* and *Paquito* were gone by 1951. By 1952, at least fifteen producers printed over forty daily, weekly, or biweekly comics.[19]

Individual comics, after about 1950, stopped trying to reach all semiliterate Mexicans. The new comic books reached toward a readily definable group: fans of bullfighting, ranchera music, romantic stories, or specific movie stars; young boys interested in science; women who wanted fashion advice; and so forth.[20] Such segmentation of the market brought an end to the era of the daily comic books, but only increased the total number of comic books printed and purchased.

Within this transformation of the comic book, there remained continuities of plot structure, imagery, subject matter, and narrative trope. These continuities help explain the comics' long-term popularity, and reveal some of the strategies that led to explosive growth and fragmentation of the comic book market in the first place. Everything that *historietas* are, they became in that initial fifteen years of wild expansion.

Constructing an Audience

What did comic book buyers get for their ten centavos in those first few years? Publishers were not sure what would make a reader keep on buying their periodicals, so every issue of the *historietas,* in their beginning, deployed multiple strategies for attracting and holding an audience. Among the most important of these were variety, familiarity, sentimentality—including an appeal to patriotic feelings—and above all, the identification of the reader with the creator.

Mexicans who bought *historietas* felt as though they were helping to create the narratives included in them, that they were participating in a communal project, rather than passively absorbing stories invented by somebody far away about distant people. This was a marketing strategy, a means of flattering the audience; but it also distinguished comic book reading from any other form of leisure activity, and it implied a connection between buying *historietas* and participating in the economic, technological, and social improvements that were supposed to characterize Mexican life in the postrevolutionary era. To read these particular comics seemed like a powerful, patriotic deed, underlining the politics of reading; their pages were also imbued with a strong dose of faith in progress and modernity. All this was accomplished through identifying producer and product with consumer.

The first successful Mexican comics—*Chamaco, Paquín,* and *Pepín*—appear to have stumbled accidently on this strategy. The new periodicals had no particular political agenda, but rather, only the intention of creating an audience for themselves and surviving in a tough marketplace. They were in competition with each other, as well as the Sunday supplements. As Armando Bartra points out, the early years of these comics saw them experimenting with innumerable methods of filling space; they retained what sold.[21] Mentioning the *mexicanidad* of the new cartoon magazines was an obvious step and, since it worked, the cartoonists kept on doing it.

When a reader picked up one of the *pepines*, she or he encountered a package stuffed with many different items, all more or less familiar to a regular reader. Any *Chamaco, Pepín, Paquín,* or *Paquito* included episodes of tragic or dramatic serial tales meant to last up to two years, and episodes of tragicomic or comic serials designed to go on indefinitely. It contained very little blank space: games, contests, puzzles, ads, and other filler packed whatever room was left between the stories. Even the top and bottom margins sported advertising or patriotic slogans.

Besides this generous dose of entertainment in every issue, *historietas* before about 1950 reached out in a variety of ways to all readers or potential readers. They invited responses through contests and lotteries, and they printed readers' letters, lonely hearts advertisements, photos, drawings, and contest entries. They even solicited readers' life stories as possible plots for new serials. Indeed, the popularity of the comic books left their producers with a constant need to fill as many pages as possible. What could be easier, or cheaper, than to print what their readers sent them? In addition to being convenient for publishers, this proved popular with the comic book audience. It made each comic book seem like a little community, which in turn, became another way to encourage readers to keep buying *historietas*.

An Exemplary Historieta

The blurring of the lines between comic book producers, readers, and characters can be seen in a random example of *Pepín* (no. 891, 21 August 1941).[22] Its gaudy lithographed cover used bright, matte, simple colors, although the rest of the issue was printed in smeary black ink. It showed a cartoon of a young woman, seated at a large desk before a window, pen in hand, looking at a folded sheet of paper. She sports heavy makeup, with green eye shadow and a flower in her hair; although her dress is tight, her modest neckline reveals no cleavage. Her hair is dark and glossy, but she has a small nose and pale skin: she is recognizably Mexican, but not mestiza. The leather-bound books on her desk and her gold bracelet add to the general impression of wealth. Behind her head floats an enormous envelope addressed to "Cumbres de Ensueño" (Heights of dreams), which is one of the continuing narratives to be found inside the cover. This picture implies that she is sending a letter to the comic strip, as many readers did. It suggests, too, that the female readers of this particular serial are upper-class, respectable women.

Pepín—like *Paquín, Paquito,* and *Chamaco*—never printed a table of contents and placed most of the information generally attached to a masthead in the middle of the magazine. All mixed the order in which serials were presented every day: editors acted as though readers needed no guides through the *historieta. Pepin,* no. 891, for instance, began abruptly with a translation of the U.S. strip, "The Phantom," a reminder of the magazine's roots in the *dominicales.* At the foot of the page, as on almost all this issue's pages, are two tiny lines of self-promotion: "PEPIN publishes the most interesting and best-drawn comics every day, which is why it is the most popular." These comments boasted of the magazines' ten-centavo price "throughout the republic" (which acted as a check on vendors tempted to raise prices).[23] Marginal advertisements helped build suspense, too, by announcing upcoming serials or contests.[24]

In turning the first page, however, the reader encountered a story in quite a different style: a seven-page chapter of the humor serial "Los Super-locos," written and illustrated by Gabriel Vargas.[25] Here, the charming blowhard, Don Jilemon, sneaks into a stranger's wake in order to scarf up the food and drink. Nothing much happens: there is hardly any suspense, almost no plot, and no punch line. The pleasure of "Los Super-locos" comes from its art. Vargas eschewed the illusion of reality. No unnecessary details clutter the page, no cross-hatching provides the illusion of depth, no gray tones stand in for color. Instead, Vargas offers viewers a pleasingly balanced collection of lines, of white and black spaces rhythmically deployed on a planar surface, that is also effortlessly decipherable as a group of people making recognizable gestures and taking characteristic poses. This offhand masterwork of composition was a feat Vargas repeated every day for decades. Except for Vargas, the artists represented in this issue of *Pepín* aimed only for clarity—a goal that they consistently achieved, but rarely surpassed.

Pages 12–19 of *Pepín*, no. 891, were filled with a chapter of the dramatic, episodic serial, "Adelita y las guerrillas."[26] Adelita, one of the few continuing characters in any of the serials that the magazine published over the years, acted as and argued for the *chica moderna,* the modern girl who desired a degree of autonomy, excitement, and affection in her life. Her story began when her father, a wealthy rancher in an unnamed northern town, was killed during the Revolution. The brave orphan met the poor but honest young soldier Juan Sin Miedo while defending the village from the bandits who killed her father. They fell in love, and he ran off to seek his fortune, to be worthy of her. Juan returned as a rich, famous bullfighter, only for the couple to be parted again when he was kidnapped by Chinese pirates. Adelita and Juan were only reunited, engaged, and able to exchange their first kiss after four years and some months of plot twists. Meanwhile, Adelita had met a Mexico City girl detective named Nancy, and became an amateur sleuth herself. Nancy, who earned her own living and was a proud, chic city dweller, was even more self-consciously modern than Adelita; the serial's action sometimes stopped for days while the two characters discussed the limits of acceptable behavior for the *chica moderna.*

At this point in the cliff-hanging saga, Juan and Adelita are visiting the ranch of her sister's fiancé to investigate mysterious beings lurking in the ancient ruins, while Nancy is coming to their aid. Driving north from Mexico City, Nancy and her fiancé, José, get caught in a thunderstorm and take shelter in a dark mansion that, unbeknownst to them, is inhabited by a mad scientist. As the chapter opens, in issue 891, Nancy is grabbed by the scientist's crazed, leprous servant. The mad scientist drags José off, leaving the servant to lock Nancy up; entranced by her beauty, he is about to kiss her—and infect her with leprosy—at the chapter's end.

This episode made no difference to the larger scheme of the tale. It was, after all, just a stop along the road to the place where the central story was suspended. (By *Pepín,* no. 901, Nancy and José had extricated themselves unharmed, and rejoined Adelita.) The delight of this particular chapter of "Adelita" lay precisely in its lack of consequence. Its author, José Guadalupe Cruz, was as great a master of the infinitely suspended narrative as Vargas was a genius of pen and ink drawing. Cruz asked his readers to follow a plot in the same way that they might watch a juggler at the circus: just how many plates can he keep spinning in the air?

The whole acrobatic enterprise of "Adelita" had an improvised quality that increased the thrill. For example, at one point he sent Nancy (unconscious, amnesiac, blindfolded, and bound and gagged in the back seat of a car) hurtling over a cliff toward her doom while Adelita watched from above, wringing her hands. The true suspense here arose not from wondering whether Nancy would survive, but in how Cruz could wiggle out of this narrative bind. The next day, Cruz solved this problem by having Superman come flying in to catch the falling car and then converse briefly with Adelita. "I don't belong here!" he complains, "I am supposed to appear on other pages of *Pepín!*" Adelita explains that,

> if Nancy died all of a sudden, the author of this cartoon would die slowly of starvation. . . . You suspect that the author of this comic book story has bats in his belfry, right? I do not suspect so any more. . . . I AM COMPLETELY CONVINCED OF IT![27]

This is certainly an unusual example of transnational cultural appropriation. Yet the manner in which Cruz calls attention to himself and to his own cleverness in solving this difficult narrative problem would have been quite familiar to his audience, and they would also recognize the scene's deliberate absurdity. To extend the metaphor, his circus act included frequent cries of "Look out! I'm going to drop something any minute now!" At the same time, by making the difficulty of the writer's quandary far more entrancing than the girl detective's dilemma, Cruz had invited his audience to think like the writer, another example of the close connections among character, creator, and consumer in Mexican comic books.

Perhaps because of his frequent interventions into his own stories, Cruz was also the first of *Pepín's* authors to become a star, and his name was used as a selling point in advertising new serials. In the chapter of "Adelita" in *Pepín,* no. 891, the last page replaced the story with a little article on "The Collaborators of José G. Cruz," including three photos of the young artists who specialized in drawing clothes and interiors, "special effects," and exterior backgrounds for several of Cruz's serials, including "Adelita." Photos of Cruz himself, a handsome young man, had already appeared several times. This, too, added to readers' double involvement in the story: they could interest themselves both in the absurd ramifications of the story *and* in the tale of how the story came to be told. This "doubleness," a strategy familiar to readers of movie magazines, was one of the techniques Cruz used over and over again in his long career as a cartoonist and publisher of *fotonovelas.* Both Cruz himself and the characters he invented seemed to step out of the page to speak directly to the reader in these episodes. But Cruz designed these discursive breaks in the narrative flow as conversations with his audience, always prefacing them with phrases like "by popular demand" or "at the request of a certain reader."

A chapter of another long-running serial, "El Alacran" (The scorpion), filled the next eight pages of *Pepín*, no. 891. El Alacran, the invention of A. Tirado, was a nineteenth-century masked crusader who, in this episode, was unjustly imprisoned by a cruel oligarch. The art and script of "El Alacran" did not meet the standard set by the rest of this issue of *Pepín*. Nothing in this chapter would hook the casual viewer. Yet Tirado had a long career, thanks to his capacity to produce page after page of graphic narrative every day. *Pepín*'s producers always had to balance the competing needs to keep readers interested, attract new readers, and simply fill pages.

The following two pages (28 and 29) contained an imported "Superman" strip. Like the segment of "The Phantom" mentioned earlier, it was printed on a smaller scale than the Mexican serials surrounding it, as if to render the North American contribution less important. The indica for this issue, also on page 29, gave no more than the address, the name of the editor (newspaper magnate José García Valseca), and the date, number, and year of the issue. Page 30 contained a numerology game, "The Message of the Stars." Using a complex set of rules, readers could unravel such harmless counsel as, "you should ask an experienced person for advice." Fortune-telling, astrology, and palmistry pages like this one were a special target of complaints by clergy involved in anti-comic-book campaigns, noted frequently in official Catholic publications as incitements to superstition or heresy. Such controversy gave filler pages such as this one considerably more interest than their mild contents might otherwise have justified.

The next eight pages of issue 891 were taken up with two chapters of a melodramatic novel by George Spitzmuller called *The Son of Santos*, set in sixteenth-century France. It was *Pepín*'s occasional practice (*Chamaco* followed suit) to offer sections of "real novels" as premiums. Consumers were supposed to pull out the pages of the novel, which were stapled into the middle of the magazine, and preserve them together, apart from the rest of the publication. To underline the idea that this was a gift to its audience, rather than just another feature of the periodical, this section was paginated separately: it began as page 5, the better to be added to the first installment of the previous day, and concluded in midparagraph on page 12. This feature, like the contests that appeared in perhaps two out of three issues, emphasized *Pepín*'s generosity: a book, after all, was a valuable object.

On page 8 of the historical-novel centerfold, a half-page advertisement announced, "Earn MONEY! making Good cartoons with the A. Tirado method." The creator of "El Alacran" was peddling his self-published book, *Learn to Draw*. The overlap between readers and creators became visible in Tirado's assumption that his audience wanted to know how to do it themselves. Another kind of overlap, between the periodical's employees and the group of businessmen they hoped one day to become, also emerged here.

On page 40, *Pepín* resumed numbering its pages sequentially with a short chapter of the serial "Chucho Duran." Like "Adelita," it was a continuing detective/adventure story; it shared the insistent modernity of the Cruz serial, with its working women, fashionable clothes, and attempts at witty, sophisticated dialogue. But the anonymous author of "Chucho Durán" lacked Cruz's narrative gift. The serial lasted less than two years—about average, by *Pepín*'s standards.

The next serial to appear was the second in this issue to have been drawn and written by Tirado. This one, describing the adventures of a group of Mexican mountain climbers, was called "Avalancha." It was better than Tirado's other work, perhaps because he was a devoted alpinist. On several occasions, he printed photos of himself atop especially tall or inaccessible peaks. He also printed obituary notices for fallen mountaineers and even acted as a kind of community bulletin board for Mexican climbers. In the middle of this chapter, for instance, on page 46, he broke off from the story to publish a tiny photo of an enormous crag, along with the caption:

> Recent climb by the "Himalaya Club" exchanges flags with our good friends of the "Tequiteptl Club," to whom, by means of these pages, we send a warm greeting.

Though few potential readers were avid climbers, practices like these helped to build a wider audience; again, we see a creator deliberately erasing the boundary between himself and his readers, between the stories and their lives.

The next serial chapter printed in *Pepín*, no. 891, was as anonymous and placeless as "Avalancha" was personal and local. The unsigned "Aventuras del Espacio" (Space adventures) was set on a nameless, and nearly featureless, planet. The editors of *Pepín* canceled the serial abruptly a few months later, after a run of less then half a year, leaving the hero stranded forever on a meteor. Although *Pepín*'s publisher did not run formal marketing surveys, reader responses, experience, and instinct told its editors when a serial was not succeeding.[28] This story differs from successful serials in its lack of connection to specific places, as well as to the history, experiences, or already familiar narratives shared by at least some audience members. Such a lack may explain the serial's failure. By contrast, many stories involving fantastic new inventions by present-day Mexican inventors, or weird monsters and mystic beings in pre-Cortesian Mexico, achieved great and lasting popularity.

As an example, even before Cruz started writing "Adelita," his detective series, "Brenty," ran in *Pepín*. "Adelita," however, was insistently local: every new adventure took place in a real Mexican region, always named and with all its landmarks shown. Brenty's adventures, in comparison, took him all over the world. The differences between Cruz's two serials map a central tension in *Pepín*. The magazine offered both the national and the transnational, the patriotic and the modern. Perhaps the greater success of "Adelita" as an independent publication in the 1950s shows what consumers preferred.

The next serial in *Pepín*, no. 891, "Cumbres de Ensueño," was a series of completely distinct romantic stories played out over six to eight weeks. Each had a shared framing narrative: they were supposedly told by or to a wise old man, who sometimes also acted in the story, but always provided an epilogue at the close of one tale ("and they are still living happily in Veracruz today") and an introduction to the next. This character could point to the moral of the story, an increasingly important function as the *pepines* were subjected to more and more criticism of their morality.

Guillermo Marin, the author of "Cumbres de Ensueño," also had a long career in the publishing industry. His stories were not particularly interesting, but he was an excellent draftsman, with a gift for inventing faces and bodies. Perhaps it was Marin's fascination with physiognomy that led him to encourage readers to send the series their photographs. Although the first one that he printed, in 1940, had been sent unsolicited, he then announced that he would print any photograph sent to him. He followed this policy until 1944, when he begged his readers to stop because he had enough to last for years, even at the rate of running four to six a day. He always addressed his readers as female, and almost every photograph printed was of a woman who appeared to be somewhere between twelve and sixty years old. The four reader photos in *Pepin* are not snapshots, but studio portraits; the women, some in makeup, posed with carefully coiffed hair, and all wore tidy, modest dresses.

More than bringing their faces to the comics, these readers wanted their lives to be included, too, and so they sent Marin stories and autobiographies. He seems to have used them on occasion: after 1942, every "Cumbres de Ensueño" story concluded both with the old man explaining the moral *and* with a drawing of the reader who had suggested the plot, in a kind of double framing device. One photo in *Pepín*, no. 891, carries the caption, "Senorita Consuelo Gomez, of Tampico, Tamps. I received your little romantic story. How grateful I am that you sent it to me." In 1943, Marin began to write himself in as the narrator's interlocutor, making himself the true star of drama, the one who told the tale to which the older man would pose a moral. This was, again, a method of including readers: if Marin could be both the real person with whom they corresponded, and a figure in the comic book, might not that also be possible for the readers themselves?

Pepín tried to connect itself to its audience (or its potential audience) by using generic stories, local settings, real people and events, and the reader contributions. Another form was stories taken directly from familiar sources—folktales, radio dramas, theater, popular song, and cinema. The last section of this issue, "Corazon del Norte," was based on a Bette Davis vehicle that had been popular in Mexico the year before. The art is undistinguished, the story uninteresting. Yet as soon as this serial ended, it would be replaced by another based on another film, *Strangers on a Train*. Narrative novelty, clearly, was not as important as the comfort of the familiar.

This, then, was the form and content that *Pepín* usually followed. *Chamaco, Paquín,* and *Paquito* also used a similar format and included similar serials. Like *Pepín*, all three, by accident or design, encouraged their readers to imagine themselves as the authors and characters of *historietas,* and to envision the *historieta's* producers as audience members and as comic book characters.

Keeping an Audience

Over time, the form that *Pepín* and its competitors used evolved to include many tactics to build loyal audiences, as well as to make readers think of them as something different from and preferable to the *dominicales*.[29] For instance, most of the *pepines* distinguished themselves by offering at least a few pages of color not only on Sundays but also daily. All of them had gaudy, full-color drawings on their front covers. For years, *Chamaco* played three pages of the humorous serial "Los Supersabios" in color on the inside front, inside back, and outside back covers. *Paquito Grande* ran two-color advertisements. Another physical feature that attracted readers was the size of the comic books. They were thick, but pocket-size and lightweight.[30] It was easy to carry them to work or school, to be read while commuting or during lunch hour. They were cheaply made, yet durable enough to be passed from hand to hand, traded, and even resold.

Comic books differentiated themselves from the *dominicales* in content as well. Increasingly, they relied on episodic serials, with beginnings and endings, as opposed to the strip format with continuing characters who might go on forever. *Pepín* dropped all syndicated newspaper strips by 1942; *Paquito* never had them; and *Chamaco* filled a steadily smaller number of its pages with them over the years. Extended yet closed, serials could be more exciting than infinitely running dramas because they held out the possibility that something final—marriage, death, repentance, punishment, wealth—might happen to the central figures. Often, six to twelve serials were included in a single comic book issue.

Usually mixing elements, the art and narratives of these serials had something to interest any possible reader. If it was set in the countryside, sooner or later, at least one character would visit the city. If its main character was male, there were sure to be chapters in which the hero's mother, sister, or girlfriend took center stage. If it was predominantly romantic, a crime, battle, or similar crisis added a little action to the blend. If it was sad, a few funny scenes livened up the proceedings. Changes in tone— from comic to tragic, or vice versa—often signaled changes in which class was on stage: for instance, in a storyline that followed a poor little rich girl, her travails would be fodder for witty commentary by her servants. Or the opposite might be true: a tragic serial whose protagonist was a working man would include buffoonish wealthy neighbors or employers. The writers and editors of the *pepines*, in other words, believed that their readers craved variety.

Yet each comic book had to build a distinct identity for itself, not only for the finite serials. One means of doing this was through a high degree of self-reference: street scenes in *Pepín* included newsstands with copies of the comic prominently displayed or street urchins reading the comic. The serials also referred to each other on occasion. For example, characters from the serial "Brenty" attended Adelita's birthday party.

Additionally, *Pepín*, *Chamaco*, and *Paquín* used contests to sustain reader interest and build the magazine's identity. Almost every issue of *Pepín* made reference to at least one contest by printing a teaser page, a list of prizewinners, or a coupon. In part, contests increased circulation by offering the audience something for nothing, and the prizes hinted at who the publishers believed to be in their audience. A 1938 "Christmas lottery" in *Pepín* handed out a motorcycle, a refrigerator, two typewriters, three sets of furniture (one each for living room, kitchen, and bedroom), an electric stove, two tuition-paid courses to study mechanics and appliance repair, a washing machine, three radios, a gas stove, a set of Lone Ranger outfits, a perfume collection, a gentleman's suit, a set of luggage, two women's outfits, a pen set, a set of watches, a boy's suit, and "an adorable and varied set of toys."[31] This list suggests an audience of aspiring, upwardly mobile, urban families, neither so wealthy as to turn up their noses at the offer of a chance to study a trade nor so poor that their homes were not wired for the electricity needed by a refrigerator.[32] Other contests presented smaller prizes to more people, as in *Pepín*'s 1941 offer of five pesos (the price of fifty copies of the comic book) to the first twenty readers every week to answer questions in Mexican history such as, "Who was the second viceroy of New Spain?"[33] At the same time, *Pepín* was raffling off watches and fountain pens in exchange for coupons that it printed daily.[34]

Contests also worked like cliff-hanging serials, dragging out over weeks or even months, and keeping readers loyal by adding an element of suspense along the way. They required active participation as well as passive hope. To take part in a contest often required clipping ten or twenty coupons, which appeared over three months or more, after several weeks of buildup. The winners would then be announced over another long span. For example, in a raffle in *Tesoros* (a weekly comic book for children), readers had to clip coupons for seven to ten weeks before finding out whether or not they had won the advertised skates, balloons, and "other surprises."[35]

Contests served another purpose: the pages that they filled, particularly when the comics printed the winning contributions in drawing or writing competitions, did not demand more artwork or script from the cartoonists.

Pepines, in the years 1934 to 1952, usually relied on ten to fifteen people to do all the writing and drawing. That could mean filling up to 64 pages every day and 128 pages on Sundays. Any additional material must have been welcome.

Most of all, contests helped the magazines understand what their readers wanted. The contests that asked for readers' drawings of their favorite characters or appreciations of their favorite serials worked as a rough kind of market research. For example, from 1939 through 1941, *Pepín* ran a serial called "Chucho el Roto," based on a nineteenth-century Robin Hood–style folk hero who had already inspired at least one movie and a radio serial. In March 1940, *Pepín* ran a contest asking for "the best, the most sincere and most clear opinions on the theme 'WHY I READ CHUCHO EL ROTO.' "[36] First prize was the considerable sum of fifty pesos (five hundred times the price of one issue), but the author of any printed answer received a peso, and *Pepín* ran one response a day for at least three months. This contest should be seen as a financial investment in reader response.

Printed entries in the "Chucho el Roto" contest included such comments as, "he was no vulgar bandit, he shared with the poor who live under the lash of vile capitalism;" "although it takes place in a bygone era, the theme portrays the social doctrine of the present day very well; really 'Chucho el Roto' was a selfless defender of the oppressed"; and "it is the story of a noble, audacious and very Mexican man who struggles against injustice, aiding the social class he came from."[37] Remarks like these may be mirrors of how *Pepín*'s editors wanted to see themselves: participants in the Revolution, representatives of *mexicanidad,* modern even when discussing the nineteenth century. Other contest entries, however, praised less high-flown aspects of the serial. One fan wrote, "if only, the way he hands out gifts in the serial, Chucho would present me with a prize for my letter."[38]

Some readers seemed to want little more than thrills or repetition, as *Pepín*'s creators knew. A few advertisements used ideological language. One described Chucho as "leaping from the most Mexican pages of the past century" and another mentioned "the naive, but spontaneous, socialism of the 19th century."[39] But many advertisements made frank appeals to presumed reader preferences for sexy stories:

Between silks and perfumes, the throbbing heart of Matilda tries to trap Chucho el Roto, wanting to submit him to the injuries of her blue blood and her money. Another danger for the firm, clean will of . . . Chucho el Roto!![40]

The "Chucho el Roto" contest exemplifies another tactic that the comic books used to construct their audience: nationalism. *Historietas* encouraged readers to see purchasing a comic book as a patriotic act as well as an act of solidarity with all other Mexicans reading them. (That was the import of the pro-government slogans in the margins of the *pepines*.) With the first censorship campaign, in 1942, this strategy took on added significance because pro-censorship forces argued that comic books harmed the nation. In response, comic books relied increasingly on devices such as running patriotic essay contests, printing photographs of editors and publishers at the side of important government figures, drawing patriotic stories of the safely distant past, and putting nationalist slogans in the mouths of popular cartoon characters.

Many cartoonists moved beyond nationalism into regionalism. Some serials carefully portrayed the sights of Mexican rural or town life in hundreds of specific locations. *Pepín* ran a contest in 1942, and *Paquito Grande* a similar one in 1949, that offered a prize to one school in each Mexican state. Story lines of "Adelita y las Guerrillas" almost always unfolded in meticulously drawn depictions of real state capitals, rural villages, and even authentic ancient ruins. Some cartoonists, on the other hand, enjoyed emphasizing their base in Mexico City. Gabriel Vargas dropped his abstract style every so often to show his characters walking past famous buildings in the capital—the Bellas Artes Museum, the Cine Metropolitan—portrayed in photographic detail. Guillermo Marin set many scenes in named, recognizable restaurants and bars of the city, and the old man who framed his stories in "Cumbres de Ensueño" often strolled through Chapultepec Park.

Every comic contained representations of both the center and the periphery of the nation, highlighting an unresolved tension that existed, of course, outside the *pepines*, too. As with the tension between Mexican and international settings that was visible in *Pepín*, no. 891, the comics did not valorize one side or the other of this division. Instead, they managed to offer something for readers from every part of the nation, no matter how they felt about their home towns in relation to the capital.

Chamaco, Paquín, Paquito, and *Pepín* also connected with their readers by making their artists and writers into stars. They printed photographs of the authors at work and advertised new serials by splashing the authors' names over teaser pages. Such teasers would run for days or weeks before the new serial began. Some contests offered original drawings by the cartoonists as prizes. The logic here was that the authors, rather than the cartoon characters, could be the focus of consumer recognition and loyalty. Even the most popular serials ended eventually, but a writer or artist often had an association with a comic book that lasted through dozens of stories.

Even models might receive this star treatment. One drawing in "Adelita y las Guerrillas" portrayed an artist gazing attentively at a shadowed, gaunt, middle-aged man, with a caption explaining that this was "José G. Cruz during one of the rest periods, conversing with the actor who plays the role of the 'dreadful' Black Monk."[41] The next four pages show scenes of the serial's production process, including the participation of Josefina Cruz D. (the author's sister and a fashion illustrator), who drew all the "suits, dresses and accessories," and was responsible for "all the women's dialogues too" in "Adelita."[42] The final panel in this sequence shows the model for Adelita herself, in "an interesting and AUTHENTIC photograph of the much-imitated and attractive star."[43]

Comic books invited readers, through a variety of narrative strategies, to imagine themselves either as characters or creators of *historietas*. Readers responded eagerly. As we have seen, they sent photographs of themselves to cartoonists. They also sent samples of their own drawings, often of their favorite characters. Marin sometimes printed contributions with his suggestions for improvement: "use more ink in drawing the hair," he told one reader.[44] But the most important way in which the comic book audience participated in the construction of the comics was by sending their life stories, as fictions or confessions, to their favorite writers, artists, or periodicals. Cartoonists responded to such gifts by inventing a new genre: the true-life romance.

Stories *de la vida real* appeared in *Chamaco* and *Pepín* long before "true-life" romances became commonplace in North American comics for girls.[45] Unlike the U.S. versions, Mexican stories *de la vida real* always claimed to be based on readers' letters. These letters, like the photographs, first came entirely unsolicited to "Cumbres de Ensueño." Readers may have been encouraged by the drawings and photos that Marin published of himself as a handsome and sophisticated bachelor with a friendly face.[46] Although it seems clear that the letters did exist, it is unclear what relationship—if any—they bore to the stories supposedly modeled on them.

Stories *de la vida real* quickly gained a wide audience. In 1943, a new women's magazine adopted the strategy, promising its audience that "vidas verdaderas" (true lives) would be presented in its articles and photonovels.[47] This narrative technique brought the magazine enough popularity to flourish for at least a decade. In 1950–52, *Paquito Grande* solicited stories from readers with a full-page advertisement that looked like a movie poster. "IS OR WAS YOUR LIFE A TRAGEDY?" it demanded, over a drawing of a beautiful young woman's wistful profile, concluding, "send it to us!"[48] A few weeks after this ad began to run in every issue, a new subtitle was added to the magazine's cover: "All true-life stories!"[49]

Once the industry was well-organized and the audience clearly defined, comic books stopped using most of the strategies described above to find readers. The era of *Pepín* and its competitors drew to a close; the numbers of Mexicans reading comic books did not decline, but after 1952, there were far more comic books available and far fewer readers per title. Running elaborate (and expensive) contests no longer made sense. The form of each genre had been fixed; readers knew what to expect. Thus, the increasingly formulaic stories no longer had to be interrupted by editorial exhortations or authorial interventions. Cartoonists no longer became stars of their own comic books.[50] *Historietas* began to aim themselves at increasingly well-defined segments of their audience, rather than offering something for everyone. Or, to put it another way, readers had learned to insist on stories just for them. Children's comics were the first specialized cartoon publications, perhaps in response to moralistic criticisms that argued that the general-audience comics damaged children, even if adults might be unharmed by them. By the early 1950s, though, consumers could choose among rural romances and urban humor comics, among comics starring superheroes, real-life matinee idols, or wrestlers.

Small reminders of the time when Mexican audiences participated in creating comic books did linger past the death of *Pepín, Chamaco, Paquín,* and *Paquito.* Photos of readers, lonely hearts columns, pen pal pages: these and similar devices still appeared, at times, on the back pages of certain comic books. Above all, the "true-life" romance refused to disappear. The comic book *Corazon* offered readers fifteen pesos for "the story of your life," to be adapted for its pages, beginning in 1955.[51] Comic books such as *Aventuras de la Vida Real* (which began publication in 1956) and *Correo Amoroso* (1960) also used the narrative device of claiming to be illustrated versions of readers' lives. The continuing appeal of stories from *la vida real* can be seen in the occasional use of the convention in contemporary Mexican comic books.[52] The stories may or may not be "true," but a reader, invented or actual, often is credited with suggesting them.[53] Of all the techniques that helped Mexicans read comic books as their own creations, "true-life" stories are a relic of the era of audience formation, and a continuing reminder of the close identification between readers and creators in Mexican comics.

Combining several strategies for audience building and maintenance, this page presents the photograph of cartoonist Guillermo Marin in several lights: as a gift to readers, as a means of reminding readers that they belong to a large group of Marin's fans, as a visual hint (given his leading-man pose) that Marin is a star, as a suggestion that Marin is a friend of the individual reader—perhaps a romantic friend—and as an opportunity to advertise his serial, "Cumbres de Ensueño." *Pepín*, no. 861, 22 July 1941, p. 51.

A month later, *Pepín* presented this photograph of José G. Cruz; like Marin, Cruz appears in the guise of young movie star—handsome and suave. *Pepín,* no. 889, 19 August 1941.

This cover of *Pepín*, no. 891, 21 August 1941, is a portrait of an idealized reader, writing—as so many readers evidently did—to Guillermo Marin's serial. It is also a reference to the current "Cumbres de Ensueño" story line, which began in Cuba; note the Havana return address on the envelope. It reinforces the idea that the stories told in this series were not invented but, rather, were reworked versions of readers' true-life adventures.

"We all have in our memories a shattered love! / and Señorita Eva Ochoa Lara of Mexico City has sent us her most interesting romantic story to be dramatized in these pages. / You can do the same . . ." Here, the reader's photograph literally has been placed in a cinematically romantic landscape. *Pepín*, no. 779, 1 May 1941, p. 58.

"IS OR WAS YOUR LIFE A TRAGEDY? . . . Then write it down simply as if you were chatting [with a friend] and send it to us!" This ad ran at least once in every issue for at least three years, usually with this illustration: the reader as movie star—young, white, wealthy, and perhaps, a *chica moderna*. *Paquito Grande*, no. 2037, 22 January 1950, p. 3.

Chapter Two

Home-Loving and without Vices

"Modernity," "Tradition," and the Comic Book Audience

 What is Mexico's national culture?

This question has been at the center of political and scholarly debate for most of the twentieth century. Indeed, beginning in the 1920s, it was the explicit project of at least some of Mexico's leaders to create a modern national culture by supporting mass media and high culture, controlling education, constructing a revolutionary mythos, and intervening into aspects of everyday life from cuisine to transportation. Although proponents emphasized the newness of such revolutionary enterprises, these projects also continued late-nineteenth-century positivist efforts to bring progress and order to Mexico—through urban planning, hygiene, architecture, and state control of poor people's behavior. Planners and politicians, both Porfirians and revolutionaries, claimed to be bringing a new nation into existence, thereby implying that before them there had been no nation at all except in the strictest legal sense.

Scholars of the 1940s through the 1960s more or less agreed that no single Mexican national culture existed. Some anthropologists—notably Robert Redfield—saw two static Mexican cultures, both presumably with deep roots in the past: one urban and modern, the other rural and traditional. Other scholars, like historian Luis Gonzalez y Gonzalez and anthropologist Guillermo Bonfil Batalla, have insisted on a Mexico of many near-independent regions, each requiring study on its own terms. These regionalist scholars tend to see national culture as an imposition from outside—if they see any national culture at all. To them, "deep" Mexico is Mexico state by state, or town by town; from their point of view, to look for cultural continuities at the national level is to participate in a process of state formation that may well be inimical to the interests of a particular region.

More recently, historians have begun looking for spatial and chronological continuities again. As Steve Stern puts it, the irony of the "*many Mexicos*" model is that, in the end, we start to notice "language and experience in common," among Mexico's regions, that is, "many *Mexicos*." Alan Knight suggests that these commonalities did not arise from the revolutionary attempt at creating a national culture, which he believes generally to have failed, but from the subsequent rise of a modern national culture created by the new consumerism that was another prominent feature of Mexican life after 1920.[1]

From the vantage point of consumer culture and mass media, there is yet another answer. A new national culture did develop after the Revolution, but it had two faces; one might even say it was comprised of two discourses. One was the set of ideas, arguments, attitudes, and metaphors related to modernity, progress, industrialization, and urbanity. The other was a discourse of tradition, conservatism, rural life, and Catholicism. Both of these discourses were equally rooted in the past, both were equally new, and both of them changed over time. Both were deployed by representatives of the government, and their opponents, at various times and for various purposes. These discourses developed in dialogue with each other over gender, work, and nation. "Tradition" did not precede "modernity" any more than modernity displaced tradition. Each required the other. And both were aspects of a single national culture that was developing throughout this period.

These discourses run through mass media in the postrevolutionary period and through the political debates that mass media inspired. Many commentators assumed that comic books—along with movies and radio—must be a modernizing force, and the language and imagery of progress certainly did figure prominently in *historietas*. Journalistic and scholarly descriptions of the comic book audience, too, came to rely on the language of modernity and urbanity. At the same time, even as comic books were elaborating on this discourse, the stories they told often agreed with and added to the discourse of conservatism. And when members of the audience got the chance to describe themselves, they chose the words, veiled assumptions, and values of "tradition."

The Experts Examine the Audience

The comic book audience was a subject of controversy almost from the moment it came into being. Mexican conservatives presumed that the *historietas* had a terrible effect on their readers, and in 1944 the Mexican state implicitly agreed by setting up a censorship office. Four decades later, critics Adriana Malvido and Teresa Martínez Arana wrote that this controversy had reinforced assumptions about the identity of comic book readers and the effects that mass media had on them: the "contempt that the majority of journalists, writers, students, researchers, art critics and government officials profess for this medium . . . leads to an underestimation of the readers, millions of Mexicans" and the image of the audience as "semi-literate."[2] This picture of the audience drew, as well, from an academic discourse that both lamented modernity and took for granted its inevitability as it described postrevolutionary city life.

Oscar Lewis (with Redfield, perhaps the most influential of all ethnographers of Mexico) saw a "culture of poverty" when he started to study Mexico City working-class life in 1943. He recorded the memories of two generations of a "typical" poor family in his 1961 *The Children of Sanchez*, noting that they had moved from the countryside—"a Mexico without cars, movies, radios or TV"—to a place and time formed by "post-Revolutionary values . . . individualism and social mobility." According to Lewis, however, these new values had destroyed the prospects of the family's second generation, for while the hardworking patriarch had "managed to raise himself out of the depths of poverty," his children had sunk back into it.[3] These new values were carried by the mass media, and comic books—alongside radio and cinema—were prominent in Lewis's account. He cites the fond memory of Sanchez's shiftless son, Roberto, that "my father had always brought copies of the comic magazines for Elena [the stepmother] and for us kids," thus unwittingly setting them up for corruption.[4] In the case of daughter Marta, whom Lewis depicts as having ruined her life through early promiscuity, her troubles began in her "tomboy" childhood when she took Tarzan as a hero.[5]

Following Lewis, other ethnographers, essayists, psychologists, journalists, and travel writers picked up on the theme of comic books as a corrupting force of modernization or, at the least, a defining trope of urban poverty. In 1984 a reporter for the *New York Times* repeated the received wisdom of liberal sociology when he presented a grim picture of comic book readers as innocent peasant girls newly arrived in the big city, working as maids, corrupted by mass media "exposing them . . . to different standards of morality," thereby rendering them vulnerable to premarital pregnancy and subsequent abandonment by family, employers, and lovers.[6]

More serious and sympathetic scholars, such as Larissa Lomnitz, drew less extreme conclusions; still, in 1977 she asserted that the "comics, photo-romances, [and] sports sheets" that she had seen everywhere in the "shantytown" she studied were "carriers of the values, norms, and aspirations of urban national culture."[7] Similarly, Jonathan Kandell connected urbanity, modernity, and media when he wrote of the growth in Mexico City's population between 1940 and 1970:

Migrants were pulled toward Mexico City by the communications revolution . . . reaching into the most isolated rural zones—that evoked an advanced, renumerative, and exciting way of life as an alternative to the static poverty of the countryside.[8]

In the 1970s, other scholars—influenced by the Chilean literary critic Ariel Dorfman—took up a new modulation of the older view of comic books as part of a modernizing wave of consumer culture, that is, as cheerleaders for capitalist materialism. They added that comic books were a form of counterrevolutionary political brainwashing. These sociologists, anthropologists, and critics identified capitalism with the United States and, thus, resistance to capitalism with nationalism.[9] For example, Dick Reavis described a migrant to Mexico City whom he encountered in 1977. This man had been a peasant activist when he lived in San Luis Potosí and, in a particularly dangerous moment, had drawn courage from imagining himself doing "what Kalimán [a popular comic book character at the time] would have done." Reavis records his own disappointment that this heroic man did not take "Fidel or Che" as a model instead.[10]

This position required some explanation, as the most popular *historietas* in Mexico were not the Disney comics that Dorfman studied in Chile but rather locally produced and descriptive, in their own way, of local conditions. Irene Herner, whose valuable 1979 study of the comic book and photonovel industries was informed by this anti-cultural-imperialist perspective, got around the difficulty by explaining that "the imperialist offensive" against Mexican sovereignty had found "native allies [in] Mexican private enterprise" who were helping to inject foreign values into the "spiritual and intellectual formation of the people."[11]

Such qualitative accounts had quantitative counterparts. Two surveys from mid-century participated in the academic construction of the comic book audience: in 1950, a Universidad Nacional Autonoma de México (UNAM) economist, Lazlo Radvayi, studied "readers addicted to comic-book Magazines"; and a professor of education at the Instituto Nacional de Pedagogia, Herculano Angel Torres Montalvo, surveyed "the literary tendencies of Mexican adolescents" in 1956.[12] Neither survey says much of interest about the audience for comic books and related periodicals, but both reveal a great deal about standard academic assumptions of the time. Both took teenagers as representative of the comic book audience as a whole while also being an especially problematic or endangered group, and assumed that mass media consumption was an urban phenomenon: so the surveys used Mexico City adolescents as the sample group to stand in for the entire audience. Both assumed that *historieta* readership would be inversely related to education, and expressed surprise when their results did not show any relationship at all. And both relied on hierarchical relationships, sending university students out to examine (generally) poorer and (always) younger subjects, while the oldest, most authoritative men designed the questions and interpreted the answers.[13]

In sum, the experts who examined and described comic book readers were all participating in a broader project: the development of a critique of Mexican modernity from within the discourse of modernity. These scholars and journalists viewed Mexico's industrialization and urbanization as inevitable, and beneficial overall, but they highlighted progress by pointing out what they viewed as its darker effects: the increasingly visible misery of poor people in the cities. At the same time, the experts sought to displace the blame for such misery from modernity itself or from modernity's beneficiaries (a group to which they belonged, after all). Instead, they moved back and forth between ascribing urban poverty to poor people's values and behavior (in this case, their passive willingness to consume too much cheap entertainment) and blaming the troublesome values and behavior on the cheap entertainment.

In comic books, as in Mexican cinema and recorded popular music in this era, the discourses of modernity and tradition formed primarily around the representation of women. The contrast between the (invented) past and the (imagined) future was played out in stories that valorized either *chicas modernas* or traditional women, but displayed both. The stereotypical traditional women stayed at home, preferably in rural areas. They subjected themselves to their husbands, fathers, and sons—or if necessary, they used deceit and manipulation to maintain the appearance of subservience. They never directly expressed a desire and avoided presenting themselves as sexual objects. *Chicas modernas,* on the other hand, obeyed nobody—except, perhaps, an employer. They were up-to-date consumers who tried to appear desirable and expected companionate marriages. They were impatient and could speak bluntly, but were honest, chaste before marriage and faithful afterward.

Mass media deployed both stereotypes as they participated in the development of both lines of cultural argument. After 1940, however—the year that marked the transition from the administration of Lázaro Cárdenas, which had relied heavily on the language of progress, to the Avila Camacho administration, which used both languages—the picture of this modern girl painted by most forms of media grew progressively uglier, while the traditional woman's portrait gained a far rosier tint. Only a few forms of popular culture (certain song genres, burlesque and variety theater, and to a certain extent, *pepines*) resisted this trend. An editorial in the *sinarquista* newspaper, *El Hombre Libre*, recognized the survival of the *chica moderna* in lyrics when it complained that "songs like 'Adelita,'" the most popular of all revolutionary ballads, "must result in moral and intellectual retardation."[14] In this period, *historieta* narratives invariably presented traditional womanhood in a flattering light. Yet they also continued to offer stories valorizing the *chicas modernas*.

It was well known that the ranks of comic book producers included some real-life *chicas modernas,* who wore suits to their offices, competed with men, and sometimes even went on working after marriage. The single most successful author of comic book scripts, Yolanda Vargas Dulché, was one such modern type. Her astonishing narrative gift lifted her from poverty to riches, beginning when—still a teenager—she submitted her short stories to newspapers. Among the many *historietas* she created were two of the most popular ever—*Memín Pingüin* and *Lágrimas, Risas y Amor;* she wrote scripts for hugely successful radio dramas, films, and *telenovelas;* and her work made her husband's comic book business, Editorial Argumentos, into one of Mexico's largest publishing companies (it is now directed by their sons).[15] Vargas Dulché also pushed the boundaries of female propriety, not only by working well past marriage and the birth of her children but also by leaving the country, as a young woman, to try her luck as a nightclub singer in Cuba.[16] Usually, the heroines of Vargas Dulché's narratives—good wives and mothers, downtrodden servant girls, hardworking clerks, and the like—did not lead lives as daring as their creator's own. For the most part, she reserved such adventures for her wonderful villainesses, like Raratonga, "a jungle queen . . . equally comfortable on her island and at the corporate headquarters of her transnational empire."[17]

The *chica moderna* as heroine was an important trope in *historietas* almost from their inception, especially in the work of *Pepín*'s most prolific writer, José G. Cruz. Whether or not Josefina was directly responsible for it, José Cruz's work in the 1930s and 1940s portrayed independent, active, powerful women as attractive and moral characters. Readers eavesdropped as they thought out loud about pressing gender questions.

In Cruz's "Adelita y las guerrillas," the *chica moderna* Nancy (the character who was born in Mexico City) often made the case for the pleasures of life as a modern girl while sometimes requiring rescue by the slightly more circumspect title character, Adelita. In a 1941 episode, the two friends discuss Nancy's romantic prospects in Adelita's luxurious Mexico City apartment as they prepare for an evening out on the town. Nancy criticizes her new beau:

> I never could fall in love with a man like him. . . . This man dreams of the classic peaceful home: to arrive at night after work and to glimpse from afar the tranquil form of his wife waiting for him in a white robe, with the newspaper ready for him in one hand and his slippers in the other. . . . He thinks of love the way my grandfather did, he is a gentleman and he will be the ideal man for it but . . . I DON'T WANT IT! I dream of love, but in another way, with a man with modern, advanced ideas. . . . The rhythm of the times requires that everything moves along with it; even matrimony itself, though still preserving some of its old characteristics, shows us new facets and a certain undeniable modernity.

Adelita replies:

> It could be that you are right in some ways, above all because you are a girl with ultra-modern ideas and character.

Nancy continues:

> If you knew where he takes me (sigh). . . . He takes me to visit his relatives!!!

Adelita:

> I can't believe it! What for?

Nancy:

> I don't know . . . maybe so that they can approve his choice. . . . His relatives asked me, no less, when I made my first communion and if my mother and father were legally married. . . . And now we are going to visit Aunt Carmela.

Adelita:

> B-but you won't go, will you? . . . So what will you tell [him]?

Nancy:

> That I want to go to the wrestling matches, even if I have to pay for the tickets.[18]

Here, José Cruz (perhaps with the help of his sister Josefina) envisions a marriage based on shared activities, sexual attraction, and emotional attachment, a marriage made solely in the interests of the couple involved. To this "ultra-modern" idea, the author opposed the "classic" picture of a marriage made to benefit the entire extended family, with the pleasure of the husband and wife being of much lower priority than the respectability and social status of everyone involved. The passage even implies some disdain for traditional womanhood, in the form of the man's snoopy relatives—though they stay out of sight. In this story, a woman can earn and spend her own money, present herself as a sexual object (throughout the scene, Adelita and Nancy are applying makeup, fixing each others' hair, and picking out fancy evening clothes), and speak disrespectfully of the older generation without feeling ashamed, losing her dignity, or suffering some horrible fate in the final chapter. In fact, the entire narrative, not only this passage, presents the case for this new picture of Mexican womanhood and new style of heterosexual pair bond: Nancy does indeed reject her old-fashioned swain.

The modernist content of "Adelita y las guerrillas" should not be exaggerated. Some of the strip's other female characters acted in more traditional ways. Adelita and Nancy were clearly portrayed as being at the far end of a spectrum of acceptable female behavior. Furthermore, they never appear to be frustrated by the limited possibilities open to women of their time and place, nor seriously annoyed by male behavior or attitudes; they enjoy being girls. And the narrative logic behind their endlessly drawn out engagements appears to have been the unexpressed idea that, when they finally married, they would have to stop having their fabulous adventures.

Yet, even with all these limits, it is easy to see how shocking the Adelita stories might have been, particularly since the pictures told the audience how attractive these new women could be, while the text constantly underlined their new, modern, antitraditional stance. Adelita also shared her name with the most famous song of the Mexican Revolution. Cruz meant her to be seen as profoundly Mexican, playing roles that other Mexican women had enacted before her, and connected to the most important events of the Mexican past. Her name told fans and critics alike that Adelita could not be dismissed as a foreigner.

Adelita and Nancy were not unique. Other popular comic and dramatic serials also presented continuing female characters who were pleasure-seeking rather than long-suffering, including the extremely successful Gabriel Vargas comic book, *La Familia Burrón*. Ten years after Nancy and Adelita held the conversation reproduced above, Vargas wrote a scene in which the middle-aged housewife, Doña Borala, mother of the comic-book Burrón family, proudly listed the priorities she shared with her teenage daughter: "We modern girls, *first* we learn to dance, flirt and smoke and then *later* to cook, to sew and to embroider."[19]

Comic book stories sometimes presented the modernist critique of urban poverty—characterizing the lives of poor people in the cities as chaotic, pleasure-seeking, and aimless—though not precisely in the scholarly mode of sociology and anthropology. A 1942 serial in *Pepín* showed a man infecting his girlfriend with an unspecified venereal disease through a single kiss, supposedly, although everyone in the story behaves as though this kiss stood for a sexual relationship. The couple dies, but the woman goes to heaven because she was "innocent" and "faithful."[20] This is an extreme case; comics rarely mentioned sexually transmitted diseases. Premarital pregnancy, however, was so common a plot device that it appears in perhaps half of all romance or true-life-story *historietas* after 1950.

Whether they emphasized the pleasures or dangers that modernity held for Mexican women, comic book narratives helped to define what modernity meant. Like movies and radio dramas, theater and dance music, and tabloid journalism and women's magazines, *historietas* showed readers how "modern girls" looked and acted, what might be expected of them, and what they might expect from the world. But even as they were elaborating on this image, the comics were also participating in the construction of a counternarrative of "tradition."

Old and New Stories in One: An Exemplary Narrative

The experts' negative assessments of comic book readers came from within the Mexican discourse of modernity. But the comic books themselves were considerably more complex in the assumptions they made about their own audience. They spoke both the language of tradition and modernity; in fact, they often managed to deploy both discourses in a single story. This can be seen in a close reading of a single serial from mid-century: "El Viejo Nido" (*The old nest*), printed in *Pepín* in brief daily installments between Sunday, July 24, 1949 and Tuesday, December 20, 1949.[21]

"El Viejo Nido" was drawn by a longtime contributor to *Pepín*, Guillermo Marin; it was written by Fernando Casillas V., whose name never appeared in the comic book before this serial began publication. Nothing distinguished "El Viejo Nido": no contests were associated with it, no advertisements mentioned it, and it was featured on *Pepín*'s cover only 8 times in the 150 issues in which it was published. Nor was it exceptionally titillating: there were no shocking sex scenes and violence consisted merely of punches and slaps, mostly in a boxing ring. "El Viejo Nido" was as close to typical as any of the hundreds of serialized narratives published in the daily comic books between 1934 and 1950.

Much of the serial's content was dictated by its form. Like the other serials running in *Pepín* at the time, "El Viejo Nido" appeared in daily episodes of five to seven pages, most divided horizontally into two panels. Each episode, therefore, rarely contained more than twelve panels. This allowed room for a maximum of twenty lines of dialogue per installment, and often far less.[22] The story had little space for verbal flourishes; instead, the pictures had to convey the nuances. Marin's illustrations informed the audience of the characters' personalities, explained what the social status of each household was, and announced the precise location of every scene. The words of "El Viejo Nido" might be pared down to a dry minimum, but its rich visual detail more than made up for any deficiencies.

"El Viejo Nido" tells a complex tale. Its complications include a large number of characters: two protagonists, eight important secondary figures, and innumerable "bit players."[23] Moreover, several secondary characters abruptly switch from being virtuous to evil (or vice versa) in the course of the action. The number of locations adds to the difficulty. The pace of the story, too, can be confusing: sometimes the events of a single day occupy several installments and sometimes months of fictional time seem to have passed in the gap between two episodes.

But in other ways, "El Viejo Nido" is quite simple. The visual and verbal language has been stripped of all complexity. The script, while perfectly grammatical, employs the most basic Spanish. It avoids subjunctive and compound tenses and uses a sharply limited vocabulary.[24] The pictures, as well, contribute to the ease with which the story may be followed. They never show one thing while the script talks about another. The artist uses a few readily understandable icons—hearts, question marks, flying drops of sweat—but otherwise eschews abstraction. The human figures and inanimate objects in "El Viejo Nido" are realistically proportioned, and drawn with the proper perspective and shading to give them a solid, believable appearance. Like the words, the pictures require very little effort (or experience with reading comics) to be understood.[25]

The plot structure of "El Viejo Nido," too, is not complicated. Readers learn of events in the exact order in which they are supposed to have happened. There are no flashbacks, flash-forwards, or dream sequences. There is scarcely a "meanwhile."[26] Yet the story of "El Viejo Nido," though told in an easily comprehensible form, is convoluted and long. At the same time that the style betrays a certain anxiety over the naïveté of the audience, the length and richness of the story reveal great faith in the readers' patience and memory.

These omissions and inclusions, simplifications and convolutions, were absolutely typical of the comic book serials that were so popular in mid-century Mexico. What do they say about the audience? The creators of "El Viejo Nido" produced a tale for unskilled readers and viewers, who had some experience at listening to long stories. And the serial (which carefully incorporated scenes of settled domestic life and youthful passion, boxing matches and fashion shows, life in high-rise office buildings and rural shacks) reached for an audience that stretched across lines of age, class, and sex.

The drama of "El Viejo Nido" revolved around a series of family crises caused by a move from country to city, a transition that nearly everyone involved in the periodical industry at this time had made. Writers, artists, entrepreneurs: all lived and worked in Mexico City, though few had been born there; all were struggling upward from poverty toward middle-class status or even the riches that a few of them attained; and all, as the industry was so new, were engaged in a different business from that of their parents.[27] The men and women who produced Mexican comic books encouraged their readers to identify with the characters and producers of *historietas*, but such identification ran in the other direction, too: to some extent, they told the stories they knew.

Three issues—gender relations, representations of modernity, and anxieties over migration—are central to "El Viejo Nido" (and, by extension, to all comic book tales from this period). Readers should come to these topics with a clear understanding of how heavily they weigh in the story as a whole. Therefore, a recounting of much of the plot of "El Viejo Nido" is in order here.

The serial begins in a small town. Other locations will be carefully specified, but this fictional place remains merely "a village [*pueblito*] in the interior of the Republic," which might be any reader's hometown.[28] Outside the front door of a tiny house surrounded by identical houses, José—a handsome young man in a suit—is making his farewells to his parents and home, as his "adventurous character" has impelled him away.[29] His gray-haired parents bless him, warn him against bad companions, and exhort him to behave well. José's mother, Julia, complains that he was the last of their children to leave—"Alvaro is there at the university in Mexico City. . . . Elvira got married"—while her husband, Marcial, reassures her that, at least, "every day we love each other more."[30]

"El Viejo Nido," however, does not revolve around José's story; readers will not see him again until the final crisis of the plot. Instead, the next episode introduces Don Refugio Suarez, a banker "with a heart of stone."[31] He will foreclose on the old couple's house unless Alvaro begins sending money home to repay the debt his parents incurred in financing his education. At the banker's house, Julia meets his beautiful, virtuous daughter, Consuelo. Consuelo, who immediately befriends the visiting debtor, asks her father to forgive the loan; he shouts back, "Get to the kitchen!"[32]

The next day, Marcial comes home with a young man named Luis. He tries to explain what Julia has already guessed:

> Neither in my youth nor when I entered adulthood was I any kind of saint. I had many faults which I am not going to try and excuse, as these are things that now have no cure. . . . I met a woman and—I don't know if I loved her or not but—the fact is that Luis— [33]

Julia interrupts: she knows Luis is his son. She has been feigning ignorance for years in order to avoid "embittering our lives."[34] Marcial wants to introduce his son into their household, since the young man's mother has died; Julia is dubious but accedes graciously to her husband's wishes.

Luis immediately alarms them by announcing that he intends to earn his living as a boxer. Once again, however, "El Viejo Nido" defies expectations: it does not become a story about generational conflict, it does not require Luis to defy his family in pursuit of his dream. Instead, the young man quickly finds work to help support Marcial and Julia, and he does more than his share of the work at home, too. By contrast, the married daughter Elvira visits only to complain about her own children and her servants. She tells her father that Luis is "a son of yours but not a brother of mine."[35] Her visiting brother Alvaro adds, "If you were to recognize all the children you have had, I suppose that this house would not have room for them all."[36]

When a doctor warns Marcial that too much hard work will kill him, Julia takes a job as a seamstress while Luis cooks the meals at home and works in a shoe factory. One night, the dutiful but ambitious young man sneaks out of the house to enter a boxing match. He meets the local boxing promoter, Chato, and with his advice, first beats the local champion and then a professional in a nearby town. Chato greets him on his triumphant return, insisting that he take to the road as a traveling boxer. Luis, indecisive, returns to his house, only to find that Marcial has died.

Elvira and Alvaro argue over who will take charge of their mother now. Julia wants to stay in her house with Luis. Alvaro, however, tells Luis to go.

Outside, Luis encounters Consuelo, who tells him that she will not enter the little house. She fears Alvaro, whose attentions she has already rejected. Alvaro and Elvira finally depart; although Consuelo reunites Julia and Luis, he decides to take up Chato's offer of a boxing tour. Consuelo bids him farewell with a tender kiss.

Luis wins bouts all over Mexico. Alvaro remains in the village with his brokenhearted mother, who believes that Luis has forgotten her. (In fact, Luis sends money and letters, but Alvaro intercepts them.) Elvira abruptly moves to Mexico City when her husband finds a job there, happy to "leave this filthy little town."[37] Her mother admits tearfully, "If I were to leave this town, I would die." Alvaro retorts, "You wish that everyone else would stay here too; but . . . there must be progress."[38]

Alvaro, too, plans to go, but he hopes first to marry Consuelo. He drunkenly tries to kiss her in front of a group of his male friends. She slaps his face and his friends laugh. Swearing revenge, Alvaro bets his friends that he can spend the night with her. He forges a note from Julia, saying that she is ill. Consuelo, defying her father's orders, rushes to Julia's house, but she is away for the night. Alvaro locks Consuelo in and hides on the patio to await his friends' arrival at dawn, in time to see her run out. Soon, the whole town believes that Consuelo has disgraced herself. Alvaro departs for Mexico City to begin his career as a lawyer, leaving his mother to face the wrath of banker Suarez, Consuelo's father.

The banker calls in Julia's debt, selling her home and forcing her to move into his house as a servant. There, she is humiliated and starved. But Consuelo assures her that Luis has not forgotten them. Even though Luis has not contacted Consuelo, fearing that to do so would anger her father, the young woman believes his promise that once he has earned a world championship (and his fortune), he will return. Julia finds consolation in religion, but she grows so hungry that she begs food from the neighbors. Someone hands her meat wrapped in an old newspaper; too tired to read it, she misses the photograph of Alvaro, with a pretty blond member "of the most distinguished metropolitan society" on his arm.[39] The family's fragmentation is now complete.

Luis, meanwhile, concentrates on his career. Since Julia never received his letters, she has not written back. Assuming that she "prefers to forget me," Luis trusts that Alvaro has remained with Julia to take care of her.[40] Thus, Luis is infuriated when Alvaro visits him in Chato's Mexico City gym. When Alvaro flees, Luis finds his office address in the phone book and confronts him. Alvaro claims that he supports Julia. He teases Luis about Consuelo's ruined reputation, giving Luis a version of the story that leaves out his own part in the matter. Luis refuses to believe it, but his ruined concentration leads him to lose boxing matches.

Chato traces his boxer's decline to the encounter with Alvaro and returns to the village to discover the truth. He finds Julia, by chance, on the street. She is delighted to hear about Luis's career, and reassures Chato of Consuelo's virtue and loyalty. Wishing not to worry Luis on the eve of his championship bout, she also claims that Alvaro is supporting her and that she is living comfortably in her old house. Chato repeats all this to Luis, who decides not to visit them until he has gained the championship.

Back in the city, Alvaro is arrested for extorting money from "unwary people" in his law practice.[41] Reading this in the newspaper, Luis rushes to the jail to bail him out. Alvaro, shamed by the goodness of Luis, confesses to his half brother that all the gossip about Consuelo was only the result of his trickery. He also accepts Luis's money to give to Julia. Luis goes away satisfied, but Alvaro thinks, "Luis believes that I am going to change, but I am not very sure. Even I myself don't know yet."[42]

Meanwhile, Julia collapses from overwork. As she lies near death, the evil banker orders his daughter, Consuelo, to "throw her out on the street."[43] Consuelo arranges for an ambulance and sends a letter begging Luis to return. Her outraged father chases the ambulance down the street through a rainstorm, then returns home and knocks Consuelo unconscious. He is suddenly stricken with pneumonia, however, brought on— the doctor explains—by rage and wet clothing. Suarez dies soon after, but torments Consuelo even from the grave: his will disinherits her, and she is left penniless and homeless.

In New York City, Luis wins his championship bout. Afterward, José, the half brother whose departure set the whole story in motion, visits Luis in his dressing room, simply to congratulate someone from his distant hometown. José is ignorant of all that has happened since his departure, but the two men soon realize their connection and form a friendship. Back in his hotel room, Luis finds Consuelo's desperate letter. He insists on their immediate departure, bringing José with him despite his protest, "I have a job here."[44]

On returning to Mexico City, Luis punches Alvaro in the head as punishment for his failure to support Julia. Then Luis sends Alvaro to collect

Elvira. At last, all three of Julia's children, along with Luis and Chato, take the train back home, where—to their horror—they find their old house boarded up and for sale. Julia, meanwhile, wakes in the hospital to discover that her illness has passed. Regretful, she asks, "Oh God, why did you not take me to you? I will only suffer again."[45]

Suddenly, her three children appear to promise her, in Alvaro's words, that "all the sufferings that I caused you, I will change to happiness—I will never be separated from you again!"[46] Luis, having repurchased Julia's home, joins the happy family in the hospital. He announces that soon Julia will have another daughter as well, and Julia replies that Consuelo, too, already "has treated me as if she were my child."[47] Alvaro assures his mother that both Luis and Consuelo have pardoned him, thus resolving her last anxiety: "I see that you have repented," Julia says.[48]

At the doorway of the family home, Consuelo and Luis kiss passionately. The last frame of the serial pulls away from the happy couple to a shot of the whole house with a sunrise behind it and the caption, "Once again there was warmth in THE OLD NEST!"[49]

Gender, Family, Location, and Class in "El Viejo Nido"

Four sets of ideas organize the plot of "El Viejo Nido": gender, kinship, location, and social class. The creators of the serial generated their narrative from the contradictions among these hierarchies of values, and the plot is resolved happily when the demands of gender roles, family duties, geographic boundaries, and social class cease to conflict with each other.

In the story, the limits on female expression and behavior are not quite as strict as they might appear on first reading. Even the bad sister, Elvira, seems to submit passively to the whims of the men, as do the good female characters. Male characters, on the other hand, act as if they were free from most social constraints: they move around the country and across international borders, they take up and abandon jobs at will, they express anger with their fists, and they engage in extramarital sex. They may even rape with impunity, if we see Alvaro's destruction of Consuelo's reputation as a veiled depiction of that crime. This apparent freedom holds for villains like Don Suarez, heroes like Luis and Marcial, and characters whose moral stature changes during the narrative, like Alvaro.

Yet gendered behavior in the serial actually conforms to more subtle patterns. All the women maintain a facade of obedience to their male relations, but they seem to feel no compunctions about acting in their own interests as long as that facade is maintained. For example, Consuelo put her reputation at risk by disobeying her father's command to stay away from Julia's house, but the serial presents this as a sign of the girl's virtues—her compassion for the bereaved, her respect for the aged and the dead—rather than a demonstration of her foolishness. Julia concealed her knowledge of her husband's second family for twenty years, but her deceptiveness is portrayed as a kind of virtue, too. Elvira excuses her departure from her parents' village by saying that she must follow her husband to Mexico City, but actually she is thrilled to leave: her display of obedience is a transparent disguise for her selfishness. Having reformed, Elvira vows to return home for good, presumably abandoning her husband—and this, too, is depicted in a positive light.

The ability of female characters to maneuver within a seemingly severe code of gender expectations depends on their places within a class hierarchy and a family circle. Consuelo, for instance, has remarkable latitude despite her strict father, until he dies and she loses both the protection of a family and her high social position. Then, she must mourn both her father and, more important, her new status as a woman "alone in the world! Alone! Alone!"[50] As she tearfully recognizes, the loss of her unlovable, tyrannical father also signifies a substantial loss of autonomy. Conversely, the male characters are less free than they appear. They have only as much autonomy as is conferred on them by their places in nongendered hierarchies of kinship and class: their behavior is controlled by their age, their family responsibilities, and their social status.

The bonds of kinship, and the debts owed by the young to the old and the old to the young, underpin many of the male characters' deeds in "El Viejo Nido." Young, single, and childless, Alvaro faces few limits until he is forced to recognize his duty toward his widowed mother. Alvaro rightly points out that his virtuous, respectable father also had a wild youth. But Marcial's youthful freedom was finite. Once he had children, he had to provide for them, including his illegitimate son. Becoming responsible for a younger generation put new constraints on Marcial's actions. Señor Suarez grows increasingly evil in the course of "El Viejo Nido," and this transformation is signaled through the banker's interactions with his daughter, which begin with rigid but appropriate concern for her reputation and end in his refusal of shelter to her. Throwing Consuelo and Julia (an older woman and, as a servant, also a person in a kinship-like relation to the banker) out of his house, the banker enacts the ultimate abdication of his family responsibilities.

Like kinship, social class controls men's behavior in this serial. Alvaro, like Elvira, finds his hometown stifling, but he cannot simply leave his family behind. Instead, again like Elvira, he justifies his absence from home by appealing to a set of values other than the ones that place kinship ties at the center of moral life. Elvira excuses her departure by citing her subordinate place in a gender hierarchy, whereas Alvaro claims the right to leave on the grounds of his shifting class position: his parents must support his migration to Mexico City because there he will become a lawyer. The virtuous Luis makes the same choice as his half siblings. The narrative presents his absence as painful to the women left behind, but Luis's moral stature is never in doubt. Indeed, the happy ending to "El Viejo Nido" depends on the money Luis earns in his championship bout. On the other hand, sometimes kinship matters more than class, as with José's abrupt (if reluctant) decision to quit his New York job in order to take care of his mother back home—a decision presented as being morally sound.

And the narrative sets up an opposition between city and countryside that is finally resolved in favor of the country, but without ever presenting one side or the other as unambiguously good or bad. The city (both Mexico City and the more dimly rendered New York City) allows space for corruption, but truly desperate poverty is found in the country. True love—both familial and romantic—is part of country life, but excitement and progress belong to the city. The characters who spend time in cities are smarter and more sophisticated, but the characters who remain in the *pueblito* are wiser. To the extent that the narrative points a moral about location, it is a double one: virtue and lasting happiness are to be found in the country, but life requires movement between city and country.

In sum, the characters of "El Viejo Nido" juggle these four sets of values, which inform their decisions, shape their lives, and control the plot in which they are enmeshed. These values—hierarchies of responsibility and deference organized by gender, kinship, location, and social position— offer no support to liberal notions of individuality nor to socialist ideals of egalitarian community. "El Viejo Nido," read closely, plays with both the modernist and traditionalist discourses that were shaping Mexican culture—and Mexican politics—at mid-century. It valorizes both city and country, change and stability, loyalty to kin and personal ambition, economic mobility and geographic immobility.

Although the engine driving the plot is the conflict among the story's four sets of values—an engine that shuts down when the contradictions are all resolved—the serial also suggests that these painful conflicts should never have existed in the first place. They are called into being by the serial's positions in time and space: its locations in the cities stand in for modernity; its location in the village becomes the site of tradition.

Modernity in The Old Nest

The version of progress in "El Viejo Nido" is not simply the changed gender roles and expectations that were so evident in "Adelita y las guerrillas." And this story used the imagery and language of modernity in quite a different manner than Oscar Lewis and the other academic experts on the urban poor and their relationship to consumer culture. Both the experts and the creators of the serial see the new, impoverished migrants from country to city as naive and impressionable, subject to corruption and even ruin. Both see that the new technology—especially in the areas of transportation, communication, and entertainment—is changing the lives of the people they depict. But though the anthropologists and sociologists generally decry these changes, the creators of "El Viejo Nido" sometimes view them as neutral and occasionally paint them as good. Moreover, while Lewis and Redfield, in particular, associated modernity with urbanity, the artists and writers of *los pepines* were equally sensitive to the class-bound distribution of new machinery and consumer goods in the countryside.

The modern world enters "El Viejo Nido" in ways both obvious and subtle, often in connection with new forms of entertainment and communication. The poverty of Julia's house is contrasted with the wealth of the Suarez home by comparing oil lamps and electric lights, but the banker's illumination is meager compared to the glaring spotlights that mark all of Luis's boxing matches. The sport's modernity is also embedded in the way that microphones, wires, and other tools of the radio trade surround every ring. Telephone booths and telephone books play a prominent role in the story; so do telegrams. Progress wears many faces in "El Viejo Nido," not all of them friendly. Medical technology appears first with the X rays that foreshadow Marcial's death, then with the ambulance that precipitates Don Suarez's attack of pneumonia, and finally, with the injections that fail to save him. Even modernity in foodstuffs receives some attention in a scene where Alvaro, having spit out the cup of chocolate that his mother had made for him, also complains, "Beans for me? But mother, only poor country people eat this stuff!"[51] Still, this is intended to show his bad character, rather than suggest that city cuisine is any improvement on country cooking.

New technology appears in conjunction with new forms of work. We never see Marcial at work in the fields or Julia laboring at home, but factory and office scenes abound. Marin depicts Alvaro's office equipment—switchboard, intercoms, typewriters—in exact detail. Luis, before becoming a professional boxer, takes a job producing shoes; his sewing machine, along with the factory inside and out, is the subject of several careful renderings. Buses and trolleys speed the characters from workplace to home; these, too, appear far more frequently and in far more detail than would be strictly necessary to convey the action of "El Viejo Nido."

Indeed, most prominent among the images of modern life are depictions of new forms of transportation. In the beginning of the story, José leaves home simply by walking away. Luis, however, first departs by bus— we see him buy the ticket—and eventually is seen traveling in taxis, trains, limousines, and airplanes. City streets in "El Viejo Nido" are crowded with cars, trucks, and buses. Scenes set in New York City even show the tracks of an elevated train. The serial's visual emphasis on transportation technology reflects a deeper connection between modernity and mobility—which was not, of course, unique to the creators of "El Viejo Nido." To identify progress with transportation was, by 1949, a habit of thought in Mexico with a history at least seventy years long.[52]

In the serial, mobility is not a question of the convenient movement of trade goods or a conspicuous display of middle-class leisure; transit stands for work-related, semipermanent migration. As such, improved modes of transportation are only partially a cause for modernist (or nationalist) celebration. The buses, trains, planes, taxis, and limousines appear slick, powerful, and attractive, but they are used in connection with some disastrous event. Marcial dies on the eve of Luis's return from his first long bus ride. Luis takes an airplane home from New York to rescue Julia and Consuelo; we do not see his (presumably happier) ride to the United States. Modern, rapid transportation signified both improved standards of living and the anguish of separation from home and family. Both these responses are part of the multiple representations of travel in "El Viejo Nido."

The name of the serial itself suggests half of its attitude toward migration—for a new generation to leave a small town is necessary and inevitable. Alvaro and Elvira might be selfish and greedy, but when they express their disdain for their *pueblito* and their intention to leave, their parents agree. Yet much of the rest of the tale, beginning with its very first scene, expresses confusion, anger, and sorrow at the absence of young people from the towns where they were born.

Some of the unhappy emotions attached to migration are given an objective focus through the difficulties of communication between the departed young people and the older generation at home. Nobody ever makes a long-distance phone call in the story, nor are any telephones visible outside the big cities: messages are sent around the little town by street urchins who carry notes. Mail, though reliable, depends on the ability of the recipient to read it. On countless occasions, Julia misses important news because someone steals a letter or note meant for her, or because she fails to notice a crucial newspaper story, devices that convey the frustrations of trying to stay in touch with distant, illiterate relatives. Even with the best intentions, sometimes loved ones simply disappear into the larger world, like José, who only rediscovers his kinsman Luis through coincidence.

The creators of "El Viejo Nido" remain strictly neutral on the moral questions raised by migration. They portray the situation of the serial's end, with all the family happily living with or nearby each other in the town of their birth, as the most desirable state. Yet they also use transparently implausible plot devices to help their characters arrive at this position. Through the unlikeliness of the happy ending, the authors suggest that most endings will be unhappy; they recognize, that is, that most of the audience will not arrive at the domestic bliss achieved by Doña Julia and her children but instead are fated to be separated and scattered by the forces of technological and economic progress.

Migration brings the characters from "El Viejo Nido" into a new world filled with novel objects and locations, but one where the same moral hierarchies apply as in the countryside. It is not city life, but the tension between the villages and the cities, that leads to distress and confusion. Spatial mobility acts here as a metaphor for social mobility: conflict is engendered when the characters literally *do not know their place*. "El Viejo

Nido," therefore, can be read as fulfilling both a practical and moral role. In practical terms, it acts as an advice manual for readers who are moving from countryside to city, guiding them through some of the most important and incomprehensible requirements of urban life. In moral terms, the serial serves to anchor readers in a conservative set of values; it tells them that the hierarchies of gender, kinship, and class that they grew up with will govern social interactions in large cities as well as tiny villages, even if spatial mobility creates (or exposes) contradictions within that set of values.[53]

Hogareña y Sin Vicios: The Audience Defines Itself

Of all the groups of people who argued about the dangers, pleasures, and profits of comic books in Mexico, the audience had the least audible voice. They spoke, for the most part, only with their centavos and pesos. Little remains of the contemporary responses of these consumers. Comic book companies appear not to have bothered with market surveys nor to have preserved reader letters.[54] Traces of the readers, however, can be found in the comic books themselves: in the readers' photos, drawings, and stories *de la vida real* that helped to fill so many pages.[55] And when we turn to the one space in comic books where readers did speak directly to each other, we find them telling some very dramatic (if radically simplified) tales about themselves.

Readers were often given the chance to publish lonely hearts or pen-pal advertisements in their favorite periodicals. The truthfulness of their voices need not concern us. The underlying values and habits of thought that were expressed—even in such a mediated form—clearly and consistently speak through the discourse of tradition that Mexican media helped to invent in this era. The discourse of modernity was not the one that readers chose to use in describing themselves and their world.

Lonely hearts advertisements first appeared around 1945 in a women's magazine, *Confidencias,* that also sometimes ran photonovel-style romances. They entered the comics in 1948, in *Paquito Grande,* a *historieta* that specialized in romantic serials. Free to both advertisers and respondents, they were a bargain as well for the publishers, as they provided a page of interesting filler in every issue for only the price of setting type and forwarding mail. And, in some cases, they must have engendered intense reader loyalty, for they occasionally helped to create happily married couples (the magazines would, of course, print wedding photos and even anniversary pictures), and in at least one instance, they really did reunite long-estranged family members—oddly enough, the "Sanchez" family studied by Lewis was brought together with some Veracruz cousins thanks to an ad in *Pepín*.[56]

Such pages of personal ads have been one of the most popular and enduring features of Mexican comic books. The appeal of the ads in *Paquito Grande* can be seen in the prominent place that the lonely hearts page held for at least three and a half years: the inside front cover. During and after the era of *Paquito Grande*'s greatest popularity, similar features ran in *Historietas* (1954–55, under the title "My Heart in an Envelope") and many other comic books. They can still be seen today, on a greatly reduced scale, in *Libro Semanal*, *Libro Pasional*, and other romance comics.

Lonely hearts advertisers sometimes shaped their brief texts into chapters from the romance serials. They represent themselves, but they also represent stock characters; they tell pieces of their life stories, but they also retell tales that they and their readers have read many times before. Here is one:

> I am Mexican, white, average height, of ordinary cultivation, 20 years old and without vices. I find myself locked up in the Mexico City penitentiary, and to remake my life I need the hand of an understanding little lady who would send me a little letter to fill me with courage and spirit.[57]

And another:

> I am looking for a friendly heart who could relieve my hours of loneliness. I am a young man but I have failed in life. If there is a reader who feels the same need for a soul like her own, write me, you will not regret it. I come from the state of Puebla.[58]

And a third:

> I want to establish a correspondence with a gentleman no older than 38, it would not matter if he was a widower with one or two darling little children as long as he had no vices, was moderately cultivated, hardworking and honest. I am 25 and not pretty, but I am friendly and have a jovial, sincere nature. I want the gentleman who writes to have the aim

of forming a firm household, which is what I pray for. I ask for your absolute sincerity and am not looking for adventures.[59]

These writers seem to be hoping to turn their lives into *historietas* as much as, perhaps more than, they yearn for companionship.

Moving beyond individual cases, the aggregate of the personal ads contains equally suggestive evidence about the mentality of the comic book audience. Between 1949 and 1952 (the years for which some issues can be found in the Hemeroteca Nacional's archive), *Paquito Grande* ran ten to twenty such advertisements in every issue, producing a completely new page twice a week. The tens of thousands of resulting advertisements cannot be taken as unvarnished fact, of course.[60] Moreover, the advertisers were a self-selected group of unattached readers, unlikely to be completely representative of the entire comic book audience. Still, these advertisements do offer a blurry collective self-portrait. Their language reveals what the advertisers, as a group, believed desirable traits to be in men and women.[61] Almost all the ads followed a strict formula and used a limited vocabulary. (This rigid form is all the more remarkable since the ads were unedited and cost nothing.) Looking at the words that advertisers choose to describe themselves and their ideal mates, certain conclusions about their values, ambitions, and worldviews become inescapable.

Religion mattered deeply; 58 percent of the ads displayed this concern by either announcing that the advertiser was Catholic or requesting that the respondent be, or both (the percentage is slightly higher for women and lower for men). Of course, far more than 58 percent of the Mexican population was Catholic at mid-century; anyone reading the advertisement could have been assumed to be Catholic. The point for these advertisers was not simply to state the obvious, but to show that they took their religion seriously—despite their involvement with comic books. As the next chapter will demonstrate, the leaders of the Catholic Church had long since created a connection in the public discourse between reading comic books and various forms of sinfulness. The advertisers who called themselves Catholics, or were looking for Catholic partners, knew that and were trying to disassociate themselves from such a connection.[62]

Moral character, along with religious affiliation, was the most important descriptive category to advertisers. "Formal"—that is, capable of behaving within the bounds of propriety—was a desirable trait for 43 percent of both males and females in describing either themselves or a mate. Other moral concerns were expressed in highly gendered language. An attractive man would be "without vices" (*sin vicios*) (61 percent of the men described themselves in this manner, while 54 percent of the women sought this in their ideal partner), and "hardworking" (*trabajador* or *muy trabajador*) (similarly, this was a self-description for 41 percent of the men and a desirable trait in a mate for 28 percent of the women). Some women (16 percent) also hoped for a "gentleman" (*caballero*). All of these terms had an economic dimension: for instance, men *sin vicios* were men, very specifically, who did not smoke or drink, and therefore, could be trusted not to waste family money.

Women's moral character mattered, too, although, the terms that described them or that they picked to describe themselves had no economic implications. Women were supposed to be "simple" (*sencilla*) (a self-description for 22 percent of the women and a trait in an ideal partner for 35 percent of the men), and "home-loving" (*hogareña*) (again, 24 percent of the women described themselves this way and 24 percent of the men described a desirable respondent as such). A few men hoped to find a "kindly" (*amable*) (6 percent), "agreeable" (*agradable*) (12 percent, with 19 percent of women describing themselves), and "affectionate" (*cariñosa*) (13 percent) mate.

Words that indirectly suggest social status overlapped the category of words dealing with morality and religion. An astonishing total of 78 percent of the female advertisers and 60 percent of the males specified their degree of education by employing some version of a phrase with strong connotations of social class: 68 percent of the women and 48 percent of the men presented themselves as "cultivated" (*culto/a* or *de buena cultura*); 12 percent of the men and 10 percent of the women advertised themselves as "not too cultivated" (*poco culto/a*). Similarly, the 18 percent who described themselves as "well-mannered" (*educado/a*) were matched by the 28 percent who called themselves or their perfect mate "humble" or "from humble beginnings" (*humilde* or *de cuña humilde*). Two percent of all respondents went so far as to label themselves "*pobre,*" and all of them were also looking for a "poor" mate. Advertisers, as a group, seemed less concerned about inflating their status than they were with finding a match neither too far above nor too far beneath them socially.

Advertisers in "Eslabones Espirituales" (Spiritual bonds) cared about looks only to the extent that appearance reflected class. Twenty-nine percent of them either felt themselves to be, or wanted someone who was, "presentable" (*bien parecido/a*), while only 9 percent called themselves or their dream date "beautiful" or "handsome" (*guapo/a*). Three percent of the men even described themselves as "ugly" (*feo*); similarly, 13 percent of the women said that they were "neither pretty nor ugly" (*ni fea ni bonita*). Their concern here seemed to be maintaining modesty while still providing potential mates with some identifying information. The fine details of skin and hair that place Mexicans in their precise spot on the racial map frequently appear in these ads, as with the 11 percent who reveal their hair texture and the 30 percent who use some variation of "brown-skinned" (*moreno/a*) to portray themselves. Another indication of the class status of most *Paquito Grande* readers is that only 9 percent of the men and 7 percent of the women called themselves "white," and a mere 2 percent of both sexes hoped for a "white" mate.

Kinship and marital status had a less consistent vocabulary than other important descriptive categories found in these personal ads; still, roughly a third of the ads referred to children or previous spouses in some way. Nineteen percent of the women announced that they wanted a man "without other ties" (*sin compromisos*), but only 5 percent of the men described themselves that way. Six percent of the men identified themselves as "unmarried" (*soltero*), but less than 1 percent of the women used the feminine form, *soltera*, with its connotation of spinsterhood, to describe themselves. Two percent of the men and 1 percent of the women said that they were widowed. Three percent of the women said that they already had children, while only 1 percent of the men announced that they wanted a childless mate. Conversely, 4 percent of the men specifically requested a "widow or divorced woman." A small number sought to reassure potential mates of their good intentions: 4 percent of the men and 3 percent of the women wrote that they were "not in search of adventures," with a specifically sexual connotation, while 3 percent of the men and 2 percent of the women declared their goals in placing the advertisement to be "serious" or "matrimonial," and another 3 percent of the men and 1 percent of the women said that they wanted "to form a home" with a new mate.

Choice of profession or leisure activity mattered little to this group. Unlike descriptions of appearance, education, or behavior, words referring to work or play did not seem to serve the secondary function of implying social class. Fewer than 10 percent of the men and 4 percent of the women mentioned what they did for a living. (Another 4 percent of the men and

1 percent of the women said that they were students.) The range of employment mentioned was quite wide, however, from small business owners and factory workers to lawyers and accountants. Hobbies and recreation mattered even less to advertisers. Only 3 percent mentioned an interest in movies; another 2 percent said they liked to dance; and 4 percent enjoyed sports. Not a single advertiser said that he or she read comic books.

This collective self-portrait should be read against the stories that *Paquito Grande* published, narratives from other comic books (such as "El Viejo Nido"), and the criticisms of comic books that were raised during the first censorship campaign. The central objection to the *pepines* was that they contributed to the corruption of the nation by showing sexually active women as well as romances that broke the bounds of propriety in various ways. *Paquito Grande* did describe such behavior, in its decorous and moralistic manner. Premarital pregnancies, usually involving secondary characters, often advanced the plots of its serials. The motor of many stories in the comic book was a relationship between inappropriate people, such as employees and employers, who insisted on making a life together despite opposition from society in general and their families in particular. Female characters often held jobs, ranging from domestic work and clerical work to factory work, waitressing, and teaching. Such comic book romantic narratives might be read as valorizing economic independence for women, affectionate relationships based on shared interests, and romantic love and sexual pleasure even for poor women, as well as across class and race lines.

The readers of *Paquito Grande* who placed lonely hearts advertisements, to judge by their own words, had absorbed none of these values. Instead, they clung to the moral code underpinning such apparently racy serials, the moral code that structured the plot of "El Viejo Nido": they believed in a firm set of hierarchies—based on kinship, class, and gender—that organized their world no matter where they found themselves. The advertisers evidently were not looking for "adventures," sexual freedom, or the thrill of vice; nor were they searching for companionate, egalitarian unions. They distinguished clearly between acceptable traits for men and women, while believing that both men and women should conform to religious and social expectations appropriate to their carefully delineated class and kinship positions.

Advertisers were willing to look for love outside their own locality; relations that began in the pages of *Paquito Grande* lacked the implicit approval of family or community. To that extent, they were as untraditional, or "corrupt," as the anti-comic-book crusaders feared. Yet most advertisers placed no importance on shared interests with a potential romantic partner, and they did want him or her to be of the appropriate social status. They did not care much about sexual attraction; thus, they did not emphasize their own or their partners' looks beyond what was necessary to ensure that no socially awkward mismatch would occur. Questions of character and morality within marriage deeply concerned them.

The men and women who advertised themselves in "Eslabones Espirituales" presented themselves as, and desired to marry, people who had avoided the vices of modernity and the big city. Perhaps we cannot believe what the advertisers said about themselves. Probably, though, we can assume that what they said represented what they wished were true and believed ought to be true. If so, to judge by this, the fears of the anti-comic-book campaigners were groundless: like the *historietas* themselves, their audience upheld deeply conservative values and patterns of life in the face of all the pressures of urbanization, migration, and industrialization. What, then, motivated some Mexicans to express profound hostility toward the comics and to fear their power to corrupt readers? That is the question that the next chapter examines.

Luis in Mexico City: buses, telephone poles, billboards, a phone booth and phone book, and the discovery that his wicked half brother has his own office in the city. *Pepín*, no. 3891, 13 November 1949, p. 31.

Chato the boxing coach visits Alvaro: filing cabinets, window blinds, building scaffolding, and more buses. *Pepín*, no. 3898, 20 November 1949, p. 7.

The uses of print: In a newspaper article, Luis discovers that Alvaro has been arrested. Newspapers convey crucial plot points on four occasions in this serial, always presented so that the comic book reader can see the newspaper story. *Pepín*, no. 3909, 3 December 1949, p. 31.

Luis and friends return from New York City: the plane flies over a recognizable block of Paseo de la Reforma, near the Alemeda Central, in central Mexico City. *Pepín*, no. 3924, 16 December 1949, p. 35.

The countryside of "El Viejo Nido": Julia struggles across the central plaza toward the church of this imaginary small town. In this artist's construction of a placeless, "typical" town, Julia wears the shawl and long skirt of a vaguely conceived rural tradition. *Pepín*, no. 3900, 22 November 1949, p. 19.

Chapter Three

The Uses of Tradition

Conservative Opposition to Comic Books

 Family, the imagined past, and the pressing need for social stability served as constant points of reference for the arguments and imagery of a traditionalist, conservative discourse that developed in dialogue with the discourse of modernity in Mexico. Throughout the postrevolutionary era, conservative Mexicans deployed these tropes as they battled against many forms of mass media and popular culture. Comic books were not the only target of conservative outrage—everything from billboards to ballroom dancing received some criticism from the right in this period—but they were a popular one, just as the *historietas* themselves were popular. Distrust and disdain for the comics was so general that, by the mid-1940s, the word *pepines* came to connote any vulgar or indecent publication.

Public outrage over the immorality of print media in general and comic books in particular rose and fell in the years 1942 through 1976, but it reached surprising heights in three periods: 1942–44, 1952–56, and 1971–76. The longevity of the fight over this specific form of mass media suggests that the battle against *los pepines* was not one that any conservative expected to win. Rather, comic books became the center of a broader argument over values, an argument against modernity, that was useful precisely because it was unlikely to close. All parties to the debate understood that the problem of morality in this particular form of media was intractable. Protesters were in no danger of winning their argument; nor would the government allow them to lose entirely or quickly. By participating in this bloodless fight, all sides legitimized each other, reconfirmed their allegiances to each other, rewrote the terms of their discourse, and reinforced the underlying values that (paradoxically) the comic book audience also claimed.

Popular culture had been used by the Mexican state as a vehicle for modernization well before the revolution. Some of the Porfirian regime's attempts at encouraging—or enforcing—progress were as much cultural as economic, as the state's efforts to regulate bullfighting at the end of nineteenth century demonstrate.[1] As mass media entered public life, they too became subjects of debate. Some revolutionary leaders demonstrated a critical grasp of the power of mechanical reproduction of imagery. Pancho Villa, for example, would restage his battles for the benefit of documentary filmmakers in exchange for some control over the representation of his struggle.[2] At the same time, the Mexican Revolution was, for some of its participants, an opportunity for cultural renovation: not only did it lead to the literacy campaigns described earlier, but it also made possible crusades against public drunkenness and gambling, among dozens of other efforts at cultural reform.[3] And the Cristero Revolt of 1926–29, along with the anti-government violence by religious rural people from 1934–38, should also be seen as a bloodstained disagreement over cultural questions.[4]

Beginning in the middle of the 1930s, debate over mass media and popular culture intensified as religious debate lost some of its stridency. Arguments over images and styles sometimes seemed to take the place of directly ideological or political debate among right, left, and center. The Partido Revolucionario Nacional, in its efforts to co-opt or suppress its opponents on the left, has often used cultural argument as a distraction or a means of offering compromise without losing power.[5] But the state has also turned this process against its opposition on the right. This chapter offers an account of the transformation of political struggle into cultural argument, as some Mexican conservatives were led from opposition to post-revolutionary modernity, to opposition to representations of modernity, to active collaboration in the state's attempts to repress those representations.

Right-wing politics in postrevolutionary Mexico formed in response to the policies of the revolutionary state. The Cristero Revolt began a long process of negotiation and co-optation, after the peasants who took up arms to defend their faith against the vehemently secular government were firmly defeated. The Catholic hierarchy agreed to resume offering sacraments to

Mexicans (and implicitly, to stay out of politics), while the government backed off from its more extreme anticlerical stances—churches were no longer to be used as dance halls, for example.[6] A brief spate of further violence followed Lázaro Cárdenas's 1936 efforts to enforce Article Three of the 1917 constitution, requiring "socialist education" for all Mexican children; and many presidential elections took place in the midst of small-scale violence, or the threat of violence. But in general, after 1929, right-wing opposition to the government was expressed peacefully.

This does not mean that such opposition was minor. The Mexican right in the 1930s was a lively, if amorphous, conglomeration. It included at least four sets of would-be leaders. First, there were the industrialists—notably, the "Monterrey Elite"—who more or less upheld the old Porfirian ideology of order and progress.[7] Their conservatism was primarily economic, rather than social. Second, there was the Catholic hierarchy, whose major goal was preserving their place in Mexican life against the secularizing revolutionary government. Third, there were the opposition party politicians, some allied with José Vasconcelos and some opposed to him as well, but all united by their futile attempts to win elections. Finally, there were the internationally minded fascists, the *sinarquistas,* who were most concerned with Mexico's foreign policies and, especially, with support for Germany in World War II.[8]

Although all these leaders had some loyal followers, a much larger group of Mexicans offered different right-wingers occasional support, shifting from one to another depending on the extent to which they agreed with the particular issues under discussion.[9] By 1940, it was clear that cultural questions were attracting the most attention from rank-and-file Mexican conservatives. As Carlos Monsiváis wrote in 1976, the right wing then developed a "series of cultural projects" that still have not been studied sufficiently.[10] In his version of events, after Avila Camacho took office in 1940, the Catholic hierarchy—which Monsiváis views as the voice of Mexican cultural conservatism—appeared satisfied with the compromise it had made with the Mexican state; yet despite the end of government-sponsored religious persecution, and the toleration of parochial schools, the right periodically brought up new demands.[11] (Monsiváis cites a 1971 movement against sexual education in public schools as an example.)[12] New demands were never narrowly political and always couched in cultural terms: even anticommunist movements avoided ideology in favor of rhetorical opposition to foreign ideas and patriotic support for national culture.

Although all rightist opposition leaders took up cultural issues at one point or another between 1929 and the present, Monsiváis is not far wrong in identifying right-wing cultural protest with the Catholic Church. Catholic voices spoke louder than any others in opposition to secular education, mass media, and other vehicles of modernity. Other potential right-wing leaders in Mexico had conflicting goals: industrial elites lost interest in cultural issues at the point where they broadened into a critique of modernity; the *sinarquistas*'s focus on foreign-policy questions was so extreme that this faction disappeared altogether after World War II. Even before that, though, more people allied themselves with Catholic political groups in the Mexican "culture wars" than with any other party to these disputes.

The discourse of modernity in the postrevolutionary era contrasted a progressive, if atomized, urbanity to a superstitious and regressive, but closely knit, rural life. But the discourse of tradition was quite different: it refused to give virtue a location, arguing for the possibility of morality in the cities. In this, the traditionalist discourse matched the experience of conservative groups. Catholic-associated conservative organizations found their most active supporters in battles over culture in Mexico City, Guadalajara, Monterrey, and other expanding cities of this period. It was relatively simple to organize newcomers into parish chapters of such international groups as the Knights of Columbus or the Legion of Decency, into national groups like the Parents' Association, or into autonomous local organizations like the Hermosillo Anti-Drug-Addiction Civic Committee. Sometimes these groups engaged in large national campaigns, like those in opposition to comic books or pornography; sometimes, like the Coyoacán parish that in the late 1930s set up its own movie theater as a morally pure alternative to the neighborhood cinema, their work was quite local.[13] Such groups occasionally held their meetings in church buildings and usually recruited through parish-based social networks; but their work was facilitated by the modern urban conveniences of transportation and communication that their members sometimes found so unsettling.[14]

Conservatives often rallied around questions related to education—indeed, so often that Alan Knight, among others, has suggested that the church, in the years after the Cristero rebellion, was deliberately confining itself to that "key issue."[15] But this is only partially true. Both leaders and followers folded a large number of concerns—especially anxieties about gender roles, sexuality, and shifting patterns of employment—into the portmanteau issue of secular schooling. Moreover, Catholic leaders, like other conservative political actors, offered their followers a variety of stances on many different (though related) cultural questions. Sometimes they joined in political displays generated by the state itself, as in the church's positive response to the nationalization of oil in 1938 or its enthusiastic support for anticommunist movements in later years.[16] And of course, they led movements against several forms of mass media, the most frequent targets being films and comic books.

It is tempting to view these Mexican culture wars as a form of elite politics, but they were more than a high-stakes word game among powerful men. Politicians and clergy may have started waves of moral panic, but such movements would have been invisibly small had not large numbers of ordinary people entered into them. Leaders tried to fix agendas for conservative action, often through well-publicized conferences that set forth lists of potential issues. But followers reacted to those issues that moved them, making only a few of the church's causes their own. All this did not happen against a static backdrop; social conservatism grew more visible as the middle class expanded between 1940 and 1970.[17] Opposition to capitalist modernity helped some Mexicans imagine a world of happy family relationships and beneficent authority. Just as the audience did, mass media's opponents forced the media to conform to their social and political needs.

What Was Wrong with los Pepines?

What was it about *historietas* that, as the medium's best historians put it, "satanized" them in the eyes of Mexicans?[18]

The most subtle arguments against comic books came from the Catholic hierarchy as expressed in the pages of *Apreciaciones*. This free weekly leaflet was produced by the Mexican Legion of Decency (which, in turn, was sponsored by the archdiocese of Mexico City) and distributed weekly at masses throughout the city. Beginning in 1933, it printed one-line movie reviews, sorting them by degree and type of sinfulness. *Apreciaciones*, predictably, disparaged representations of nudity, "free love," and divorce; even the implication of sex, as in "inappropriate dancing" and "daring clothes and poses," was censurable. It cautioned readers against depictions of beliefs other than Catholicism in its strictest sense, so that images of "superstition or atheism"—along with movies that dealt with monsters, witches, or the supernatural—were proscribed. The Legion of Decency also disapproved of crime or violence, even if displayed in a moralistic context. Some of its criteria for categorizing mass media were broader; *Apreciaciones* warned against "morbidly sentimental" films, films inspired by "false social, moral or religious ideas," and those set in a "cruel, repugnant atmosphere." [19] In the ten years that it described films, however, *Apreciaciones* rarely issued calls to action, even against the movies that it saw as advocating mortal sins; instead, the leaflet simply told its readers what to avoid and why. The only time *Apreciaciones* departed from this passive stance was when "education" was at stake, as when it urged a boycott of theater owners who had allowed minors to see *Star Spangled Rhythm* or *Frankenstein Meets the Wolf Man*.[20] But in 1943, the legion adopted a wider focus. While continuing to object to the same sorts of representations, it began editorializing against comic books as well as movies. *Apreciaciones* declared "an absolute boycott of those indecent magazines," announcing "we will destroy as many copies [of *Pepín*] as we can." [21]

Through *Apreciaciones,* the Legion of Decency advocated a very different response to comic books than it had to movies. It argued that religious authorities could help audiences distinguish between safe and harmful films, but that comic books had to be controlled by the state. This reflects the legion's understanding of the different processes by which movies and *historietas* were produced and consumed.[22] While parents might keep their children out of movie theaters, they could not keep them from borrowing comic books from their friends. Indeed, protests against comic books often focused on their ubiquity in Mexican life. *Apreciaciones* cautioned in 1945, for example, that a new comic book was giving away sample copies "inside boxes of chocolates . . . comic books that are of the same type of *Paquín,* already condemned by this Legion." [23]

Comics also raised new issues for the legion. Above all, it objected to the soap-operatic Mexican serials printed in *Pepín* and its competitors. *Apreciaciones* criticized melodrama far more often than comedy, yet sometimes borrowed the language of melodrama in order to make its criticism, recounting heartbreaking tales of the terrible fates suffered by those who read *historietas*. One priest reported that

a poor mother came to see me, dissolved in a sea of tears—"Father, please, what can I do with my son . . . he's done something really crazy, a barbarity." . . . He is now a young father, and in the home of a poor woman of the people, the daughter of the maid: a new victim! *We are reminded* of the obscene and squalid comic strip that has been offered in *Pepín*—they don't sow so much evil in vain![24]

Through a long series of articles like this one, *Apreciaciones* asked its audience to pressure the government to ban *pepines*. The leaflet argued that it was bad enough to imply that sex was part of the story, but even worse to write the stories in such a way that readers might sympathize with any of the sinning characters. *Apreciaciones* located the inherent danger of mass media not in their advocacy of any one ideology but in their promiscuous openness to interpretation. Comic books were not bad because they caused or represented social change, but because media, in themselves, were an evil thing.

This line of argument disappeared as the censorship debate broadened. The notion of media in general as morally threatening was rarely articulated; instead, protesters limited themselves to specific words, plots, or pictures to which they took exception. In regard to comic books, the only complaint about the dangers of the medium as a whole was that comic books might be physically damaging because their poor printing could cause eyestrain. Sometimes comic books were even praised as a form by the very crusaders who most wanted to see them banned: protesters acknowledged that the *historietas* were an easily accessible form of printed material in a newly literate society.

At the same time, the objects of debate shifted. *Apreciaciones* considered media—especially comic books—a threatening influence on male behavior, as in its tale of the unwed father above. Other protesters said that comic books endangered women and children, ignoring their supposed effect on men. The argument for banning *los pepines* became a protest against the shape of Mexico's future, as represented by its children. Most of all, it grew to oppose the gendered aspects of postrevolutionary modernist discourse, as it protested the images of appropriate femininity that the comic books contained.

The most ordinary expressions of anxiety over mass media tended to be the least clear about the difference between objecting to comic books themselves and disagreeing with the social changes that comic books depicted, recognizing both as aspects of the same modernist discourse. One anguished parent's 1944 letter to the president about comic books showed him projecting everything he feared for his daughter's future onto the *pepines:*

> The campaign against illiteracy has occasioned much favorable comment. . . . All the same, there is a disagreeable reason to wish that our youth did not know how to read: the publication and massive circulation of pornographic "Magazines" such as PEPIN. . . . Youth of today . . . use extremely vulgar and precocious language, and their behavior passes the limit of misdemeanor, up to and including crime. All this is due to, there is no doubt, the corrupting influence of these indecent publications, in which they read illustrated lessons of all vices and the most shameless acts. . . . Today's paper published a report that the editor of one of these squalid publications that is weakening and poisoning the national soul, has been fined a thousand pesos. . . . The FIRING SQUAD would be too little as a punishment for the deeds of those criminals; so a fine of a thousand pesos is . . . "as if a cat lost a single hair." . . . I have had to take my youngest daughter out of school because I have learned that one of her female classmates rents for one cent, to the other girl students, "Pepín" and others of these little magazines. Better that my daughter lose this year's schooling, than that they turn her into a prostitute. Next year I will have to make the sacrifice of sending her to a private school, where with true zeal and full justification, they guard against those magazines reaching the hands of the girls.[25]

The letter's author, Luis G. Villalpando, expresses almost every anxiety raised by the censorship campaign, including many that would be heard again in subsequent attacks: the connection between education and immorality, the especially sexual nature of comic books, the danger posed to women and children, the link between comic books and crime, the substitution of complaints about mass media for complaints about education, the demand for stronger action by the state, and the perceived relation between mass media and national weakness.

Many such complaints were specific and detailed. Some offered a careful critique of a single objectionable story, as Villalpando did: he enclosed a few pages torn from a *Pepín* as evidence, describing it as "a sentimental comic strip of two lovers, in which she tells him the great news that soon he will have a son engendered in a ditch." As Villalpando may have known, this was the last episode of a serial that had run for months and the two characters were a married couple reconciling after countless travails. The pair embrace, but do not kiss; the writer assiduously avoids the word "pregnancy," along with any direct mention of sex. In fact, even the most daring of these stories never showed sex acts and seldom implied that sex had taken place. Villalpando's objection to this scene may have been less to the implication of sexual activity than to the female star, who pursues her husband when he has strayed, walks alone on the beach, wears makeup, cuts her hair short, and sports a new, tight, fashionable dress. She is, in short, too much the *chica moderna.*

What the letter does not say is almost as important, since the possible lines of argument that it ignores also failed to interest other anti-comic-book crusaders in the 1942–44 campaign. Even though Villalpando asserts that they present a danger to the nation, he does not equate reading comics with becoming a foreigner. He is not complaining about cultural imperialism. Instead, Villalpando's argument is that comic books are agents of modernity and that modernity is bad for Mexico. This can be seen in his accounts of how he and his daughter acquired their *pepines.* She—the object of Villalpando's fears—innocently accepted one given to her almost freely by a trusted peer. He—who expresses no concern about his own moral purity—purchased his "from a used-book stand on the street," in order to send a few exemplary pages along with his letter. To Villalpando, men are already constructed as sexual and enmeshed in the dirty business of wage labor, but women and children can be separated from it. The asexuality of women and children, and their distance from the capitalist marketplace—their fragile "purity"—guarantees the stability of the family, the nation, and the whole moral universe. He sees comic books as a modern, or modernizing, threat to the cohesion of the Mexican family and, thus, to the Mexican nation.

The argument over comic books was not a struggle between the sexes, but it only makes sense in the context of a wider debate over the representation of gender during this period. In that context, it is interesting to note that almost all the pro-censorship protesters between 1942 and 1976 were male (even those who only went so far as to join a group of people sending a telegram to the president), while a large minority of *historieta* producers (from publishers to writers to newsstand operators) have been women. *Pepín* and its competition often portrayed precisely the type of modern women whom Villalpando loathed.

The *pepines* were participating in a wider cultural debate over what was appropriate for women. In the Revolution's aftermath, the nature of Mexican femininity was much questioned. The state's education projects and public celebration of a new female citizen joined with the new consumer culture in widening the range of acceptable models for appropriate female behavior, and some women eagerly accepted and extended this spectrum. Women portrayed new ways for themselves to be family members, workers, and citizens. As *soldaderas,* as industrial workers, as teachers, and as athletes, they marched in parades.[26] As famous or infamous artists—painters and patrons, actresses and hootchy-kootchy dancers, novelists and comic book scriptwriters—they provided models for female behavior. Celebrities and ordinary *mexicanas* together invented the figure of *chica moderna,* who was young, educated, and proud of her emotional and financial independence.

Alongside this new stereotype, another stock character entered the Mexican imaginary to act as a counterweight: the silent, virtuous, and long-suffering Mexican mother who never left her home. In the terms of the modernist discourse, the imaginary (rural) wife and mother was someone whom one might pity or admire, but nobody would ever want to be her. This image had remarkable durability: as late as 1974, a feminist psychologist described this "stereotypical Mexican woman" as "self-abnegating," "servile," and sexually frigid.[27] The task of the traditionalist discourse was to change the light in which these female figures were seen. It could, as Villalpando did, turn the *chica moderna* into the hapless unmarried mother, a victim of her uncontrolled desires. And after 1940, as the state adopted this traditionalist discourse, the figure of the good mother was also recast: she became a patriot. This invented woman—peaceable, wise, patient, and unselfish—was much in evidence, for example, in the rhetoric federal officials used as they granted women the vote in 1953.

When female conservatives spoke, they sometimes allied the image of the good woman of the past, "whose role was [to be] gentle, loving, and pleasant," with the good woman of the present,

> of whom much more must be asked: a double, valiant role is demanded of her; first, as in bygone days, within the limits of her own family; second . . . [and] no less feminine, to guard others' homes, with the highest aim . . . of fighting for the preservation of the Catholic Faith![28]

The author of this editorial from a Catholic women's magazine, while urging women to participate in church-related cultural and moral campaigns, was also suggesting that new times had created a new way to be a good Mexican woman. The discourse of tradition did not require a return to the imagined past, but instead offered a moralistic response to modernity that included (yet was not limited to) the world it described as traditional.

Two newspaper columnists got to the heart of the matter in February 1942. An anonymous female journalist protested the brand-new observance of Mother's Day: it not only revealed the influence of North American culture on Mexico, but also insulted women by not celebrating their other achievements, including *soldaderas'* military accomplishments. She claimed such masculine privileges as marching in parades because "we revolutionary women . . . could have passed for men." [29]

Her male colleague disagreed, writing:

> In general, our women gave their contribution to the people's cause in tears, in self-sacrifice and pain. . . . They died next to their husbands in order not to depart from their sweetly feminine role. [30]

The next week, he explained that his "repugnance" for armed women sprang from an encounter with a *soldadera* who had tried to kill him during the war, and he explicitly connected such behavior to comic books, melodramatic narrative, and the popular press:

> Those manly women feel themselves to be truly superwomen. [But] I have seen, a hundred times, abandoned wives, tricked and even martyred by their husbands, triumph with sweetness, with patience, with self-sacrifice, virtues essentially feminine. . . . Despite the enormous amount of propaganda . . . the Mexican woman is no criminal. [31]

These journalists' quarrel, in other words, asked, Was the ideal *mexicana* the good citizen and good worker, or was she the good mother and self-sacrificing wife? Was a bad woman one who declined to leave her household to participate in the revolution's modernizing project, or was a bad woman a manly, dangerous *soldadera*? Images, narratives, and arguments like these shaped the content of comics as well as the debate over them.

The First Episode of Moral Panic

The first two waves of moral panic over comic books coincided with periods when Mexico's most visible politicians seemed to uphold conservative social values. The most famous of such openings toward the right was the choice of Avila Camacho as president in 1940. He implied a (partial) repudiation of revolutionary anticlericalism early in his term when he proclaimed himself a Catholic and publicly questioned the morality of coeduation. The president also projected a public image as a rather prudish family man—as in his wife's well-publicized insistence that a nude statue of Diana the Huntress, newly placed on a central Mexico City avenue, be draped in a loincloth—and, thus, as a participant in the discourse of tradition.[32]

Gestures such as these amounted to a sign of willingness to hear conservative complaints on cultural questions, lessening political strains without forcing a complete rejection of Cárdenas-era social policy. Avila Camacho's policies, like his public image, were chosen in an attempt to prevent the violence and threats of violence that had marked previous presidential administrations. His administration definitively abandoned socialism as a goal or method, taking as its aim, instead, the preservation of the state and the ruling party. At the same time, "modernity" and "progress" remained important motivating factors in shaping government policy—as they had been long before the Revolution. Thus, Avila Camacho moved government resources from land redistribution and other agricultural initiatives into industrialization. And state cultural policy shifted away from attempts to build a new, nationalist, revolutionary high culture for the masses (as with the state-supported muralist movement). Rather, Avila Camacho's administration concentrated on control of and collaboration with mass media: not only did comic books and other periodicals fall under government supervision in 1944, but state censorship of film scripts began in 1941.

Well before the 1942 start of the first concerted campaign against them, comic books had already earned a reputation for immorality. Efforts to deal with this perceived problem had already begun, but these attempts were couched in the language of progress and modernity. In 1937, a political response to the sudden popularity of *historietas* was initiated with the production of an alternative children's periodical called *Periquillo estudiantil.* Much as Catholic conservatives would in the Avila Camacho years, the men responsible for *Periquillo* hoped to

> arrest the nefarious action that raises up the editorial houses without scruples with their publications of so-called "funnies" that contain only noxious stories of gangsters and lowlifes.[33]

But *Periquillo* was a modernist, revolutionary response to the problem of mass media, as its imagery emphasized: the first issue's cover art depicted a group of heroically muscled foundry workers.[34] The new periodical cost ten centavos, the same as the *pepines*. Unlike them, however, it lacked excitement; its stories told of mild mischief and good deeds enacted by middle-class children. It also included a dose of math lessons inadequately disguised as funny-animal stories. All in all, it seemed insufficiently lurid to survive long in the competitive business of *pepines*.

Still, either their intentions or political connections garnered *Periquillo's* editors some extra help: two weeks after this first edition, President Cárdenas himself requested that the governors of every state buy subscriptions to be distributed to poor families in their regions. The governors ordered 14,000 pesos worth of subscriptions from *Periquillo's* traveling salesmen in November 1937, but the magazine lasted only five issues: the governors and the federal bureaucracy did not pay for their subscriptions.[35] Thus ended the first of many efforts to provide an alternative to commercial comic books for Mexican children, and the first organized response to the perceived moral failings of the *historietas*.

Whereas *Periquillo* had joined conservative revulsion against mass media with revolutionary puritanism, more successful "clean" comics aimed at children were advertised to conservative parents in *sinarquista* and Catholic publications. These comics were often supposed to "instruct," but unlike *Periquillo,* they also took care to entertain and to match the production values of commercial comics.[36] Many of these alternative children's periodicals had financial support from the church. *La Cruzada* received a subsidy from "an organization of Roman Catholic clergy"; in 1945, Catholic parishes competed to see which women's groups could sell the most subscriptions to *Piloto*.[37] Such publications rarely achieved even a small percentage of the *pepines'* popularity, but alternative, traditionalist comics for children reappeared with every successive wave of public concern over the morality of print media.[38]

The first real campaign against comic books began as the work of a few Mexico City organizations in 1942–44. It appears to have inspired no mass demonstrations, unlike the 1952–55 censorship campaign; and unlike the 1974–76 crusade, it did not convince tens of thousands of citizens to send telegrams and letters to the government. It was easy for an uninformed observer to ignore the political roots of this first campaign. In 1943, Dorothy

Adelson, a North American journalist covering the growth of the comic book business, did not even remark on the conservative Catholicism of comic books' enemies: she simply listed them as

> educators [who] point out that teachers cannot keep the attention of a class that is reading comic books . . . [and] intellectuals concerned with the cultural future of Mexico.[39]

This outsider was impressed by the class status, rather than the social views, of the crusaders for censorship.

But in fact, opposition to this form of mass media moved across class lines while remaining confined to people in rough ideological agreement with each other. The first group to actively oppose the existence of comic books in Mexico was the large, powerful, and extremely conservative Acción Social. Every year, representatives of its regional chapters met in Mexico City to listen to speeches from bishops and vote on new nationwide plans of action. Its 1942 meeting officially decided to concentrate the group's efforts on purifying print media, but it had already taken steps in that direction by urging parents to prevent their children from reading "this class of literature." In February 1942, the campaign commenced in Mexico City with the submission of a project to the Department of the Judiciary "to restrict the sort of publications that ought to be considered morbid," asking specifically for a ban on "publications . . . that are a school of crime for juvenile spirits." The next step was to persuade the city libraries not to stock "the novels, leaflets or children's comics . . . [that] are considered dangerous for youth." Acción Social presented *pepines* as a threat peculiar to modern urban life: "dangerous" comic books were those "published in the Capital."[40]

Within a few weeks of the 1942 meeting, a trickle of letters requesting the abolition of comic books began to arrive at the president's office. At least two or three such letters every week—usually signed by several people—came in from all over the country for the next two years.[41] Probably no organized campaign produced them (the numbers are too low to suggest that), but the letters do resemble each other somewhat. They rely on similar arguments, most likely repeating statements heard in church homilies or read in newspaper editorials and Catholic periodicals.

Other conservative groups were slower than Acción Social and la Legión Mexicana de la Decencia in actively taking anti-media positions.[42] One Catholic group, the Family Action Section of the Union of Mexican Catholics, did eventually join the campaign. They, too, complained about the number and availability of comics, arguing that it was up to the Mexican government to ban or censor *historietas*. In a January 1944 leaflet, they warned parents against letting their children read "los 'pepines,' 'paquines' [and] 'chamacos.'"

> Many have plots . . . so immoral that they would not even be tolerable for adults; it is quite common that the drawings are dangerous to purity and not in a small way. . . . other comic books foment delinquent acts such as, for example, organizing bands or gangs of youth that dedicate themselves to causing damage and mischief to whole neighborhoods. . . . The child used to reading funny-books is made INCAPABLE of serious reading. . . . The few words of such presses can hardly be grammatical (SLANG, most of the time). . . . Being allowed to read the immense variety of such comics prevents—as is obvious—young scholars from paying careful attention in class.[43]

The Family Action Section was arguing that the comics (appealing in part, as we have seen, because of their representation of social change, modernity, and progress) were, in fact, an obstacle to upward social mobility.

The *sinarquistas* were committed to the idea of the nation as a single, patriarchial family; they blamed national weakness on the weakness of ordinary families. So their version of the argument against comic books did not request government help for families that were unable to protect themselves from the onslaught of mass media. Instead, the *sinarquistas* reversed the equation: they demanded that the government protect itself, and the youth who were its proper responsibility, from its own corrupt or incompetent parents. This line of reasoning began with the contention that reading comic books distracted young people from their studies and turned them into "criminals . . . a burden on society," explaining that this happened because "fathers are too preoccupied by business and mothers are too interested in their bridge games."[44] Therefore, the *sinarquistas* concluded, the government must ban comic books.

Although smaller numbers of protesters involved themselves in this first campaign than in the one a decade later, those who did take part seem to have felt strongly about the issue. Not all of them belonged to the urban elite and not all of them were intellectuals; they did not always limit themselves to such polite protests as letter writing and leaflet distribution. For example, one Mexico City "cacique" (as a newspaper called him), who ran the large market in Villa de Guadalupe, took advantage of his position to "persecute and bother the vendors . . . of Mexican periodicals." He was so outraged by the presence of comic books, magazines, and tabloid newspapers near the basilica sacred to the Virgin of Guadalupe that he insisted that "the inspectors and policemen available to him" close down newsstands and "in cases in which the aggrieved vendors have raised a protest he has detained them arbitrarily." [45] A public health inspector, similarly, used his position of authority to act against comic books: he made the presence of *pepines* the most prominent part of his report on "unsanitary" conditions in a Mexico City high school, threatening it with closure. [46]

Avila Camacho's government backed away from enforcing socialist education and sexual education in the public schools without ever openly repudiating the policies of earlier governments; at the same time, it attempted to mollify conservatives by echoing their protests against mass media through the mouths of public-school teachers and bureaucrats. This process of co-opting the conservative discourse on media allowed—or promoted— the appearance of a split in the state's lower ranks. Education Secretary Octavio Vejar Vazquez attributed the deficiencies of "the current generation" to a moral failing on the part of their parents. Consequently, youth

> have NO willpower; lack ideals, have no taste for the noble and unselfish things of the spirit; do not love work and lack patience for it; are possessed by an ardent desire to experience life and only have ambition to attain power and material things.

A schoolteacher named Luis Morel Suarez arranged to have an open letter to the president reprinted in a Mexico City paper, in which he quoted Vejar's words; Suarez, however, blamed this declension on the vile influence of *Paquín* and *Chamaco*. [47] In this case, the education secretary spoke from within the modernist discourse, with its emphasis on the state as the voice and arbiter of morality. The conservative voice, meanwhile, belonged to the schoolteacher, who turned the blame away from parents and toward mass media. Paradoxically, Vejar was widely understood to be a conservative (and his policies certainly were less "socialist" than those of his predecessor), while schoolteachers were perhaps the segment of society most committed to revolutionizing Mexican culture and society: this exemplifies the malleable, almost playful nature of the dialogue between the discourses of conservatism and modernity.

Similarly, a union local of teachers from Oaxaca split its argument for a complete ban on comic books between the modernist and traditionalist styles of government rhetoric. It began: "*Chamaco, Pepín* . . . etc. contravene the ideology proclaimed in Article 3 of the Constitution." But it continued in a tone that allied patriotism and conservatism: "those magazines . . . [cause] grave damage to NATIONAL UNITY in this hour of crisis for our FATHERLAND."[48]

A few left-wing educators and intellectuals moved beyond forming a coalition with social conservatives on the issue of comic books. Rather than simply joining in public clamor against the perceived social effects of locally produced *historietas,* they formulated the first complaints against global mass media. Strenuous objections to the popularity of Walt Disney's animated cartoons and newspaper comic strips were expressed in a debate over the possible creation of Disney films specially designed to aid in the 1944 literacy campaign. Some of the arguments seem to have been taken straight from the anti-comic-book campaign, such as a suggestion that Disney animators would represent girls from "our humble classes" as if they were "senioritas americanas," thus destroying "the natural courtesy of our Indians." The central issue, however, was neither female sexuality nor the fear of modernity, but a kind of cultural protectionism: Mexicans "are masters of our own culture. . . . [Therefore,] the education of Mexicans must be the exclusive work of Mexicans!"[49]

Commenting on the same Disney literacy project, the *sinarquista* newspaper, *El Hombre Libre,* agreed that the project represented "the peaceful conquest of Latin America by Uncle Sam."[50] But this was in the context of the ferocious support of the *sinarquistas* for German, Spanish, and Italian fascism; in 1944, they took every opportunity to warn readers against any doings of the United States. Their main objection to the project arose from the collaboration between the Mexican education bureaucracy, the U.S. government "Good Neighbor" film project, and Disney: the content of the films is never mentioned in the half-page article.

In general, conservatives believed transnational media to be safer than local products. In 1947, *Apreciaciones* printed a "Protest" against a Mexico City movie house that had put together a children's program with two Walt Disney movies, which is an admirable thing to do; but between the two showings they have put a MEXICAN NEWSREEL with scenes from a swimming pool.[51]

With the exception of the *sinarquistas*, the nationalist preoccupations of left-wing media critics made no difference to right-wing social crusaders who actively approved of Disney. The moral purity of North American cartoons remained a popular assumption among Mexican conservatives, as can be seen in a 1957 essay on the publishing industry: "Cartoons [such as] Bugs Bunny . . . may at least partially displace the native cartoons. They are decidedly more wholesome in nature and are much better suited to the young reader."[52]

By then, social conservatives had long since realized that the mere existence of government censorship of comic books would not be sufficient to impose their moral strictures on mass media. Doubts about the new censorship law surfaced, in fact, as soon as it was promulgated in 1944. The conservative Catholic newsletter *Acción feminina* carried a short, dry report of the new regulations, without any commentary. But the same issue, and most subsequent ones that year, carried articles advising mothers to check carefully on what their children were reading. And *Acción feminina* went on printing advertisements (in fact, the only advertisements in some issues) for an alternative, "morally sound" children's comic book.[53]

El Hombre Libre, meanwhile, took a cynical tone in reporting on a "Conference against Vice" that a number of conservatives had organized in Mexico City in support of this new government initiative. It described the conference as

> another assembly in which pretty speeches are made . . . but real solutions to the problems are replaced by half-baked propositions that will not fix anything. . . . It is something that the worst sources of degradation have now been condemned but . . . the designated norms [for comic books] are not sufficient.[54]

El Hombre Libre's doubts turned out to be reasonable ones. Little visible change would be seen in mass media after the initial conservative victory, the founding of la Comisión Calificadora.

Industrial Self-defense and State Response

In 1944 it seemed as though the government really might act to suppress comic books. Despite guarantees of press freedom written into the 1917 constitution, conservatives were not asking for anything unusual when they called for strict censorship of print media. Informal (sometimes violent) government controls on the political content of the press were well known to exist.[55] (And some conservative papers publicly denounced such forms of censorship when it affected their interests.)[56] A complete ban on comic books appeared perfectly feasible, since the campaigners argued that the comic books were a danger to the state's projects of education and modernization, if not to the state itself. But the first campaign against comic books failed to reach its goal of eliminating the funnies from Mexican newsstands altogether because it faced active and effective, if quiet, opposition; in the end, the government acted in an attempt to satisfy both supporters and opponents of mass media.

Response to the censorship campaign was muted and indirect in the pages of the comic books themselves. In *Pepín* and its competitors, the level of nationalism and implied affiliation with the government and the ruling party rose dramatically in 1943, remaining high throughout the following decade. For example, the comics began to print pro-military, anti-Nazi, and patriotic slogans at the bottom of every page in early 1943.[57] The *pepines*, however, made no direct appeal to their readers to save them from Acción Social and its allies.[58] Nor did they organize, as far as can now be seen, on an industry-wide level.

The publishing industry did not respond directly to its critics because there was no need to do so. The same publishers produced comic books and Mexico City newspapers, and these newspapers were important government supporters; sometimes, too, newspapers acted as mouthpieces for individual politicians, none of whom were at all likely to risk offending publishers by shutting down their profitable businesses.[59] Publishers could use their personal connections to high-level government officials to oppose the censorship campaign. The publisher of *Pepín*, José García Valseca, also owned a large string of powerful regional newspapers and was well known to have used them in supporting President Avila Camacho's rise to the top of his party and the government. García Valseca's working life began as a chauffeur to the president's brother, rumored to be the silent partner in all of the publisher's later enterprises.[60] Romulo O'Farrill, the publisher of *Chamaco*, had an even closer tie to Avila Camacho: in 1942, he married Hilda Avila Camacho, the president's niece.[61] With the reasonable belief that they had nothing to fear from censorship campaigners, publishers did not bother to respond to them directly. What mattered, then, to both publishers and protesters was not their relationship to each other, but their separate relationships with the state.

Other, less powerful voices loudly opposed a ban on comic books. Newsstand operators, organized by the Syndicate of Periodical Vendors in Mexico City, sent dozens of letters with hundreds of signatures to the president, all more or less repeating the same set of facts. Their most important point, that the vast majority of comic book buyers were adult men, responded to the conclusion of many that comic books and related media were dangerous to women and children.[62] Vendors also maintained that comic books were a mainstay of their business and, as a group of loyal clients, claimed the protection of the state, using language that already seemed out of date. One group of vendors from San Cristobal de las Casas, Chiapas, alleged that the crusade to eliminate comic books was the work of "anti-democratic elements. . . . We say anti-democratic because to leave off selling said magazines would greatly damage the interests of one of the MOST HUMBLE CLASSES OF THE WORKERS," adding that 80 percent of their profit came from selling comic books.

The vendors offered a compromise:

> We agree that those illustrated magazines which carry in their pages comics lacking in any instructive content . . . should be prohibited; those that suggest, promote, incite and exalt vice, sin, corruption, moral dissolution, because the pernicious influence of such publications could make an honest person's face turn pale. But, basically instructive magazines, magazines for recreation that tend toward moral teachings, which are the majority of them, always deserve official and private support.[63]

The government agreed. This was, in the end, the solution held out by the state to those who would prefer that comic books disappear altogether: only consistently immoral magazines would be banned.

In January 1944, the secretary of public education announced a "project to purify children's literature." As described to the newspapers, a new law would set up a committee to study and report on books and publications for young readers, but reporters were assured that lawyers from the Department of Public Education would "eliminate from the text [of the law] . . . any aspect that could be interpreted as unconstitutional or restrictive of freedom of expression."[64] (These lawyers appear, in fact, to have written the law in its entirety.)[65] The 1917 constitution did absolutely protect freedom of the press, yet the legal issue was sidestepped by the new law; it did not propose prepublication censorship but, rather, only to punish those that stepped outside legal limits after they published and distributed comic books and other publications, more or less on the model of libel law. By the time the regulations were promulgated, children's books had fallen outside the scope of the purification project. Still, all illustrated periodicals except newspapers — no matter who was reading them — fell under the purview of the new law.

On March 11, 1944, the president authorized "the Regulations of Illustrated Magazines in that touching on Education." It was supposed to solve the comic book problem to the satisfaction of all parties after it went into effect on March 19. At least in theory, the law answered some of the major objections of social conservatives: it banned representations of crimes, texts, or pictures "which offend modesty or custom," as well as slang. (As *El Hombre Libre* complained, however, the regulations did not demand "a strict respect for the religious beliefs of the Mexican people.")[66] The law also responded to left-wing concerns about global mass media with a clause banning comic books or magazines "which provoke disdain for the Mexican people, their abilities, or their history."[67]

Had the law done what it promised to do, it might have stilled conservative anger and anxiety over comic books. But it did not "purify" comic books; moreover, it seems that this was never its intention. The new Comisión Calificadora had no clear powers of enforcement: it could levy fines, but not require that the judiciary collect them; it could ask that publishers submit to interviews, or even be arrested, but could not compel the police to make these arrests. And in its first few years of operation, despite the splash of publicity that had greeted its founding, the commission had a tiny budget. It ceased to function at all in 1947, during the Alemán administration, having failed to make a noticeable impact on the content of *historietas* or any other periodical.

So Mexican crusades against comic books — and eventually, against magazines in general — continued because of the successes, and the failure, of the first campaign. The 1943–44 campaign succeeded on three levels.

First, it attracted worldwide attention and imitation. It helped inspire, among others, campaigns in Cuba (1944), Colombia and Venezuela (1955–56), and Peru (1976) against North American and Mexican comics.[68] The second—and more encouraging—success of the Mexican anti-comic-book campaigners was the creation of the government censorship commission, despite its shortcomings. Finally, the campaign against comic books helped create a rhetorical arsenal—imagery and arguments about family, femininity, and politics—that could be reused when conservatives took up the battle against mass media again.

Yet the second and third campaigns against comic books in Mexico did not grow from the successes of the first so much as they sprang from a sense of failure. The censorship legislation never put the comic book industry out of operation and, in itself, never drove a single publisher from the field. In fact, the censors often complained of their powerlessness. By extension, it must have appeared to the thousands of Mexicans who protested against comic books that the censors' activities had not resulted in much, either.

Subsequent Moral Panics

Conservative frustration with *las historietas* reappeared in public discourse not long after a new president, Adolfo Ruiz Cortines, took office in 1952. Between 1952 and 1958, his much-reported emphasis on government responsiveness and cleanliness, coupled with his eloquent silence on more radical topics, was taken by conservative groups as an opportunity to press old grievances and make new alliances with the state.

Three factors distinguished the first wave of moral panic over comic books from the second, which ran from 1952 to 1956. To begin with, participants in the first campaign aimed, variously, at the replacement of immoral comics by moral ones, strict government censorship, or the complete elimination of *historietas*. By 1952, however, a mechanism for censorship already existed, so that people agitating against periodicals had a specific goal ready-made for them: they wanted the commission to do its job better. The second distinction was in the scope of the campaigns. The first wave of complaints about periodicals focused on comic books, particularly on their youngest readers. The second wave of concern encompassed comic books, but also covered true-crime tabloids, scandal sheets, and men's magazines. Finally, the first and second movements against periodicals differed in the sources of their inspiration. The first campaign resulted from the conjunction of elite clergy and politicians looking for a safe issue, ordinary Mexicans who needed a target for outrage over wider social issues, and an administration responsive to this type of protest. On the other hand, the second moral panic appears to have been initiated by the state itself, with the 1952 reintroduction of the commission. Conservatives attached themselves to this cause only later.

Despite the governmental origin of this second movement against comic books, Catholic leaders sometimes spoke as if the government—rather than producers or consumers—was responsible for objectionable print media. The bishop of Toluca, for example, on being appointed head of the Mexican Legion of Decency in 1953, remarked that only "civil authorities" could "put a stop to" comic books. (In contrast, he asked Catholics to avoid the "immoral spectacles" of cinema, rather than demanding that the state censor movies.)[69] Ordinary people adopted a more conciliatory tone, but also turned to the state to solve the perceived problem, like the letter writer who addressed President Ruiz Cortines as "the Doctor who knows how to apply the rapid and efficient cauterization that is required."[70] Not only was this an appeal to the state as the remedy for this wound to the body politic, but an appeal couched in the language of the modernization discourse, with its deep respect for expertise as the source of authority.

Some men appear to have made an avocation of the struggle against immorality in print media. They, too, relied on the state to cure the social ill that worried them. One such moralist, Antonio de Ibarrola, led a group called the National Commission to Moralize Society between 1954 and 1958. He and his group searched Guadalajara for offensive periodicals and then sent them on to the classifying commission, complete with details about where and when they were purchased.[71] He met with his senator, urging him to carry on the struggle in Mexico City against "unclean" periodicals.[72] And he continued to work with his group after his term as leader of "the National Commission," scouring Guadalajara as late as 1961 for pictures of half-dressed women and stories involving adultery.[73]

The first and second movements against immorality in print media tapped a similar vein of dismay and fury among middle-class and working Mexicans who lacked the time, energy, or capacity for obsession that characterized the men of the National Commission to Moralize Society. While the state used the classifying commission to mollify these exceptionally dedicated antipornography crusaders, it also had to communicate with the much larger number of people who did not focus their attention on comic books yet, to some extent, shared the views of Ibarrola and his friends. As the second wave of moral panic crested, the government turned to newspapers as a means of telling outraged citizens that the state was on their side. It announced when fines had been levied by the classifying commission (though not when the fines were later waived), and it responded to published comments, letters, or editorials. Government officials warned reporters of "a huge number of comic books that attack morality" or "de-Mexicanize . . . our young population."[74] Articles like these helped create the erroneous impression that a conservative critique of mass media could have an impact on the contents of Mexican magazines.

Politicians knew that ordinary Mexicans wanted racy periodicals suppressed. Citizens often made some small gesture of affiliation with this second wave, without becoming deeply involved. As in 1942–44, a steady trickle of mail conveyed to the president how widespread such feelings were.[75] These letters often cited leaflets and sermons to which the government felt compelled to respond. Additionally, the government was the target of a small letter-writing campaign organized by the Confederation of National Chambers of Commerce: between March 25 and May 22, 1955, twenty-five local chambers sent petitions requesting that "frankly immoral magazines" be suppressed.

In these petitions, the Chambers of Commerce congratulated "the University students of Mexico" for initiating the new anti-comic-book campaign.[76] They were referring to the right-wing youth group Movimiento Universitario de Renovación Orientada, or MURO ("wall"), which in fact, did not originate the second moral panic about comic books, but certainly was among its most visible participants.[77] MURO publicly burned "indecent magazines"—especially the widely circulated men's magazines *Vea* and *Vodevil*—at open-air meetings that involved hundreds of people. They also encouraged male high school students to organize similar bonfires in symbolic defense of their female peers from the temptations of sex and crime.[78] Novelist José Agustín recalled MURO's adherents as "fascist youth" whose persistent chanting of slogans made them "the worst pests at the University."[79]

As with the first wave of antipornography activism, this second movement died down without really changing the contents of Mexican newsstands. It did elicit a few years of vigorous activity from the classifying commission, but the new censors' sincere efforts at eliminating immorality in print media all came to naught. For a few years, the men from Monterrey and Guadalajara who were most active in organizing against offensive periodicals collaborated with the censors in searching for and prosecuting such publications. But by 1960, most such activities had ceased. In the next decade, right-wing opposition to media was barely expressed at all.

The volume of moral outrage over magazines increased again in 1971, but the third wave of moral panic occurred in a very different political climate. The first two times that public opposition had been voiced, conservatives were taking advantage of state openings toward the right. This third antipornography campaign, on the other hand, articulated conservative discontent with a presidential administration that was making overtures toward the left, at least on a cultural level.

Luis Echeverría's administration faced a dramatic challenge: it had to respond to the traumatic events of 1968, during which President Gustavo Diaz Ordaz had ordered or allowed the slaughter of student demonstrators at Tlatelolco by the military after a stunning series of radical marches and protests.[80] In 1970, Mexico's leaders perceived their task as rebuilding the appearance, at least, of national unity and political stability. Thus, they repressed radical groups, sometimes violently. At the same time, however, President Echeverría announced a democratic opening, made a display of support for Chilean socialism, freed students who had been jailed in the aftermath of the Tlatelolco debacle, and claimed to have loosened strictures on artistic—though not political—expression.[81] The situation was complicated by perceptible weakness in the PRI: the ruling party's internal unity was strained and the economy had stopped growing, which made the party's usual co-optative tactics much more difficult to practice. Oppositional politics, consequently, grew fiercer.

Conservatives took on the government over many cultural and educational issues in this period, while also engaging more directly in oppositional politics. The most dramatic conservative action was a paramilitary attack on student protesters that killed ten (with, at a minimum, government collusion). Conservative cultural interventions included a scathing critique of print media, comic books among them. Other targets included the filmmaker Alejandro Jodorowsky and several avant-garde theater companies.[82] Educational issues raised by conservatives included "communist" teachers and the illustrations in a new set of government-sponsored text-books.[83] Other issues of the day—notably, opposition to divorce, birth control, sex education, and abortion—could loosely be grouped under the rubric of "family values." All these cultural campaigns had deep roots in conservative protests going back to the 1930s. This time, however, they were articulated not because the state appeared open to compromise, but because the state appeared weak enough to challenge. This was the context of the third wave of public opposition to comic books in 1971–76.

Unlike earlier crusades, this movement left relatively few traces of itself in the newspapers. It produced nothing like the public bonfires of the 1952–56 campaign; unlike the 1942–44 movement, it produced no new laws. When the crusade was mentioned, it was usually in the midst of a longer list of conservative demands. But more Mexicans were involved in this movement to purify print media than had ever before taken up the issue. They seemed invisible because their actions took place within the bounds of their existing relationship with the state, rather than in the wider public sphere. That is, this moral panic was articulated entirely in the government's terms: by citizens individually or in small groups, appealing to the state in language they believed the state could understand and to which they trusted it would respond. At the same time, though, these citizens not only voiced dismay at the content of comic books, but at what they saw as the government's deliberate refusal, over a thirty-year period, to give conservative calls for censorship more than lip service.

During this third wave, at least 2,571 telegrams protesting comic books, photonovels, and pornography were sent to the president between February 1972 and October 1973. Most were signed by groups of three to five friends or relatives, but a few came from small-town Rotary Clubs or Chambers of Commerce. In other words, some ten thousand citizens participated in this telegraphic campaign for censorship.[84]

That this was an organized campaign is indicated by the degree of uniformity in the telegrams' content. Each repeated some variation on one of eighteen slogans. Some slogans continued the old emphasis on censorship as a question of education: 252 read, more or less, "The morality of our children matters more than coddling millionaire pornographers." Seventy-two others combined this theme with the issue of cultural imperialism, writing, "North American youth lost to pornography. Help Mexico avoid an equal tragedy." But most of the telegrams conveyed more anger with the government than the publishing industry or foreigners. One hundred and thirteen informed Echeverría that "so much pornography is making a joke of your presidency," while 189 requested that the president visit a newsstand "to understand what troubles us." Protesters believed that the government could cure the perceived ill if it wanted to, so that 246 demanded that "Mr. President" or "authorities" simply "apply the law."

Some citizens involved themselves more seriously in this third campaign. They formed antimedia groups, like the Guadalajara Alliance for Social Improvement, or set up subcommittees of existing organizations, like the Lion's Club of Leon and the Hermosillo Anti-Drug Addiction Civic Committee.[85] In a few cases, they entirely changed the purpose of existing groups, as in the revised goals of the Group for the Moral, Civic, and Material Improvement of Guadalajara, which had been publishing a local version of *Apreciaciones,* the conservative Catholic movie guide, since 1962, but switched its focus to organizing against comic books in 1972.[86]

Some of these groups used fairly sophisticated tactics to make an issue out of government inaction. In one popular maneuver, protesters gathered the most offensive materials they could from local newsstands and attempted to ship them to the president. Since local post offices would usually refuse to accept packages labeled as pornography, protesters could then complain about the central government's deliberate ignorance of the problem. Echeverría received at least 174 telegrams as a result, with variations on the message that "authorities refuse consignments of magazines. We respectfully request that you order civil servants to do their duty."

Protesters also tried good faith collaboration with the classifying commission, sending detailed lists of offensive publications for the censors to track down.[87] For the individuals and groups involved in this campaign, the president had become the enemy, yet the commission was still an ally. Conservative groups, as partners in this alliance, gave speeches and wrote articles in praise of the commission (even as they complained about the rest of the government), and organized public meetings that commission members were asked to address.[88] They even traveled to Mexico City to meet with the censors on occasion, as did five leaders of an Aguascalientes group who passed "an enjoyable afternoon" at the commission offices in discussion of their mutual interests.[89]

By the end of 1976, however, the classifying commission had ceased to make overtures to right-wing groups and was not responding so agreeably

to their complaints. The content of Mexican comic books and other periodicals did change somewhat, but without diminishing the sexual references to
which conservatives objected the most. Both the critical telegram campaign,
and the insider strategy of participation in government censorship attempts, had failed. The tone of mistrust and anger adopted by the telegrams
now spilled into public discourse. A well-publicized meeting of the National
Assembly of the Unión Nacional de Padres de Familia (one of the oldest and
largest conservative groups) in 1976 made three demands: two were related
to education, but the third insisted that government "functionaries and employees who have authorized the circulation of hundreds of pornographic
magazines" be "unmasked."[90] At last, the state could no longer use the censor's office as an instrument to incorporate cultural conservatives into itself.
Conservatives' profound distrust of a particular president had expanded into
a more complete rejection of the entire system by which Mexico was ruled.

Stabilizing the Discourse of Tradition

As the following chapters will show, the government interventions that resulted from conservative protests did change the content of Mexican comic
books, photonovels, and related media. These changes had little to do with
conservatives' goals, however, and so similar protests against consumer
culture in all its forms still occur, as in the recent, angry responses in Monterrey and Guadalajara to billboards advertising Playtex lingerie.[91] Yet the
conservative campaigns against print media had other consequences, more
important if not more direct.

The political openings through which conservative leaders moved—the
opportunities to express and build dissent through cultural protest—also
created and extended a space for the formation of an antimodernist discourse that many more people than just conservative politicians found
useful at times. This traditionalist strain in political language, mass media,
and daily interactions offered Mexicans a set of images and arguments with
which to describe, embroider on, and contest the realities they faced. At the
same time, this repertoire, which began as a rather vague alternative to the
state project of modernizing *lo mexicano*, evolved into a coherent critique
of the PRI's one-party rule and eventually became the basis of a platform
for a popular conservative party, the Partido de Acción Nacional, or PAN.

In so doing, the traditionalist discourse had to move beyond rewriting the idealized Mexican woman to revamping Mexican citizenship for both sexes.

This discourse worked by setting up funhouse-mirror inversions of the modernist stereotypes of femininity. It offered new options for gender-appropriate behavior and attitudes open to women (and perhaps also to men): they could find some cultural support whether they chose to think of and present themselves as *chicas modernas* or as suffering mothers. Furthermore, everyone who read comic books, went to church, went to school, listened to the radio, or watched television heard and saw the terms of both discourses; so anybody who adopted the imagery and arguments of one discourse would have understood the other's critique of their position.

This, then, gives most representations of either position their playful—almost kitschy—quality, visible in everything from the sarcasm of telegrams against pornography addressed to the president to the exaggerations of the dialogues between the comic book characters Nancy and Adelita. The disagreements are deadly serious. But those most involved in them knew that the symbols of their disagreements could easily, quickly, be turned against them. A change of perspective could transform the political protester, acting in legitimate defense of her family, into the foolish, complacent housewife. The brave, patriotic girl detective could also find herself described as the fragile, unprotected, danger to respectable society. The participants in these arguments acknowledge this with no more than a slight twist of rhetoric, a wink of the cartoon character's eye. But we can see it, too, in the complicity between the two sides—their willingness and ability to go on speaking to (as well as about) each other—which, after all, is what kept Mexican society intact throughout the postrevolutionary era.

Here Gabriel Vargas abandoned his usual spare style for a detailed and exact sketch of the nation's most important art museum, which at the time—as the drawing suggests—was exhibiting a Diego Rivera retrospective. *Paquito Grande*, no. 2093, 8 August 1950, p. 62.

The corner newsstand, complete with comic books; all the periodicals pictured here were part of the Novedades chain, as was the *historieta* in which these panels appeared. *Chamaco*, no. 5805, 1 January 1955, p. 8.

This was back-page filler for a horror comic; it complains, humorously, that it is impossible to get help from local governments in coping with the irritations of city life. The particular irritation here is noise from neighbors' radios. *Sombras*, no. 3, 28 November 1953.

Chapter Four

The Uses of Failure

La Comisión Calificadora, 1944–1976

 La Comisión Calificadora de Publicaciones y Revistas Ilustradas lacked the power to stop comics and other periodicals
from printing offensive pictures, using proscribed language,
or telling upsetting stories. Yet the commission mattered; it
had other jobs to do. It acted as a buffer between the increasingly powerful media corporations and their critics, and it helped protect
the Mexican market from foreign publications. The censorship commission—as long as it did not completely fail—served less tangible purposes,
too. It helped keep a dialogue going between modernists and traditionalists
over mass media, popular culture, and national identity; and it ensured the
government a central, mediating position in that dialogue. This process can
best be seen in the commission's relationship with the traditionalist critics
of media, who generally concentrated on symbolic questions—on pictures
and words—rather than more material issues: their efforts were met with
just enough success to prevent them from giving up, but not nearly enough
to satisfy them. Conservatives who remained interested in media issues
found themselves acting as auxiliaries to the commission; they became
part of the state rather than opponents of it. Thus the interactions of the
Mexican government with the popular entertainment industry, and with
the industry's fiercest critics, worked to maintain a political and economic
status quo: Gramscian hegemony made visible.

'Gov't co-opts this

In Gramsci's formulation—this is its greatest attraction for students of cultural politics—hegemony does not require deliberate plotting by the powerful to oppress the powerless. It does not demand collusion by the elite, or even consciousness. Although the men who created and supervised the commission did not intend to do anything except censor offensive comic books, in doing so, they followed the most deeply ingrained patterns of behavior of Mexico's political elite. They avoided confrontation, they delayed following through on their commitments, they never took sides in cases of open conflict, they were wary of enforcing laws when such enforcement might have infringed on the interests of their supporters, they co-opted popular protest, and they tried to include as many interest groups as possible in the broadest possible coalitions under the control of the government. Following such patterns, these men defeated their own stated purposes, but they upheld their political party's dominant role in Mexican politics. At the same time—for better or worse—they aided in the preservation of Mexico's social and political stability.

A Brief History of la Comisión Calificadora

When President Avila Camacho announced the formation of a new office charged with censoring comic books, a committee of lawyers from the Department of Public Education (SEP) was charged with writing the rules that would become the official regulations for comic books. Once the new law was promulgated on March 11, 1944, these lawyers became advisers to the censorship commission, and the secretary of public education chose the commissioners. The commission, although under the supervision of the SEP, was defined legally as an interdepartmental committee whose members would be drawn from several different branches of government, including the powerful interior ministry (Gobernación).

Commissioners quickly broadened their duties to include inspection of all illustrated periodicals. The unpaid commission apparently did not function at all between 1948 and 1952, after which it was revived to respond to another censorship campaign.[1] The commission included representatives of the ministry of education, the administration of Mexico City, and the judiciary, along with members from the SEP and Gobernación; after the laws regulating the commission were reformed in 1951, a delegate from the periodical industry also joined, and commissioners began collecting a moderate salary. Throughout this period, the secretary of public education supervised the commission and approved any new appointments to it. A third wave of public outrage over provocative magazines, in 1972 through 1976, also elicited a burst of activity from the commission.

The regulations that the original committee wrote remain essentially unchanged. The classifying commission was mandated to weed out comic books and magazines that discouraged devotion to work or study, or encouraged laziness and faith in luck; portrayed their protagonists succeeding in life by breaking laws or disrespecting established Mexican institutions; provoked disdain for the Mexican people, their history, or their abilities; used dialogue or texts with slang, offended "modesty and good manners," or were contrary to the "democratic concept." These strictures also included any published photograph or drawing that, in itself, infringed against the code.[2] Thus, in the process of writing the regulations, the scope of the commission's interests expanded from comic books that children might read (the original concern raised by conservative protesters) to any periodical sold in Mexico; and it is only after this expansion of the commission's legal mandate that protesters began to raise questions about other kinds of print media, like sports papers, true-crime tabloids, collections of song lyrics, and eventually photonovels.

The rules allowed publishers complete freedom on a provisional basis— that is, they were allowed to print what they liked until the inspection period was over, as long as a copy of every issue was sent to the commission. The commission, in turn, was required to promptly grant or refuse licenses to the publishers on the basis of their inspection. After the 1951 revision of the law, the regulations required two certificates: a title license, signifying that the title itself was not immoral and could be sent to the copyright office, and a content license, certifying that the contents of the publication infringed no rule and it could go on publishing unchanged. Title licenses usually were granted immediately. Almost all publications eventually received content licenses, too, but these sometimes required weeks or months of extended discussion within the commission, as well as between the commission and the publisher.

The commissioners, in theory, had enormous power. They were entitled to levy moderate fines and request that federal judges send stubborn editors to jail; they also could ask that the government paper monopoly deny cheap, subsidized newsprint to outlaw publishers, so that one racy publication could potentially put a whole company out of business; they could withhold certification of a licit title so that no copyright could be granted; they could request that the post office deny publishers permission to use the mails at low rates, or at all; and they could ask the Mexico City police to collect fines from or arrest newsstand operators who dealt in banned publications.

But the commission could not enforce its rulings. It could announce draconian punishments, but it needed the courts and the federal and local police to impose the penalties. The commission did not usually receive such support. This lack of reliable power of enforcement is the clearest evidence that the politicians who wrote the laws that brought the commission into existence never intended for comic books, or any other form of periodical, to be completely suppressed by this highly visible public body.

Commissioners

The men and women who staffed the commission struggled with the moral and political questions raised by the goal of controlling the content of mass media: they believed in the urgency of their task. The first commissioners seem to have been chosen less for their devotion to the hard work of setting up a new bureaucracy than for their public reputation for morality.[3] For example, Amalia Castillo de Ledon had already made a name for herself as the president of a group of elite Mexico City women (El Ateneo de Mujeres de México) and an enthusiastic supporter of Avila Camacho's literacy campaign.[4] After 1952, the classifying commission demonstrated even more personal involvement in the business of comic book censorship, as evidenced in the memoranda they wrote and in the statements they made in their private meetings. Many of the commissioners took a sincere interest in their task and expressed genuine outrage at some of the publications which they supervised.

Over the years, the commission's makeup has remained remarkably stable. Its members, as representatives of the branches of the executive, were supposed to resign every six years, at the end of each presidential term. The key membership of the commission, however, often outlasted changes of administration. Fernando Ortega ran the office from 1944 through 1958. A lawyer who helped write the 1944 legislation creating the commission, Heraclio Rodríguez Portugal, represented Gobernación on the commission from 1952 through 1955, and then represented the Federal District through 1957, when he became legal adviser to the commission. These men formed a link between the first and second incarnations of the classifying commission, but newer members also tended toward long terms. A representative of the Procuduría General, Gonzalo Hernandez Zanabria, sat on the commission from 1952 through 1976. Javier Piña y Palacios both presided over the commission and represented the Department of Public Education on it from 1952 through 1965. María Lavalle Urbina advised the commission in 1956, then represented Gobernacíon from 1957 through 1964. A comic book publisher, Octavio Colmenares Vargas, represented the interests of the magazine industry from 1958 through 1965, and again from 1971 through 1975. A few members lasted a year or less.[5] Yet for the most part, there was much more continuity than change in the makeup of the classifying commission.[6]

La Comisión Calificadora did not occupy a very distinguished position in the federal bureaucracy, to judge by its minuscule budget. Commissioners never received the yearly salary due them until 1953; even then, it was a paltry 7,200 pesos a year. In 1957, the president of the commission received a raise, to 12,000 pesos a year. Salaries were not raised again until 1972, despite a 1965 memorandum from the commission to the secretary of public education calling their earnings "ridiculous."[7] The commissioners usually held other jobs; still, judging by the amount of written material they left behind and the schedule of commission-related meetings they kept, they put in a significant amount of time working for the commission (perhaps as much as twenty hours a week), for which they were poorly reimbursed.[8]

Most commission members never attained a high political rank.[9] For the most part, the commission was a backwater of Mexico City civil service, a source of part-time, supplementary work for career bureaucrats and politicians. Perhaps the commission sometimes acted as a dumping ground for politicos whose inability to distinguish between such serious problems as career advancement and trivial matters like the moral purity of the body politic had fatally irritated their mentors; the documents that the censors produced, full of conflict and dissent, certainly do not suggest that all of them were smoothly professional, diplomatic members of the governing elite. Moreover, the positions that censors took in their meetings frequently failed to represent the interests of the governmental sector that had placed them on the commission. Some representatives of the SEP—who might be expected to be the most sympathetic to nationalist critiques of media— in fact, were among the most moderate and least active censors; some representatives of the publishing industry were strong proponents of strict enforcement of the censorship regulations.

The routine work of la Comisión Calificadora de Publicaciones y Revistas Ilustradas—registering publications, collecting small fees, mailing out certificates—went forward in the midst of a surprising amount of strain and anger. Commissioners squabbled with their direct superiors over the procedures they were to follow and the money they were owed. There were more subtle tensions, too, between the government as a whole and the commission in particular over the goals of the censorship project and how they were to be carried out. The commissioners felt other pressures from publishers, some of them with powerful political connections.[10] They also suffered when spasms of public indignation against print media required them to excuse their apparent inactivity.

Besides all these external stresses, commissioners disagreed sharply with each other on some basic questions. Some members argued on the basis of a strict social traditionalism, so that the periodicals that most concerned them depicted or suggested sex, atheism, religions other than Catholicism, divorce, crime, and working women. Other censors spoke for a modernizing revolutionary nationalism, so the periodicals that most troubled them seemed to denigrate the Revolution, the government, or even Mexico; sometimes they simply fought against the idea of commercial culture itself, saying that any periodical intended to make a profit was a social ill. A third group of censors would use the language and imagery of either discourse to protect the interests of publishers, and sometimes spoke directly on behalf of transnational capitalist culture. Beyond these general distinctions, strains arose between censors who sincerely hoped to rid Mexico of periodicals that offended them and censors who took a more relaxed view of the commission's project. The guidelines the classifying commission was supposed to follow led to bitter arguments. All the commissioners complained that the regulations failed to give them the power to wipe out precisely the magazines against which they received the most complaints; but some commissioners felt that they should work on changing the law, while others believed that the law as it stood could be stretched to cover the most egregious cases, and still others argued for interpreting the law strictly.

In the beginning, from 1944 through 1946, everyone involved seemed to have agreed on the commission's goal: to prevent *Pepín* and other comic books, as well as Sunday newspaper supplements, from depicting acts or images that offended people. Other periodicals were, at most, secondary considerations. Vexed problems of definition—what is an offensive act or image?—were left dangling. The constitution forbade prior censorship, but that legal consideration was never raised, even by the publishers. Nobody stopped to worry about whether the new law designed to empower the commission actually enabled it to meet those ends, as long as the commissioners and their superiors could claim to be making progress toward the goal of cleaning up the *pepines*.

After the first epoch of their existence, however, the commission splintered over both means and ends. For example, a basic disagreement between its pedagogic purpose, as represented by Jose Guadalupe Nájera, and the legal norms that guided the commission, as seen by Rodríguez, came up in 1953. Nájera had evaluated a cowboy comic named *Llaneros Valientes*. He reported that it was

> of North American origin. Frequent reading of it by children will lead, with time, to the deformation of the Mexican character. . . . its stylized language and attitudes indirectly promote disdain for the Mexican People.

He was, that is, claiming that this comic could be declared illicit through a loose interpretation of the section of the law making promotion of disdain for the Mexican people censurable.

Rodríguez disagreed. He remarked:

> the report on *Llaneros Valientes* is not based on anything that specifically contravenes the Regulations . . . but only in considerations of a type common to all magazines of North American origin, many of which have already been approved by this very Commission.[11]

He wanted the commission only to deny licenses to publications when they contained a picture or text that specifically infringed on one of the regulations, narrowly defined.

Such divisions persisted within the commission throughout the rest of its history. The most profound differences lay between those who expressed a sincere wish to protect Mexicans from corruption through mass media and those whose actions seem to have been motivated by their regard for the best interests of the publishing industry. Other splits divided censors offended by almost any North American publication from those more willing to judge U.S. media on a case-by-case basis. Commissioners who believed in following the law to the letter expressed sharp disagreement with those who wanted to act in its spirit, or what they believed to be its spirit. Some censors focused on details: they found certain words, individual frames in a comic book, or even styles of typography troubling.[12] The rest argued on the basis of broader, more philosophical issues.

Underlying these persistent quarrels, however, was a degree of unity. All the commissioners agreed that at least a small degree of state control over the media was necessary. And all saw a need for more direct enforcement of their edicts; none of them ever said that they felt the commission was powerful enough, while almost all complained of inadequate cooperation from other government agencies. None of the censors subjected Mexican publications to a scrutiny as intense as that undergone by U.S. comic books.

Practically every imported magazine faced more stringent enforcement of regulations than their local competitors. This may have been due to foreign publishers' difficulty in understanding and negotiating the local system—unlike locals, they took bureaucratic requirements seriously, always paying fines promptly and sending representatives to respond to the commission's requests for interviews. Foreign publishers certainly lacked the essential local connections. On the other hand, many of the war comics and cowboy-and-Indian magazines that ran into trouble with the commission were projects of powerful Mexican conglomerates that had bought the license to foreign characters from their U.S. creators. Presumably, these conglomerates should have known how to prevent the commission from doing their interests much harm. Commissioners' stubborn pursuit of publications originating in North America suggests the strength of the commitment to cultural nationalism that both traditionalists and modernists shared.

This shared ideological commitment sometimes set the commissioners apart from other politicians. In 1957—a period when the Mexican government's relations with the United States were friendly enough—the commission produced a document completely at odds with the tenor of the times. They sent a letter to the secretary of public education warning him of a comic book called the

> "Illustrated History of the United States." . . . The U.S. Information Service is distributing . . . a work in our own idiom . . . which would be most attractive and interesting to children. . . . More dangerous even than territorial conquest obtained with blood and fire is this other, achieved quietly and gradually, through a silent infiltration that makes itself master of the conscience of an immature generation, promoting in them the blind imitation of that which they erroneously consider a model civilization.[13]

They had to admit that this publication did not break any of the rules governing magazines, but they requested that the secretary make an official protest to the U.S. ambassador all the same.[14] The secretary ignored their letter, as he ignored so many of their outbursts.

This was an extreme example of the commission's nationalism. More routinely, and without any need to involve other bureaucrats, they denied title licenses to publications with English-language names.[15] And they set up what obstacles they could even to perfectly translated North American comic books. Doing so required a certain ingenuity. But its dealings with other representatives of the Mexican state called for even more bureaucratic cleverness from the commission. They sometimes negotiated the labyrinth of government with admirable skill.

The Commission and the Government

At first, the new censorship commission interpreted its regulations as a mandate to inspect every issue of every comic book in circulation. A 1945 report from the commission to the secretary of public education described the process: censors called on editors of comic books and Sunday supplements, asking them to

> cease publishing those comic strips that had been pointed out to them as immoral, suppress the worthless nudes, correct the vulgar language and the use of slang, and make the printing more legible. . . . [But] some continued to publish comics that fell within the scope of the Regulations. . . . Official notice was sent . . . requiring them to meet with their

inspector [a commission censor] again. . . . It was agreed that the magazines would submit the "boards" of every story before publication. . . .
Since then, the members of the Commission have been checking the
"boards," weekly rejecting a large number of them and making suggestions for the improvement of the moral and cultural suitability of other
comics that they are able to publish.

The report added that one Mexico City newspaper's Sunday supplement
and three comic books had been threatened with thousand-peso fines, and
that fines of three and five thousand pesos had been levied on two other
publishers.[16] The censors' scrutiny of publications for children, particularly,
was detailed and intensive. They went so far as to forbid a Mexico City
newspaper from publishing paper dolls in its Sunday supplement, calling
them "naked people for dressing up."[17]

Commissioners and publishers alike soon learned that few of these careful judgments would ever be enforced. From 1944 through 1953, of all the
violations of the law governing magazines that the classifying commission
tried to prosecute, only seven got as far as the courts. Of those, two had all
charges dropped at that stage and three had more serious charges reduced
to the level of misdemeanors. Four editors were forced to pay fines, but
none were jailed. The prosecuting attorney's office told the infuriated commission that one law-breaking editor simply could not be found in order to
be brought to court.[18] After 1953, the secretary of the commission gave up
on even trying to track the court cases that were supposed to result from
violations of the law regulating the censors.

The commission could not always count on the most basic material support from the Department of Public Education, where it was housed. In the
lapse of years between 1947 and the reestablishment of the commission in
January 1952, it lost not only its office space, but many tangible and intan-
gible assets as well. As late as October 1954, Javier Piña y Palacios was still
trying to furnish offices, recover files, and regain some communications
capacity.[19] He reported to the other commissioners:

The Semanario de Cultura Mexicana was granted permission to occupy
our offices. . . . The telephone that used to be listed under the name
of the Commission is now listed under the name of the Semanario . . .
[and] various furnishing were missing, including two typewriters, a file

cabinet, and more. . . . The only item of furniture remaining is a desk stuffed with magazines in no order whatsoever, neither chronological nor alphabetical. . . . Correspondence is not received in this office or even in the department.[20]

A series of incidents reveal how little aid the commission could expect from the rest of the government, even within the Department of Public Education. The commission's secretary received copies of the first edition of two comic books, *Hechos Heroicos* and *Desfile de Historietas*, in May 1953. Both were translations of U.S. comic books containing much blood-splattered imagery of saintly blond Yankee soldiers slaughtering sneaky, twisted, dark-skinned communist Koreans. A majority of the classifying commission had already expressed the opinion that the entire genre of North American anticommunist Korean War comics was, at best, unwholesomely violent and, more likely, a thinly veiled attack on Mexico itself.[21] In this case, Commissioner Nájera was assigned to formulate an opinion on them. He presented his report to a June meeting of the commission:

> In children and youth, this type of reading arouses the aggressive instinct, the contagion of war that rules certain foreign countries. . . . They present deformed ideas of heroes and heroic action. . . . They are open propaganda for foreign political interests.

The usual practice of the commission was to vote in whatever way the censor reporting on the publication in question recommended. Yet Commissioner Rodríguez pointed out that the commission had just voted unanimously, on his recommendation, to license *Heroe en el Cielo*, another Korean War comic book from the United States of precisely the same type as *Desfile de Historietas* and *Hechos Heroicos*. He had not liked *Heroe en el Cielo*, but had found nothing in it that was specifically forbidden by the law. Rodríguez, therefore, voted against Commissioner Nájera's recommendation. The rest of the commission voted with Nájera and the two comics were declared illicit. At the same time, however, they were passed to the other commissioners for further study.[22]

A month later, Commissioner Hernandez gave the second report on the two Korean War comics. Like Rodríguez, he too was a lawyer with a long-standing connection to the commission; unlike Rodríguez, he rarely spoke at its meetings. He told his colleagues,

Professor Nájera is right. . . . this sort of reading should not be permitted for children, though for older people it makes no difference. . . . Rodríguez is right too, because there is no legal grounds to deny these publications the right to circulate. . . . I think that it is possible to accept this type of magazine . . . [despite] a true commercial tendency.[23]

He supported Rodríguez, in other words, while also clarifying the basis for their decision: a publication's commercial (as opposed to educational) purposes should not be held against it.

Rodríguez and Hernandez did not sway their three colleagues. The commission decided to refer the matter to outside experts, but the advice they sought was that of the Instituto Nacional de Pedagogia. Commissioner Nájera was this institute's president. Predictably, when the institute finally reported on *Hechos Heroicos* and *Desfile de Historietas* in September 1953, their opinion was strongly negative. The commission then used the expert opinion as a shield for its actions, voting again—this time unanimously— to deny licenses to the two comic books.[24] By that time, their decision had created a small public fuss, during which the censors showed a united front despite these deep internal divisions.

As it happened, the aggrieved publisher of *Desfile de Historietas* and *Hechos Heroicos*, Eduardo Trueba Urbina, was not without resources with which to fight the ban on his comics. That October, he sent a telegram to President Ruiz Cortines requesting clemency; he pointed out that the Congress on Inter-American Journalism was soon to be held in Mexico and censorship of his publications would shame a government that was about to celebrate Mexico's free press at this Congress.[25] At the same time, his brother Alberto, a senator, gave an impassioned speech in the Chamber of Deputies questioning why the classifying commission picked on comic books while allowing "pornography" like *Vodevil* and *Vea* to remain on the newsstands. The Mexico City newspaper *El Universal* reported the speech and ran an editorial supporting it.[26] The commissioners looked foolish, consequently, through no fault of their own: they had long since refused licenses to all the magazines that Trueba mentioned on the Senate floor. They requested that the secretary of public education meet with them to discuss the whole affair.

When Secretary Ceniceros met with the classifying commission in November 1953, he did not so much discuss their troubles as give them a pep talk. It was incoherent and verged on the contemptuous. The secretary reiterated and defended the process by which banned publications were or were not brought to justice. The president of the commission, Piña y Palacios, asked Secretary Ceniceros whether this cumbersome procedure could be modified to allow the commission to give names of illicit magazines and law-breaking editors directly to the Mexico City police. Ceniceros replied that,

> The Commission clearly fulfills all that is contained in the procedure and to us it falls to appraise the given circumstances, with respect to the procedure, suitable to follow: . . . if there are other roads to follow to obtain the same result, in relation to the interests who believe that they might be damaged, to know where we might go so as not to provoke a reaction from other people who might be in analogous conditions. . . . The Commission should not for any reason lose heart, thinking that what they do is useless. . . . A certain rhythm must be followed to realize the work, we are going to continue with the procedure as given, creating a propitious climate. . . . Just because the newspapers act precipitously does not require we of the Secretariat to do so.[27]

In short, the answer to Piña y Palacios's request was no.

This was too much for Commissioner Nájera. As Secretary Ceniceros was promising to inform the press should a pornographer be apprehended and tried, he interrupted, "What is the point of reviewing magazines and presenting our opinions if it serves no purpose?" Ceniceros tried to soothe Nájera by saying, "The President is aware of the work of the Commission, we have leafed through these magazines together," and returning to his promise of publicizing the commission's labors. Nájera again interjected, "Then we will see ourselves judged by political elements and by the public in general, having given them the impression that the Commission is inept."[28]

This time Ceniceros ignored Nájera. He repeated himself: the commission should go on with its work, the commission should not overstep its bounds, the commission should trust him. He added that these comic books, since they were defended by a politician, were a special case, "so one would not recommend a controversy." With that, he left.[29] The commission, overlooking this strong hint, never did grant licenses to *Hechos Heroicos* and *Desfile de Historietas*.[30] The comic books went on publishing without certificates of licitude and a court case against the comics moved gradually forward as a result. But Trueba Urbina never faced any punishment for flouting the law; in fact, he won an appeal in the First Circuit Court six months later.[31] Whether because of the controversy associated with them or in spite of it, neither comic appears to have sold well or lasted long.[32] Trueba Urbina's publishing company survived and thrived. The next time he requested a license for a translation of a North American comic book, the commission gave him one—although it added a long list of suggestions for the periodical's improvement.[33]

The argument over these two comic books provided the last occasion on which the commissioners would challenge their superiors openly. They persisted in trying to uphold the law as it stood and even tried to have the law rewritten to boost their powers: in February of 1954, they wrote up a new set of regulations that would have clarified the questions of what was or was not illicit; substantially widened the category of forbidden words, pictures, and themes; and strengthened the commission's powers of enforcement. Commissioner Rodríguez presented the proposal to Secretary Ceniceros, who simply ignored it.[34]

The commission never had another chance to complain when the rest of the government withheld support. After 1953, their communications with the secretary of public education and the president, for the most part, went in a single direction: the senior officials asked the commissioners to reply to citizens annoyed by various publications and the commissioners dutifully responded by sending soothing letters to complainants. It seems as though la Comisión Calificadora was useful to the government only as a buffer between the publishing industry and conservative citizens.

The Co-optation of Conservative Protest

La Comisión Calificadora de Publicaciones y Revistas Ilustradas had a fair amount of success in filling a role that never was assigned to it directly: it absorbed the fury and distracted the attentions of some politically organized social conservatives. This shock-absorbing function prevented social conservatives from doing any damage to a culture industry that was, in turn, an important supporter of the state.[35]

Yet the censors' good faith attempts to cooperate with organized groups of citizens upset by certain periodicals consistently ended in frustration for all concerned. The number of magazines and comic books published in Mexico boomed in the 1950s; rather than closely examining every one, the classifying commission concentrated on a few. For the most part, they worried about high-circulation comic books and tabloids depicting violent crime or warfare, particularly those imported from the United States. Such reading material seems to have given little concern to any other readers. The commissioners also spent a certain amount of time chasing down those periodicals about which they had heard complaints: low-circulation, soft-core pornography.

The first instance of la Comisión Calificadora responding directly to complaints from social conservatives occurred almost immediately after its reestablishment in December 1953. The Mexican Legion of Decency sent the commission a petition requesting that two girlie magazines—*Eva* and *Can-Can*—be banned. The commission resolved to pursue these publications to the best of its ability. From the Legion of Decency's point of view, the commission's best turned out to be not very good. *Eva* and *Can-Can* had never applied for licenses, so the commission's belated decision to refuse them was meaningless. Nor was a plea to the post office to withdraw their second-class mailing licenses of any use, since these magazines were not sold through the mail. The commission required the editors of *Can-Can* and *Eva* to appear for an interview. Although nobody ever answered the commissioners' letters at *Can-Can*, the editor of *Eva* showed up for a meeting, offered the censors some unsatisfactory excuses—"I did not know that these regulations existed"—and promised to reform.[36] (In the end, he neither cleaned up the magazine nor paid the 5,000 peso fine the commission levied.) The publishers seemed unmoved by threats to cut off their supply of government-subsidized paper, either because they had friends at PIPSA, the newsprint monopoly, or because their magazines were printed in the United States.[37] The commission quickly exhausted every legal recourse available to it and referred the problem of *Can-Can* to the Mexico City chief of police, on the grounds that the magazine also violated the laws governing all printed material in Mexico by not printing the names and addresses of the publisher and editor. The censors hoped that the police would then enforce the *Ley de Imprenta* by confiscating all copies of *Can-Can* from the newsstands. There is no evidence that this ever happened. The commission reported to the Legion of Decency on all their attempts to stifle *Eva* and *Can-Can,* but the legion's directors must have noticed that for all the activity, little was actually accomplished.[38]

In the decades that followed, groups of social conservatives—often associated with the Catholic Church—made more persistent attempts to cooperate with the commission, or to force it to do its job. The classifying commission was highly sensitive to such efforts. For example, in 1954, the commission spent an entire meeting discussing the Legion of Decency's recently settled complaints and a new, related problem:

> Hernandez Zanabria reports that . . . the National Press is going to initiate a campaign against pornographic magazines. . . . A well-directed campaign of this sort might bring very good results, but it is necessary to move ahead of it. . . . Rodríguez proposed that the Commission initiate the campaign before the newspapers do.[39]

As it happened, the rumor of an impending morality campaign in the papers was false. A year later, however, a single newspaper article covering an anti-comic-book speech made by a member of the Consejo Consultivo de la Ciudad de México again led the commission to call a special meeting in order to discuss the same projects.[40] And in 1956, the classifying commission met especially to consider how to reply to antipornography editorials published in three regional newspapers.[41]

The commission tried to include groups involved in antipornography campaigns in its work, making them sympathizers instead of adversaries. Usually these efforts at incorporation required little more than a letter. One typical note from the president of the classifying commission, written in March 1972 in response to a complaint from the Matamoros Committee for the Moralization of the Social Atmosphere, read in part:

> Being conscious of the legal limits of this Commission, I cannot do less than receive with gratitude collaboration such as that which you have offered. . . . Let us know which publications, in your judgement, are destroying the moral, education and cultural principles on which the Mexican family is based; however, it should go without saying that the classification of what is pornographic or obscene is the job of the judicial authorities.[42]

In a single paragraph, this letter delicately conveyed everything the Mexican government might wish an angry social conservative to believe:

that the state was responsive to and agreed with private complaints against mass media, that there were inescapable limits on state action against mass media, and that, all the same, decisions on whether and how to control media (including decisions on what words or pictures were objectionable) were best left to the state. No wonder that a month later, twenty-two copies of this triumph of rhetoric were sent out to complaining groups like the Guanajuato Lions Club, the Guanajuato Knights of Columbus, the Hermosillo Civic Anti-Drug-Addiction Committee, and the Potosí Sports Club.[43]

Sometimes the commission offered more than a vague expression of sympathy to conservative social groups. For instance, in 1971—another period of heightened public concern about pornography—the commission invited the leaders of an Aguascalientes group to come to its offices, bringing with them a collection of offensive magazines purchased from Aguascalientes newsstands, to discuss their shared concerns.[44] At the same time, the secretary of the commission was helping a group of Guadalajara conservatives—the Committee of Mental Health and Social Orientation—to pursue a case against the publishers of marriage manuals (*Guia Intima del Matrimonio*) and feminist novels (a translation of Joyce Elbert's *Crazy Ladies*) with the copyright office.[45] The commission also reexamined two magazines, sent to them by the Guadalajara group, that had been declared licit in 1969.[46] Both remained legal, as the commission's letter to the Guadalajara conservatives circuitously put it, because

> in aesthetics there do not exist any universal values that determine with precision the limits of each and every one of the concepts that we refer to in settling this kind of problem.[47]

Occasionally, conservative groups decided to adhere themselves to the classifying commission, declaring themselves—for example—"una Junta Auxiliar de la Comisión Federal," as the Central Group for the Civic and Moral Betterment of Ciudad Juárez did in 1955, or the "Comisión de Revistas Ilustradas de Guadalajara," as some members of the Group for Material and Cultural Improvement of that city did in 1954.[48] More often, however, the classifying commission attempted to absorb its conservative critics into itself, whether they wanted to join the commission or not. For instance, the Group for the Moral, Civic, and Material Betterment of Guadalajara, in the period 1971–76, constantly sent telegrams and letters to the commission explaining precisely which banned publications could be seen on local newsstands. Why, they asked, was the classifying commission not doing a better job?[49] The commission responded in 1976 with a flowery certificate of appreciation, impressively stamped and sealed: "You are sincerely congratulated for the commendable work you have developed, alongside the state and municipal authorities . . . [to aid] the members of this Commission."[50] The commission insisted on treating the Guadalajara group's members as collaborators, no matter how they felt about it. This was an old pattern: in 1955, Commissioner Hernandez Zanabria recommended that Guadalupe Zuñiga de Gonzalez, national director of Acción Social, be invited to attend commission meetings, "with the objective that [Acción Social] join in the work of the Commission."[51]

The commission's incorporation of complainants into itself even extended to hinting, every so often, that the commission and the conservatives were allied against the government. In a 1955 letter to the Huixtla (Chiapas) Chamber of Commerce, Commissioner Piña y Palacios wrote that "this Commission has taken the most drastic measures against that genre of publications, but its actions have been forcibly limited by the powers that the current law grants it."[52] To underline the point about its limited powers, the classifying commission printed up copies of the law governing it, to be sent to its most frequent correspondents.[53] This might be seen as the logical extreme of the commission's participation in co-opting the enemies of the state: it became so identified with its antagonists that it almost forgot the nature of its allies.

All this work—airing opinions, writing letters, sending telegrams, reading newspapers, holding meetings, constructing alliances—never helped drive Mexican publishers, even publishers of pornography, out of the marketplace. Nor did it strengthen conservative social groups, nor improve the political position of la Comisión Calificadora or its members. In the end, all it did was reinforce the role of the state as the mediator in every political or social transaction in Mexico.

Censorship and Political Stability

The first comic book censorship campaign began early in 1943; the most recent, in 1972. In this thirty-year period, the comics audience grew, the comics themselves improved production values, and more comic book companies published more comic books than ever before, but the style and content of Mexican comics did not change much. Moreover, the personnel of the comics remained the same, implying that a run-in with the commission was not likely to cost a cartoonist his or her livelihood. Whole new genres of periodicals appeared—ranging from photonovels, which were little different from the original comic books, to girlie calendars—and most of them infringed on the same regulations that the *historietas* did. The commission made no progress toward the goals of the anti-comic-book crusades. They did not even make pornography unavailable.

Yet the commission did perform three crucial roles for the Mexican state, even if none of them precisely fit the commission's job description as given in the law governing it. First, it helped articulate and preserve the discourse of cultural nationalism, emphasizing *lo mexicano* and resistance to international cultural forces. Even during periods when the rest of the Mexican state was more likely to use the transnational rhetoric of progress and modernity, the commission acted as a nationalist (and to a certain extent, anticapitalist) voice. Second, by raising barriers to translated U.S. magazines that were slightly higher than those faced by local publications, the commission helped prevent cultural imperialism even as it formulated the argument against it. Third, the classifying commission provided a mechanism by which conservative protest could be channeled and co-opted by the state.

The case of la Comisión Calificadora de Publicaciones y Revistas Ilustradas, in short, exemplifies the Mexican state's brilliant gift for self-preservation: even the most ineffectual node of the federal bureaucracy acted to protect the government from potential dangers inside and outside Mexico, avoid damaging the interests of the government's allies, and give as many citizens as possible some stake in the process of government without offering them any real control of the outcome. The genius of the system is that nobody had to reach a conscious decision, either in setting up the classifying commission or at any point thereafter, to act in bad faith. The legislators who orated in favor of moral purity, the lawyers who wrote the regulations, and the bureaucrats who supervised the commission simply had to act as Mexican politicians usually do. They spoke much but said little, reassured all parties that the government was in perfect agreement with them, placed many layers of government agencies between themselves and any ordinary citizen, and ensured that the power of enforcement remained concentrated in the hands of a relatively small number of people rather than belonging to the numerous subbureaucracies that proliferate under such a regime. This explains why the tale of la Comisión Calificadora fails to provide a satisfying villain, much less a hero: as a rule, to keep the system working, the use of power in postrevolutionary Mexico had to be not only invisible to outside observers, but practically unconscious on the part of the powerful participants.

The line between *historietas* and other types of periodicals has never been clear. *Historietas* evolved out of newspapers and always included some print content; the same companies produced *historietas* and most other kinds of periodicals; the same newsstands sold them; and the cartoon and photonovel format appeared in many other kinds of periodicals. Here, in a page from a women's magazine, a continuing comic strip shares space with an article on table manners. This issue also contains chapters from two serialized photonovels. *Historietas* typically formed part of the contents of women's magazines in the 1940s and 1950s. *Tu y yo confesiones*, no. 113, 29 July 1955, p. 10.

Photonovels, until the 1970s, often mixed photographs and drawings to achieve their effect. Artists also used movie stills, newspaper clippings, publicity shots, maps, mass cards, and any other materials that came to hand. The backgrounds were almost always drawn in, rather than photographed, as this saved the expense of decorating sets. Here, the photograph of two actors in an empty room is nearly obliterated by drawn-in additions, including stripes added to the woman's dress. This scene came from a melodrama (loosely based on an Agustín Lara song) that appeared in a weekly women's magazine, along with recipes, movie star gossip, short stories, panel cartoons, and fashion tips. *Paquita de Jueves*, no. 923, 1 July 1948, p. 3.

The line between *historietas* and soft-core pornography could also be blurred. Here is a page from a serial, "Born to Be Bad," that occupied the last twelve pages of each issue of an ostensibly religious comic book, *La Sagrada Familia*. The cover of this issue featured some sheep, a goat, and Isaac and Jacob; the first sixteen pages tell of the miraculous birth of Mary to St. Anne. *La Sagrada Familia*, no. 8, 3 January 1972, p. 21.

Chapter Five

Comic Books Respond to Their Critics, 1944–1976

 Comic books and other disreputable periodicals flourished in the decades after official morality was supposed to be imposed on them. The number of *pepines* increased wildly, as did the number of readers. But the period Irene Herner calls "the Golden Age" of Mexican comics—roughly 1935–50— had ended: they had grown increasingly moralizing, sentimental, patriotic, and predictable.[1] Conservatives did not care how dull Mexican comics were becoming; they still bemoaned their images of violence and sex. And the comics paled in comparison to the newer, related genres of soft-core pornography, photonovels, and true-crime tabloids. By the mid-1950s a determined shopper could find four or five magazines featuring artistic photographs of naked ladies or bloody corpses on any Mexico City newsstand.

No matter how hard it tried, la Comisión Calificadora could not protect the public from photonovels telling tales of women in prison, comic books presenting bank-robbing vampires from beyond the grave, true-crime tabloids uncovering a string of sex crimes in Tijuana cabarets, or photography magazines offering advice on how to pose nude models.[2] The commission's lack of enforcement power helped create this situation. But the ingenuity of entrepreneurs and the power of large publishing businesses also contributed to the seeming ineffectuality of the commission.

Paradoxically, the critics of periodicals, inside and outside government, helped to shape the content of Mexican media even though they lacked sufficient power to enforce their demands for complete censorship. Publishers responded to public outrage and state pressure in both subtle and obvious ways. They sometimes replied to common arguments against their products in the contents of their comic books and other periodicals. Sometimes, too, they answered the specific legal issues raised by the censors, occasionally in dry legal language, but often in highly emotional terms. Complaints about comic books and photonovels influenced the kinds of imagery periodicals used, the words they employed, and the stories they told. Even when they did not design their work for the approval of their critics, publishers learned what topics and styles to avoid. This may help explain why the comics became so drearily formulaic in the years after the first censorship campaign in 1942–44.

Some editors and publishers went to considerable trouble to put their cases to the commissioners, suggesting that they believed it to have some power over their publications after all, a belief that influenced the content of comic books and magazines more than the commission ever could have done directly. Interactions between commissioners and publishers produced a rich cache of documents in which producers of questionable magazines defended their work. These businesspeople sometimes seemed willing to say anything to the commission in order to protect their profits. Often, they borrowed rhetoric and ideas from the censors, as well as from the conservatives who campaigned against them. At the same time, the publishers—like their antagonists—remained strictly within the bounds of a national argument over modernity, capitalism, and cultural identity. Anybody involved in any dispute over popular culture or mass media had no option but to put their interests forward by taking up some position (it hardly seemed to matter which) within the larger discourses of tradition and modernity.

These words did not float free of material reality. Like other Mexican industries in the boom years of 1940–70, the publishing business faced stiff competition from the United States; like other local businesspeople, Mexican publishers used nationalist rhetoric to encourage the government to protect local markets from foreign encroachment. Such language—meant to build national consensus around a kind of state capitalism—appeared not only in the context of Mexican publishers' relations with censors, but also publicly, as in the 1952 *Jueves de Excelsior* article that warned that the recent "invasion" of U.S. magazines such as *Life* and *Reader's Digest* threatened

Mexican jobs.³ The notoriously "positive and stable relationship," in Roderic Camp's words, between government and industry was constructed through acts that were discursive as well as economic.⁴ This relationship was just as important as the formal barriers to foreign investment built up in the 1950s in creating the conditions in which Mexican business could flourish, for good or ill. The dealings of Mexican magazine publishers with their critics in the government is a small, but telling, portion of that larger story.

This chapter examines three aspects of the publishing industry's response to its critics, both inside and outside the government. First, it reviews the rhetoric publishers employed in advertising their products, pointing to their adaptions of the language of progress, modernity, and nationalism in reaction to a conservative critique. Second, it looks at an extreme example of publishers' ability to evade the law and even use it to their own advantage: the Lombardini brothers, comic book and pornography publishers who flourished for decades despite public notoriety and many encounters with the censors. Third, this chapter takes the left-wing cartoonist and writer Rius (Eduardo del Río) as another case study. Rius's career—both his run-ins with the state and his troubles with the publishing industry—demonstrates the limits on political expression in comic books, and the subtle power of the combined forces of state and capital.

Comic Books Respond to the Audience

Comic book artists and entrepreneurs spoke in favor of comics in the pages of the *pepines* themselves. *Historietas* insisted on their own value as a positive good in Mexican life, as educational tools, moralizing forces, creators of national unity, and protectors of the body politic. As Modesto Vázquez Gonzalez, the manager of a successful comic book company, explained in 1981, "SOCIAL SOLIDARITY" became the most important "moral aspect of comic book magazines."⁵ Publishers searched for moralistic and patriotic— but still profitable—content; in so doing, they turned away from imitations of U.S. comics and developed distinctly Mexican genres.

Nationalist, modernist rhetoric worked on several levels. It responded directly to critics inside or outside the government, but it also reached the audience for cheap entertainment; thus, it was an important form of self-promotion. It helped comfort consumers who might be concerned about the effects that the comics and similar periodicals were having on them or their children. It differentiated locally made periodicals from foreign competition, suggesting why readers should prefer one or the other. To the extent that it stabilized the content of *historietas,* it enabled publishers to offer readers a predictable (and therefore desirable) product, as standard-ized as a bottled soda. To the extent that readers also participated in the discourse of progress, modernization, and *lo mexicano,* it helped creators invent generic stories that satisfied the audience.

Sometimes comic books explicitly replied to common criticisms. Their advertising slogans alluded to their local origin, defending them from any accusation of cultural imperialism. One periodical noted in its indica, "this is an ORIGINAL magazine, made by Mexican writers, artists and technicians for Latin America."[6] Another went to the trouble of taking out a copyright on the subtitle, *Revista Infantíl Mexicana;* sometimes, too, it boasted "made only by Mexican personnel" on its masthead.[7]

Comic book evocations of *lo mexicano* occasionally showed a certain wit. In 1952–53, the horror comic *Sombras* presented a series of one-page humor pieces by Guillermo Marin. In one, a Mexican couple is showing a visiting Martian their kitchen, which he has already devastated in a futile search for something he cannot describe. The housewife shows him a can: "Chiles!" exclaims the alien, "This is what I was lacking! Now my people can come to the Earth for food!" The woman wonders, "Can you tell us what sort of food you want them for?" The alien shrieks, "We use them to cover the bad flavor of human meat!"[8] The plot came straight out of countless American, British, and Japanese science fiction movies and television shows. But, as the story refers to the most distinctive Mexican flavor, it comments on cul-tural imperialism. Marin poses a question: Is he a local artist brainwashed by foreign stories or a proud Mexican turning foreign stories to his own purposes? The story itself might suggest that sharing local culture with outsiders could be dangerous. "Ay!" the housewife moans in the last frame, "now the Martian is going to eat us!"

The care taken to appear Mexican did not always extend to the content of the comics. "*Dulce Amor,* the complete Mexican photo-novel," boasted one weekly's cover; yet the editor, when called before the classifying commis-sion, defended her work by pointing to the transnational literary culture in which the magazine participated. *Dulce Amor*'s contents, she said, included photonovel versions of *Bodas de Sangre, A Streetcar Named Desire,* and *Othello* to "give to the lower middle class . . . the books they do not read."[9]

The photonovel was selling itself to the public on its *mexicanidad,* but its author was quite willing to put forth a completely contradictory defense of her work in private.

Publishers' choice of subject matter itself seemed designed to protect publications from complaint and connect with the audience's national pride. The pre-Cortesian past proved useful to publishers as a means to present half-clad women and copious gore in an unquestionably patriotic and educational context. An advertisement for *Leyendas* underlined its nationalist theme, calling it "the magazine that presents the most beautiful tales created by the imagination of our peoples" while depicting a muscular man and bosomy woman in scanty "indigenous" costumes with a pyramid in the background.[10] The cover of the respectable children's comic *Tesoros* pictured national hero Cuautemoc on top of a pyramid in much the same outfit.[11] And *Joyas de la Mitologia* ran an advertisement for a fancy pen that deployed the same imagery: over a photo of an Olmec stone head, it read, "CLASSIC/the ballpoint with the beauty of traditional style."[12]

The more recent past, from Porfirio Díaz through Lázaro Cárdenas, offered trickier subject matter. Representations of highly charged events could easily alienate some segment of their audience by making heroes of one side and villains of the others.[13] But the Revolution—a subject combining violence with patriotism—proved irresistible. *La Rebelión de los humildes* luridly portrayed the campaigns of Zapata and Villa while calling itself "a publication which brings dignity to the Mexican comic book."[14] Another comic, *La Verdadera Historia de Pancho Villa,* met with unusually stiff resistance from the classifying commission for its "distortion of historical facts": the commissioners urged its writers to add footnotes and a bibliography to every issue.[15] Similarly, a José G. Cruz comic book called *Rosita Alvírez,* set in the nineteenth century, offended literal-minded readers who missed the presence of historical figures like Juárez and Porfirio Díaz.[16]

Another unsubtle but patriotic theme was biographies of present-day Mexican heroes and celebrities. Such *historietas* narrated the lives of local stars in as sexy and violent a manner as a loose interpretation of the facts would allow. Saints, athletes, movie stars, musicians, and the great figures of the Revolution all had comic books based on their lives, but their accomplishments took a backseat to their love lives and the crimes or battles they had witnessed.

An obvious source of biographies was the lives of the saints, a mine of violent, sometimes sexual narratives that were at the same time un-questionably moral. Adding nationalist to religious sentiment, publishers preferred stories of Latin American saints and Mexican clergy. Comic books such as *La Sagrada Familia, Milagros de Cristo,* and *Fray Escoba, San Martín de Porres* had pious-looking covers that hid lurid pictures and gruesome stories.[17] Athletes, too, were important subjects of nationalist "true stories." Wrestlers, bullfighters, boxers, and soccer players starred in their own comic books; the *El Santo* photonovel—on the life and times of the most famous of all wrestlers—was the greatest of José G. Cruz's successes, run-ning from 1953 through at least 1974 and at its peak selling 900,000 copies three times a week all over the Spanish-speaking world.[18] Finally, cinema provided many heroic figures. Maria Felix starred in her own photonovel—advertised as "the story which the most beautiful actress in the world cre-ated personally for you, reader, of an incident in her daring life unknown until today"—as did Tin-Tan and Jorge Negrete.[19] Pedro Infante was the hero of at least three.[20] *La vida y los amores de Pedro Infante* tried to avoid offending public morality or Infante's more conservative fans by taking the figure of the dead Infante in heaven as their narrator; the photonovel had him commenting ruefully on potentially shocking episodes.

Publishers used specific Mexican locales along with famous Mexicans to underline the patriotism of their comic books. A 1955 story in the comic book *Los Supersabios* had its protagonists participate in an international auto race across Mexico, so that recognizable scenes from several different states appeared in every issue. The author added to these local settings the element of Mexican competition with the United States by naming the favorite in the race "Invincible Jack Superman of Indianapolis." (The gringo lost.)[21] *Fotomisterio* emphasized its local origin by adding a note at the bottom of the first page thanking the owners of the Mexican buildings in which the stories were produced:

> We are very grateful for the collaboration of Sasa Seminuevos Autos, the brewery "El Popo" of Coahuila and Merida, and most especially the exclusive sanitarium and maternity hospital . . . of Dr. Ismael Mendoza Fuentes, located in . . . Colonia Del Valle.[22]

Even imported *historietas* sometimes attempted to appear local: in an early issue of *Pepín,* a translator had the Lone Ranger shouting "For Téxas and México!" as he rushed to the aid of flag-waving U.S. troops menaced by short, dark, mustachioed villains in sombreros.[23] *Dick Tracy*'s translators went to the trouble of interpreting names, as well as dialogue, so that the character Sparkle Plenty became Lucerito Brilliante. They even changed the signs on buildings, turning a drive-in movie theater into the "Auto-Cinema 'El Bosque'".[24]

Some publishers implied agreement with their opponents by distinguishing their own "healthy," "clean," or "moral" product from the rest. They tried to attract readers and deflect criticism with the vocabulary of modernist hygiene and, more rarely, traditionalist morality. One publishing house, Sociedad Editora America, advertised itself in 1957 with the line, "SEA . . . YES IT IS A HEALTHY magazine."[25] A second publisher of translated U.S. comic books claimed that its products were "safe and moral for youth."[26] Another peddled "healthy entertainment for the whole family."[27] Editora de Periodicos La Prensa urged buyers to carry its publications "to your home WITH COMPLETE CONFIDENCE."[28] This publisher even contended that some comics from the United States might have as patriotic a purpose as any Mexican *historieta,* in its advertisement for *Clasicos Ilustrados:*

> Safe reading that educates, cultivates and delights. That which previously was the privilege of people who are well-to-do or highly educated, now is accessible to every social sector. LA PRENSA . . . continues its patriotic labor of cultural diffusion.[29]

Local comic books, too, often emphasized their moral content as well as their *mexicanidad.* And their publishers looked for symbols of powerful authorities to prove their moral worth. By the mid-1950s, every comic published by SEA advertised that it had been "approved by the SEP," a coy misinterpretation of the meaning of a license from la Comisión Calificadora.[30] Similarly, the children's comic *Tesoros* announced that it had been "authorized" by the Monseñor Luís Martinez, archbishop of Mexico City, and "classified as EXCELLENT" by the Mexican Legion of Decency.[31]

Even such racy material as *Minicarcel de mujeres*—a comic book so daring that its artist hid behind the pseudonym "B. Historietista"—made what moral claims it could. Although it frequently showed women in their underwear and referred directly to adultery, premarital sex, incest, and prostitution, it also began and ended most episodes in the women's prison, so that readers could be certain before the story began that the protagonist would eventually suffer for her crimes. In a typical issue, the body of the story would be in a flashback, often as a confession to a priest.[32] A similar narrative device placed both reader and author in the role of moral judge, as in *Pepín's* advertisement of its "audacious and different" serial *Salon de Baile* (Dance hall) as "a story the every mother should read, so as to avoid some of the dangers that surround your daughters in the turbulent life of the city."[33] Thus were moral standards upheld, even in the most objectionable comic books. In this context, the label "suitable for adults" or "for adults only," applied by publishers to their most daring creations in the vain hope of warding off conservative complaint, seems like an admission of defeat.[34]

The last of this set of tactics employed in the content of comic books to answer or evade criticism seems to have been directed at the publishers' political enemies: the comics occasionally chose to emphasize their government connections. *Pepín* ran a feature in 1940, for example, in which it all but equated itself with the Mexican state, announcing a

> Patriotic Contest . . . for the students of every school in the nation. We will give the finest silk flags to the winning Schools . . . with the aim of contributing powerfully to the campaign for the growth of national pride, increasing in our children the sentiments of veneration, respect and love for the patria and the national flag, and with the motive, also, of celebrating during the month of September the glorious anniversary of national independence.

In this contest, students were to "vote" for the flag by sending a card or letter to *Pepín;* whichever school in each state produced the most votes would win a flag and also have their school photo, taken with the state's governor in attendance, printed in *Pepín.*[35] The most extreme case of flaunting political connections, however, came when *Tesoros* began printing photographs of its editors meeting with political luminaries or their families, such as Miguel Alemán Jr. (son of the president); various subsecretaries of Gobernación, Hacienda, and Educación Pública; Archbishop Martinez; and Jaime Torres Bodet, the ex-education minister who was head of UNESCO at the time.[36]

When a comic book or photonovel found itself under unbearable pressure from the classifying commission and the public at large, there was one final defense. It could fold. Sometimes editors who took this last step even informed the commission that they had done so in the interests of public morality, as did the Cabral Flores family when, in the midst of an antipornography campaign, they ceased publication of the humor magazines *Esto es sexo ja ja* and *Los mejores cuentos de Pepito.*[37] Afterward—as Irene Herner described in her 1979 study of the industry—the offensive publication could reestablish itself with a new title but almost identical contents, staff, distribution, and audience. This cycle could be repeated as often as necessary, until the energy of an antipornography movement had been completely dissipated.[38]

These, however, were only indirect responses to criticism. Publishers rarely replied directly to the complaints raised about comic books and other periodicals by social conservatives. They preferred to deal with the classifying commission, allowing (or forcing) it to defend them to the outraged public.

Comic Books Respond to the Government

Even before the founding of la Comisión Calificadora, publishers of comics and other morally questionable periodicals maintained strong connections with the Mexican government in order to stave off censorship initiatives from the public. In 1943, Editora de Periódicos La Prensa—then producing the daily paper *La Prensa,* with a much-criticized Sunday comics supplement—invested in a new, full-color printing press. Luís Novaro, director of the firm, invited President Avila Camacho to attend the gala ceremony inaugurating the expensive machine, providing the occasion to print photos placing the president and the corporation in close conjunction. At the same time, Novaro offered a 50 percent discount on printing costs for textbooks to the secretary of public education, writing, "LA PRENSA IS NOT SEEKING FINANCIAL GAIN, but only . . . to serve the Mexican Nation."[39] Novaro, in other words, traded a fiscal loss on the printing jobs for future favors from crucial government figures.

Publishers' connections to politicians and bureaucracies took on a more specific form after the 1944 founding of the classifying commission. Editors of offensive publications used a variety of strategies to achieve three related goals: they wanted to continue printing their magazines without trouble from the law, with the maximum possible freedom to push the boundaries of the socially acceptable, and the seal of government approval implied by the official license of the commission. They risked fines, loss of copyright, loss of postal privileges, even jail, to reach these aims. But this was a reasonable bet: publishers almost always won.

From the very beginning, writers, editors, and publishers who dealt with the commission refused to accept fines and reprimands. They tried to argue their way out of them, often successfully. Publishers usually told the commission that they were respecting the spirit, if not the letter, of the new law. In 1945, the humor magazine *Don Timorato* requested that a fine be suspended because the editors had not

> been informed of the law's existence: Our magazine is not, nor does it try to be, one of those which offends morality, or in any way violates the law. . . . Although ignorance of the law is no obstacle to a sanction, we have proceeded in good faith.[40]

Nine years later, the editor of the girlie magazine *Eva*, Manuel Enrique Castrillon y Rodríguez, made similar excuses to the commission: "He was ignorant of the fact that it was necessary to print the date of publication . . . [and] is unacquainted with the [rest of the] Regulations."[41] He, too, was forgiven.

Sometimes, to the great annoyance of the censors, publishers tried to ensure that their products would be eligible for commission certification by asking for comments on new projects before they were in press. As this amounted to unconstitutional censorship prior to publication, it would have been illegal; worse, it would have created an enormous amount of work for the commissioners.[42] Commissioner Rodríguez responded to one plea for guidance as follows: "The Commission will not serve as anyone's tutor."[43] Publishers had to take their chances.

Unlicensed and law-breaking publishers found ways to evade censorship or punishment. They relied on a handful of tactics that seemed to work over and over. Almost all declarations to the commission ended with the editors vowing that they would never infringe the regulations again. Beyond that, editors had four types of reasons why they should not be fined and should be allowed to continue publishing their periodicals: they blamed somebody else, they claimed injustice, they made a variety of economic arguments, or they insisted that their publications were not merely harmless, but healthy, educational, or patriotic.

Passing the buck was a favorite technique. Publishers blamed editors and editors blamed nameless freelancers, who, they would assure the commission, had been dealt with severely. For example, Carlos Vigil defended his comic book *Torbellino* by claiming that

> Number 358 . . . was illustrated by another artist who is not the usual one and the female figures were represented in a somewhat vulgar form. . . . [T]he new adventures of the principal character will have, in the future, less violent and sensual characteristics, and will take care to preserve high artistic and literary quality.[44]

Similarly, Manuel Flores, editor of the sports magazine *Velo-Poster*, explained that his periodical had published pictures of naked women only because,

> Having been absent from the country . . . [I had] left Luis Arenas Rosas in charge of the publishing house . . . who without consent printed a series of photos with naked women. . . . [I] had already given instructions . . . [to reprint] the best posters that we had published this year, but not in any way those with naked women . . . and not those that could serve for minors, juveniles and tasteless people to find, one way or another, some bad use to which the photographs might be put.[45]

Occasionally, publishers blamed forces beyond their control, conveniently outside the country. *Cortejos Romanticos* was denied a license because the comic's typography and orthography were imperfect, but the publisher argued that these flaws were the fault of a printing plant in the United States, "where the personnel do not speak Spanish."[46] The Mexican publisher of the U.S. comic *Dollman* (memorably described by the commissioners as "entirely North-Americanizing"[47]) tried a similar approach, apologizing that he was unable to change anything about the publication because "we receive it already printed, we cannot do anything to them here, [or] change anything."[48] This argument never convinced the commissioners to grant a license or rescind a fine.

A second type of argument used by publishers in trouble with the classifying commission was the complaint that their particular publication had been unfairly singled out when other magazines had been allowed to get away with worse. Castrillon y Rodríguez concluded his list of excuses for *Eva* by observing that it was "in competition with *Vodevil* [so] it would have to be, if not more daring than, at least more or less similar to *Vodevil*."[49] Twenty years later, Benjamin Escamilla, editor of the photonovel *Casos de Alarma,* sent the commission a list of twenty-six comic books and photonovels that,

> without carrying on work for the benefit of society, as we have done, still enjoy a license, even though they do not refer to real facts and they give way to flights of imagination, a thing which we consider nefarious for the reader.[50]

As an infuriated newsstand operator wrote to a tax collector, with whom he was arguing over what was and was not a tax-exempt "educational" periodical, it was difficult at times to distinguish a moral from an immoral publication, much less to guess why a licensed publication might suddenly be deemed less legal than any other. "Which magazines or periodicals are considered to have cultural goals, and which are not?" he asked.[51]

A third type of appeal was made on the basis of economics: publishers sometimes claimed that it was their right to make a profit. While they might agree that their products were vulgar, they vehemently disagreed with the implication that education or moral improvement was their responsibility. In a 1957 meeting, José Rubio Castilla—director of the true-crime weekly *Prensa Roja*—and his lawyer Rafael Curiel tried this capitalist argument on the commission with mixed success. Curiel urged the commissioners "to consider the economic project of this man [Rubio]. I do not justify it as a good periodical, but it is for . . . a type of person who asks for nothing but this." Rubio added, with notable bitterness, "We have to use the magazine as a commercial medium in order to be able to sell it. If the government would subsidize us . . . we could write philosophy, good philosophy." Commissioner Nájera, as he usually did, rejected the idea that making a profit, in itself, justified any kind of publication that did not violate a specific regulation. He responded, "the mercantile spirit that guides the editor is . . . completely immoral."[52]

Rather than debating the abstract wisdom of the marketplace, those who argued on economic grounds usually spoke in terms of economic nationalism, claiming that it was good for the nation if they made a profit. Often they excused their businesses because they employed Mexicans, as the publisher of a comic book called *El Goleador Misterioso* did:

> A group of cartoonists make this magazine and it feeds approximately five families, besides the dealers and people at the printers. . . . It is the

first time that we have had the opportunity to earn a little more than that which an artist of comic books usually earns as an employee.[53]

Publishers had a second argument grounded in economic nationalism: they sometimes cited their need to compete freely with foreign magazines. For instance, Raymundo Ampudia, president of the Chamber of Commerce of the Publishing Industry, met with the commission in 1967 to request that

the articles [of the Regulations] be modified . . . to be in accord with the modern sense of freedom that obtains in other countries . . . [and] that the Commission should be more tolerant of Mexican publishers . . . [and] that the Commission prohibit the circulation of pornographic periodicals published in foreign countries.[54]

Finally, publishers occasionally argued that their contents were positively beneficial to their audience or the nation. Those who reprinted translations of North American comics often told the censors that, as their products had been wholesome enough for other nations, they should be clean enough for Mexicans, too. The editor of a photonovel called *Tu y Yo* pointed out that its stories, produced in France, "had also been published in other lands, such as London, Paris, and Rio de Janeiro, under different names"; a U.S. comic book company wrote that their romance comic, *Cortejos Romanticos,* "has been circulating without any problems in Spain and all the Latin American countries, including Cuba, Argentina and Uruguay."[55]

Conversely, the periodicals that printed the work of Mexican cartoonists indignantly questioned the patriotism of censors who tried to interfere with the self-expression of Mexican artists. This argument worked, at least once, in favor of the high-quality, highly popular comic book *La Familia Burrón.*[56] This *pepine* was denied tax-exempt status in 1955;[57] in 1956, the commission received complaints about its use of slang and "bad language."[58] The commissioners decided that the complaints were justified: they objected to the portrayal of "a lying mother, who . . . despoils the neighborhood of useful household objects and employs as instruments of her handiwork her very own children."[59] Yet they also decided not to pursue the case, reasoning that they should leave *La Familia Burrón* in peace because it was "a Mexican magazine in which Mexican artists participate."[60]

The members of the classifying commission clearly recognized tired excuses and weak arguments when they heard them, often reacting with exasperation and sometimes with sarcasm. At one point, for instance, an editor appeared without an appointment at a commission meeting to plead the cause of a comic book entitled *Leyendas de la Bruja Maldita,* which had been denied a license. The commissioners refused to speak to their visitor, preferring to send him a letter that told him, haughtily, that "the law does not grant the Commission the capability of reversing its own decisions," without bothering to add that the law did not forbid them to reverse their decisions either; indeed, they did reverse their decisions on a regular basis.[61] Despite signs of annoyance with particularly offensive publications, the commission usually seemed willing to rethink their objections and to compromise with any Mexican publisher who promised them that his or her periodical would be reformed.

This ability to negotiate existed because all the parties involved shared the ideology of nationalist modernity, using the same language, metaphors, and arguments to express themselves. They might disagree over specific issues—most notably, over whether turning a profit was in itself immoral—but they almost always came to some conclusion that, at least temporarily, met everyone's minimum requirements. Even in the most extreme cases of publishers coming into conflict with the laws, this set of shared understandings made some resolution possible. And the need to negotiate, in turn, reinforced the power of the modernizing discourse.

The Case of the Lombardini Brothers

A variety of techniques helped publishers refute public criticism and evade many of the punishments the commission had hoped to mete out to them. But what was the effect of constant negotiation with the classifying commission over the long term? Sanctions from the commission do not appear to have had a significant effect on the content of most local publications. At most, fines or the threat of fines may have pushed some marginal producers—publishers with no government connections and little access to capital—toward cleaning up the content or changing the titles of their periodicals. This might, in turn, have limited their access to an audience. But these marginal producers were precisely the publishers who had the smallest audiences in the first place. From the point of view of the audience, the commission's efforts could have had little appreciable effect. From the point of view of the government, the interests of all its constituencies were being met while it was also reinforcing the tendency of the print media to "project a sense of well-being and prosperity," and avoid serious criticism of politicians or policies.[62]

The commission's most direct impact on the content of Mexican periodicals came to be its use as a barrier to foreign publications. As the commissioners frequently lamented, they rarely had legal reasons to deny licenses to translations of U.S. periodicals.[63] They managed, nonetheless, to set up formidable obstacles to the legal publication of certain magazines, abetted by the ignorance or arrogance of some North American publishers. Translated comic books printed by experienced Mexican publishers always received legal certification eventually, but sometimes would suffer costly delays; Mexican printers of truly raunchy foreign photonovels and genuine pornography from abroad never submitted their products for the commission's consideration, thus avoiding trouble—at least until they became the target of citizens' complaints.[64] But some of the largest U.S. publishing businesses both insisted on retaining control of their products, even in translation, and viewed the licensing process as impartial and a necessary prerequisite to publishing in Mexico: these are the publishers who faced truly formidable hurdles in Mexico.

Such foreign businesses, lacking adequate local ties or knowledge and burdened with too much respect for the letter of the law, might delay publication for years while waiting to complete their paperwork properly. *Playboy* magazine, for example, spent a decade—including eight years in which their Spanish-language edition was not distributed in Mexico—attempting to fulfill the requirements of the licensing process. Their English-language edition, submitted in late 1960, was rejected a year later on the grounds that it was not in Spanish.[65] After five years of futile wrangling conducted through Mexican lawyers, the Playboy corporation finally took on a Mexican publisher as a partner in the enterprise early in 1967. Unfortunately for them, they did not choose a partner with a great deal of experience in the licensing process: it took the Mexican corporation a further six months to discover that they had to begin publishing a Spanish-language *Playboy* before they could find out whether or not they had infringed on the commission's regulations. The Mexican version of *Playboy* did not reach the newsstands until 1968.[66] At that point, predictably, the commission denied the magazine certification, writing that its "articles of great cultural profundity" did not excuse the illegal photographs of women it also contained.[67]

Playboy sued and won in the Federal District courts, but lost before the Mexican Supreme Court late in 1970.[68]

The Spanish-language *Playboy* is available, if poorly distributed and quite costly, on central Mexico City newsstands today. But the length of time in which it was *not* published in Mexico, its capitulation to a Mexican partnership as the sole means of working through the bureaucratic process, and the profit-cutting legal expenses to which it was put are all examples of the kinds of obstacles the commission could put in the way of foreign publications trying to enter the Mexican market. These walls went up, too, in front of *Esquire, National Lampoon,* and *Rolling Stone,* as well as the Korean War and cowboy-and-Indian comics discussed in the previous chapter.[69] Such barriers had a function that was never the intention of anyone involved in the censorship process: they protected the market for locally made periodicals, especially locally made pornography.

Mexican publishers had the advantage of proximity and personal relationships, as well as a much stronger grasp of how the system was supposed to work and how it really functioned. Even in the most extreme case, that of the Lombardini brothers, these advantages proved overwhelming. The Lombardinis were marginal figures in the industry.[70] Their businesses survived for decades without making them rich. They seem to have had few ties to powerful people; they published the raunchiest, least appealing trash.[71] Yet somehow, the Lombardinis stayed in business while *Rolling Stone, Playboy,* and *Esquire* lost out. How did they do it?

The long careers of the Lombardini brothers, Sergio and Hector, exemplify how easily some publishers could avoid conforming to the law. Most of the time, the Lombardinis faced no trouble at all from the government. During moments of heightened public outcry against immoral media, particularly 1953–57 and 1972–76, the Lombardini family did become subject to fines and other forms of state sanction on their publications. None of it, however, reformed Hector and Sergio Lombardini—much less drove them out of business. It only forced them to resort to a certain amount of chicanery in front of the commission.

Hector was the first publisher ordered to appear before the reformed classifying commission, in March 1953. He had a slightly murky connection to the men's magazine under discussion, *Vodevil.* Lombardini appeared, along with two lawyers, as the representative of the editor (one Señor Mendez, according to the masthead), who may or may not have existed:

The President of the Commission . . . asked if Giberto Mendez actually existed. . . . Lombardini replied that he did and could be found in El Paso, Texas . . . that [Lombardini] only is given the magazine to censor it, to take out that which seems inappropriate, that the material is given to him by a boy at [the magazine's office on] Paseo de Reforma 21 . . . and he gives them back to the boy there once they are censored; that he acts simply as a censor, that he does not know who the responsible party might be. He does not know where the profits go, they must go to Señor Mendez. The Commission indicated that their office on the Paseo de Reforma did not exist. Lombardini replied that it did exist. . . . [H]e believes that the Director of the magazine has representatives in Mexico City, photographers etc., who do not have any contracts but have made informal arrangements with Mendez, who is his personal friend and that Mendez does not give him [Lombardini] any salary, that they all work out of pure friendship.[72]

This interview was not the last time that a Lombardini would allow a (possibly imaginary) Texan to take the blame for him, but the story never seemed to work. The confusion of identities would eventually extend to a muddle between Hector and Sergio, even though they operated two apparently distinct businesses, each with separate home and office addresses.

In this case, the commission reported Hector to the courts and asked for his arrest, but three months later no action had been taken.[73] By the end of August, Commissioner Piña y Palacios reported that he had referred the matter to Secretary Ceniceros (head of the Department of Public Education). Ceniceros, however, seemed quite uninterested in the problem—even though the secretary reported receiving a complaint about a magazine called *Pigal* ("one of the same type as *Vodevil*") from the president himself.[74] The case was soon dropped.

Sergio first appeared before the commission three months after his brother. In July 1953 Sergio came with an apology for the bad language in a comic book he edited called *Los Tres Miteros*. No fine was imposed after he promised to reform.[75] Sergio had more trouble with the commission in 1955 when, for the second time, they denied his true-crime tabloid *Nota Roja* a license. He claimed that "he had been thinking that, without it ceasing to be *Nota Roja*, it could be more moderate and also include international news." More plausibly, he said that he had been expecting *Nota Roja* to be licensed because two similar tabloids (*Policia* and *Suplemento Policia,* both published by large Mexico City newspaper corporations) had been. He added that he had suspended publication for two months, but if the commission did not act soon, he would unilaterally resume printing the tabloid.[76]

Nota Roja was still on the newsstands in June 1957, when the commission fined Sergio 5,000 pesos for violating every provision of the law regulating periodicals.[77] This was a significant sum; *Nota Roja* sold 10,000 copies a week at one peso each, so the fine represented half a week's gross income. A few months later, Sergio tried to talk his way out of the fine by meeting with the commission to repeat the usual excuses:

> It is the only way of life we have. We have done everything possible to do what you told us and to remove everything that seemed bad to you. . . . A few things, yes, like this business of using vulgar language, are the fault of the writer who is accustomed to writing for the people, many times I have begged him to change his way of being. . . . We have taken everything from the newspaper *La Prensa.* . . . Mr. Santaella [the powerful publisher of *La Prensa*] gives us the material and we make something new out of it.

Commissioner Rodríguez rejected these arguments, including the attempt to ally *Nota Roja* with the respectable *La Prensa.* He also brought up Sergio's previous promises, saying,

> Not only have you ignored us, you have started up [the tabloid] again. . . . the narration of crime by informative daily papers . . . does not have this spirit of apology for sin, as you do when you make a magazine especially about crime, and you agreed with us about this. That is why we allowed you the publication of just those issues which were already prepared. Now you tell us that you not only take the news from informative periodicals, but also fictionalize them and give them a morbid character.

Lombardini, having failed to impress the commissioners with his ties to Santaella, tried another approach, emphasizing the wholesomeness of the commission-approved sources from which *Nota Roja* plagiarized. In so doing, he cheerfully contradicted himself: "We publish [stories] taken from American magazines that are sold here in Mexico City which is where we buy them," he claimed. This moved none of the commission members.[78]

Then, at the end of the meeting, another question arose. Commissioner

Hernandez repeated Rodríguez's comment that Lombardini had promised, in 1955, not to continue "repeating the same errors." Sergio replied, untruthfully, "That was not me, that was my brother." Hernandez insisted that "the person who was here . . . introduced himself as Sergio Lombardini." Sergio, who had taken an oath to reply honestly to the commission's questions, said again, "Since two months ago my brother has not been with me [but] it was he who came and I believe a little latter he left the magazine."[79] Whether or not this exchange fooled the commission, the fine was never collected. Sergio changed the name of the publication to *Prensa Policiaca* and the whole process began again; the "new" tabloid was immediately denied a certificate of licitude, but no further action taken.[80]

Meanwhile, Hector Lombardini may or may not have continued publishing *Vodevil*. It certainly remained in business. *Vodevil* could still be purchased in Mexico City in 1955, although it no longer printed the names or addresses of its editors, publishers, or printers.[81] In July 1955 Hector tried to remove suspicion from himself by appearing unannounced before the commission as a concerned and knowledgeable citizen "in order to investigate who are the persons who currently are distributing the pornographic magazines *Vea* and *Vodevil*." This time, he called the mysterious editor in El Paso Senor Muñóz rather than Señor Mendez, but otherwise his story was the same as it had been in 1953. He also took the opportunity, in an offhand manner at the end of the meeting, to ask the commissioners whether they would declare *Nota Roja* licit, "so that the Syndicate of Vendors would sell it."[82] Clearly, this request was the true motivation for his visit. The fact that the Lombardinis decided to ask for this privilege reveals the full extent of the commission's power: they could not prevent the Lombardinis from publishing more or less what they pleased, but they *could* hinder them from making the highest possible profit.

This was the worst trouble the classifying commission ever managed to cause the Lombardinis. As the mid-1950s outcry against pornography subsided, the brothers went more quietly about their business. In 1965 through 1968, they added a few titles to their list of publications — *Colección HL, Dramas de la Vida, Vida en Broma,* and *Teen,* all weekly comic books edited by Hector, and *Corridos Mexicanos,* a luridly illustrated collection of song lyrics, edited by Sergio.[83] In April 1970, just before another antipornography campaign began, Sergio started publishing a humor weekly with single-panel cartoons featuring seminude women, *Pico Pico.*[84] After the magazine received a provisional license, however, Sergio (now using the more Mexican-sounding name Sergio Lombardini Silva) apparently never sent the commission any new issues for further supervision.[85]

Once the new antipornography campaign was in full swing, Hector ran into slightly more trouble than his brother. *Vida en Broma*, started in 1965, had become increasingly more daring, and the commission resolved to do something about it. They called Hector in for an audience in September 1971. As usual, he promised to reform.[86] Javier Cu Delgado, the president of the commission, decided six months later that the comic book had grown still more offensive.[87] He recommended that *Vida en Broma* be declared illicit and that Hector be fined 5,000 pesos. This fine actually was collected in early 1972.[88] By then, inflation had rendered it a much smaller penalty than it had seemed when Sergio evaded a 5,000-peso fine levied on *Nota Roja* back in 1957.

In sum, all these interactions between the brothers and la Comisión Calificadora amounted to very little. The Lombardinis were never silenced, either by bankruptcy or jail. If they sometimes folded one publication—either to avoid further legal conflict or because it had not found an audience—they soon started another, often quite similar to the first. They may sometimes have printed relatively respectable, deeply nationalist periodicals like *Corridos Mexicanos,* but from the beginning to the end of their careers, they also profited from lurid works like *Nota Roja* and *Vida en Broma.* The Lombardinis' case reflects the absolute incapacity of the commission to prevent the publication of true-crime, pornographic, and other types of magazines that they despised, so long as those magazines were Mexican.

"Viva la LIBERTAD JA JA JA": The Political Boundaries of Mexican Comic Books

The real limitations on periodicals turned out to be political. This did not, however, take the form of politically motivated censorship of specific issues, although such censorship certainly has existed in Mexico. The classifying commission, at least during the period under examination here, stayed well away from political censorship; for example, they refused a request from Jewish leaders in Mexico to withdraw certification from an antisemitic periodical on the grounds that the commission had no legal reasons not to license it, although their sympathies clearly lay with the complainants in this case.[89] On another occasion, when the commission had been asked to prevent the tabloid *American en Gráficas* from attacking the government of Venezuela, they reminded the procurador general that they could take responsibility only for judging the "morality or educational goals of publications."[90]

Rather, the commission had a direct effect on the ideology of mass media in Mexico through something wider, more amorphous, more pervasive, and perhaps in the end more powerful: the enforced refuge in cultural nationalism that no Mexican periodical could evade. State intervention in the publishing industry combined with conservative criticism of it to set up barriers through which little foreign competition could pass, but beyond which no profitable local periodical could go. Yet almost all successful popular magazines, and certainly all comic books, paid for this protection by joining in the discourse of (post) revolutionary modernity and national progress. There was no safe way to combine profitability with a sweeping critique of the state, of ethnic or gender hierarchies, of economic injustices.

Nobody planned for comic books (or the discourse around them) to have these political functions. Neither did anyone successfully resist the impersonal pressures that made Mexican mass media what it is. Was an oppositional *historieta* ever possible? The most sustained attempt at such counterhegemonic comics, made by Rius, ended in failure. To analyze the reasons why he lost contact with his audience is to understand the strength of the forces shaping Mexican popular culture. The process through which comic books took shape may not have been unstoppable or inevitable; but it proved to be far stronger than the cartoonist who tried the hardest to resist it.

Eduardo del Río, whose pen name is Rius, was and is—unlike most people involved with the comic book industry—a committed, active member of the Mexican left. His work has reflected that affiliation through its constant note of solidarity with the oppressed at home and abroad, agitating against the PRI, the United States, the Catholic Church, and various manifestations of the class system. Del Río belonged to the intellectual left associated with the universities and student protests of the 1960s, so that he has also taken up such countercultural topics as drugs, vegetarianism, alternative family arrangements, and Zen. Yet the uniqueness among cartoonists of his political position, and his own insistence on that uniqueness, should not obscure the ways in which Rius's career was absolutely typical of that of any talented, ambitious cartoonist.[91]

Eduardo del Río was born in 1934 in Zamora, Michoacán, but soon moved, with his mother and three brothers, to Mexico City.[92] After grade school, del Río went on to spend seven years in Salesian seminaries, where his teachers may well have warned him of the dangers inherent in comic books.[93] In any case, he decided, upon leaving the seminary, to become a cartoonist. As a young man, he learned about the business by working for a comic book distributor while trying to get his political cartoons published regularly.

Del Río first appeared in print in 1954; he was already using the pen name Rius. By the late 1950s, his distinctive look was in place: he used a fine, flexible line of unvarying thickness, with little cross-hatching and no other shading, leaving plenty of white space. This style gives no hint of academic training; it is not meant to portray its subjects accurately, but simply to make them recognizable. If it did not have such practiced delicacy, it would be crude. Rius hid his considerable skill behind a screen of amateurishness: his drawings were as far removed as a graphic artist could get from the cartoonists of *Pepín*'s glory days, who made such deliberate efforts at impressing their audience with their abilities. José G. Cruz boasted in "Adelita y las guerrillas" of the hours he spent sketching from life and A. Tirado advertised drawing lessons by mail; both men were trying to connect with consumers by emphasizing their own status as trained professionals. They presumed that their audience could identify with them as educated workers. Rius's art also allowed his audience to identify with him, but only because he persuaded viewers that he was no more trained or talented an artist than they were.

Rius "contributed to almost all the newspapers and magazines in Mexico" as a young artist while developing his spare, witty style.[94] In 1955, he succeeded the brilliant Abel Quezeda as a political cartoonist for *Ovaciones*, a left-of-center Mexico City daily. In 1959, *Ovaciones* published a Rius cartoon showing Francisco Franco—in drag—taking a paseo on the arm of Dwight Eisenhower, an image so striking that copies were passed among journalists in Spain; the editor of a right-wing Madrid daily, outraged, sent a copy of the cartoon to Mexican president López Mateos, along with an angry letter denouncing the laxity of Mexican libel laws. (The editor had confiscated the clipping from a bulletin board in his office, but not before an anonymous newspaper employee had scribbled on it, "Viva la LIBERTAD

JA JA JA.") [95] The young cartoonist was blossoming into an effective irritant of authority figures. But to annoy the powerful is not the same as teaching, organizing, or inspiring the weak: Rius turned away from political cartoons in newspapers and toward the most widely circulated print medium in Mexico. He began to draw *historietas*.

In 1964 Rius joined a breakaway group of artists and writers from *Ovaciones* in putting out a magazine. His contribution, a *historieta* called "Los Supermachos," earned immense popularity and quickly became a comic book on its own. The new magazine withered away while *Los Supermachos* joined a publishing group, Editorial Meridiano, which also published guides to family planning, girlie magazines, and kung fu journals. (The manager of Editorial Meridiano, Octavio Colemenares, sat on the classifying commission from 1958 through 1965, and again in 1973 and 1974.) Within a few years, Rius has claimed, 200,000 copies of *Los Supermachos* were sold every week, making it one of the more popular comics in Mexico at the time. [96]

By 1967, however, Rius felt pressured by his editors to tone down his politics. He quit, charging censorship, and started up another comic book, titled *Los Agachados*, with the support of a new publishing house called Editorial Posada. *Los Supermachos* continued with new artists, but soon lost about half its readership. [97] *Los Agachados*, though it never earned the popularity of *Los Supermachos* at its peak, did eventually overtake it in sales. Editorial Posada also has done a small but steady business in reprinting thematically related collections of back issues in the style of Rius's *Para principantes* books.

The *Para principantes* books—beginning in 1969 with *Cuba Para principantes*—were the logical extension of the didactic, information-packed *Los Agachados* comics. These clear, clever introductions to present-day events and problems quickly earned an international reputation; Rius's "infolibro" on Cuba was translated into English, French, and German within a year of its first Mexican publication. The *Para principantes* books, although also published for the most part by Editorial Posada, were neither priced nor distributed in the manner of comic books, and so they never sold in the same massive numbers as *Los Supermachos* or *Los Agachados*. Nonetheless, most of them remain in print and seem popular in urban resale markets. Indeed, Rius ceased working on *Los Agachados* in 1971 in order to concentrate on making books. [98]

One compliment to the power of *Los Agachados* and the first of the *Para principantes* books was the strength of government opposition they faced. *Los Agachados* earned its license from the classifying commission, but in 1968 and 1969, both Rius and his publishers had trouble with the state:

> Not only was there a conspiracy to deny the editor paper [from PIPSA] and to menace the printers, and to boycott the distributor, but there were also other things that happened. There was a kidnap attempt and then I was successfully kidnapped. The police kidnapped me, they gave me to the army . . . in 1969. . . . So finally they gave me a sort of simulated execution by firing squad to threaten me so that I would not continue with [my work].[99]

Strikingly, this all happened despite his publisher's good political connections, including his seat on the commission. No other cartoonist so infuriated politicians; and nobody else in the comic book industry would have had the nerve to go on after such an incident, as Rius did. It is worth noting that the agents of attempted censorship here were not the classifying commission, but the police and army.

This history of activism and risk-taking has caused Rius's work to be seen as lying outside the categories into which comic books usually fall. His visual style reinforces the idea that Rius is somehow different from the average creator of *historietas:* he relies much more on the conventions of single-panel political cartoons than the formal devices of romance or adventure comics. Rius himself has encouraged readers to think of his work as radically different from other *pepines*. Looking back at *Los Supermachos*, he said that he created his first comic book to "counteract the negative impact he perceived Mexican and imported American comic books were having on the reading public."[100] Notwithstanding his own experiences, in 1983 he was able to joke:

> Mexican comic books—stupefying, sentimental, and in the worst taste— are an insult to the so-called "eighth art," deserving . . . the guillotine or the firing squad from the Secretaria de Educación Publica, to protect the mental health of the Mexican people.[101]

More seriously, he said that he had looked at the three best-selling Mexican comic books of the 1960s—*Kalimán, Memín Pingüin,* and *Lágrimas,*

Risas y Amor—only to figure out how not to do *Los Supermachos;* as early as 1964, he would say in 1979, he believed that they were "totally alienating to people."[102] Statements like these are more than one cartoonist announcing his superiority over another; they are deliberate attempts to lift his own work, metaphorically, off the newsstand where more vulgar *historietas* are displayed.

Despite the trouble that Rius took to distinguish his work from "bad" popular comics, all three of the projects that he undertook in the 1960s— *Los Supermachos, Los Agachados,* and the *Para principantes* series—strongly resemble other Mexican graphic narratives. Certainly, they could be described as a set of steps away from the ordinary publications with which they shared newsstand space or as a set of steps toward Rius's eventual radicalization of graphic narration. Among other remarkable innovations, he subtracted continuing characters, added collage elements, and played with the devices of textbooks such as tables of contents, bibliographies, and even footnotes. Like many other experimental cartoonists of the past thirty years, he has also juggled various arrangements and styles of the little boxes that frame standard graphic narratives, before abandoning them altogether. Rius's art today overlaps the definitions of illustrated book, comic book, and something altogether new. This was not the case, however, when he began his first comic book.

Los Supermachos not only seemed like an ordinary comic book, but it fit within a well-defined subgenre of popular Mexican comics, too. It told the story of the daily life of a large group of people, from all parts of society, in a small imaginary rural town. The continuing characters spoke in slang and had recognizably local skin tones and clothing, but otherwise were not too different from the familiar stereotypes of other serials. These characters, who enacted the requisite complex plots, included the usual sexy single women, good mothers, kind priests, greedy bishops, authoritative professionals, city slickers, patriarchal landlords, and hardworking poor men. The plots wove through various political topics, including elections, state violence, and currency devaluation, which would never have appeared so plainly in any other comic book. Yet the easy replacement of Rius by anonymous artists when he left Editorial Meridiano suggests that his precise political stance was not the most important feature of the comic book to the publishers. And the loyalty of many *Los Supermachos* readers, after

Rius's departure, indicates that they, too, cared less about the fine points of political analysis than about the characters, drawing style, and sarcastic tone of the comic—which all remained more or less consistent.

When Rius began *Los Agachados* in 1967, he invented new characters who strongly resembled the cast of *Los Supermachos*.[103] The campesino Nopalzin became a central figure: by asking ignorant questions of his friends—the used book dealer and schoolteacher—and by eavesdropping on the local police and bartender, he learned about the topic of each issue. Often, episodes began with some foolish notion—a society for the preservation of Mexican machismo, for example—that Nopalzin must be persuaded to abandon.[104] Nopalzin stood in for the reader, the real object of *Los Agachados*'s pedagogy. Usually, though, at the end of each thirty-six-page comic book, Nopalzin was no less ignorant than before. For him, each episode finished with a shrug and a joke. *Los Agachados* kept Nopalzin blithely stupid, but assumed that the readers underwent a more permanent change through hearing what Nopalzin heard.

Over the years of writing and drawing the comic, Rius came to use these characters less and less. Early on, he was threatened with a legal suit by Editorial Meridiano for continuing to use characters from *Los Supermachos*. (His former publishers still held the copyrights.) Although this may have discouraged him from using particular characters, it did not stop his use of continuing figures and a story format to convey information. Perhaps he stopped working with this formula because it worked less well for certain topics Rius wanted to cover. For instance, he dropped it in one 1973 issue to give a brief history of European clothing—a subject it is hard to imagine Nopalzin asking questions about—substituting collage illustration and a first-person voice.[105] Perhaps, on the other hand, Rius simply got bored with the formula he had been using to produce a comic book every week, almost single-handedly, for almost a decade.

But in moving away from the standard narrative forms and visual style of *historietas*, Rius lost his audience. Only one marketing survey was ever made of his readership, in 1967, as he was searching for a publisher for *Los Agachados*. Even then, he was sorry to find that most of his readers were

students, [and] after that certain middle-class professionals—doctors, engineers, teachers—and then to a small degree workers and peasants, one percent or something like that. I already knew it. I had more or less imagined it from the kind of letters I received and the people that I saw on the street buying the magazine. Those were my readers: students, and certain people of the middle class with certain political worries.[106]

Rius was already failing to find readers from outside the middle class, as he had hoped to do. Moreover, his total audience declined throughout the 1960s. *Los Agachados* never equaled the circulation of *Los Supermachos;* the *Para principantes* books—though most were reprinted many times—were usually published in editions of between 3,000 and 10,000 copies. These print runs were quite large as books published in Mexico go, but tiny compared to the readership of either *Los Agachados* or *Los Supermachos.*

This decline in total readership probably indicated an increasingly middle-class audience as well. Moreover, the loss of the working-class audience reflects decisions Rius made, as if he had resigned himself to speaking only to a particular segment of the Mexican population after about 1965. He stopped drawing stories; he stopped drawing continuing characters. Instead, he began using much denser and less idiomatic texts, finally abandoning the comic book format altogether in favor of more expensive, less inviting, and less well-distributed books.[107] In some sense, this was an abandonment of his audience, too.

Having failed to create a popular left-wing alternative to *historietas*, Rius turned to analyzing why that task should have been so difficult. He produced a series of books that offered his own global history of graphic narrative, combining political analysis with aesthetic appreciation. They mixed informed praise for some of the best artists with tips for young artists, but largely, they were an attempt to arm his readers against the ideological dangers of the medium. He complained about the influence of "historietas yanquis," and included examples from Disney and other North American comics to prove his point.[108]

Rius saved his harshest words for the complex system that produced and controlled Mexican *pepines.*

> Mexican comic books . . . have been left in the hands of the worst merchandise-peddling publishers, who, *in complicity* with our educational authorities, make only comics that are alienating and in bad taste, pornographic and disgustingly sentimental, and they sell millions of them.[109] (italics in original)

He did not accuse artists and writers of deliberately making state-sponsored propaganda. Instead, he pointed to the ways in which the government and media were so bound up with each other as to be almost the same thing. Producers of *historietas*, as Rius had discovered, would have had to abandon all self-interest in order to create oppositional popular culture.

The only solution that Rius could imagine was effective state intervention: he wanted the regulations governing comic books to be enforced. He hoped that "if there were no crap on sale, the public would consume better comic books, which would benefit them."[110] Rius had moved the left-wing critique of comic books away from the cultural imperialism argument and back toward a critique that the fiercest right-wing opponents of comic books had shared with a few of the censors themselves. In other words, comic books corrupted their readers because they were themselves fatally corrupted through their capitalist origin; their audience, an otherwise blank slate, needed to be protected from the mass media that created (consumerist) desires.

The cost of reaching a mass audience, or even attempting to reach one, seems to be participation in a discourse that has by now solidified into only a few, inflexible arguments and counterarguments. Rius's appraisal of the situation has not, so far, helped him create the types of oppositional narratives that might reach a truly broad Mexican audience. Instead, he now makes books for the university-educated art audience.[111] He even accepted government financing for a brochure series on ecological issues illustrated in his inimitable style; arguably, he has himself become complicit with the Mexican state.[112]

The Cultural Context of Historietas

Rius was not the only Mexican who tried to turn the conservative form of the *historieta* to radical ends, although he was the most successful. More recently, there have been attempts at lesbian-feminist, punk, and art comics, all more or less modeled on North American underground comics.[113] Like the *Para principantes* books, all have been costly, far larger than the pocket-size standard for Mexican comics, and available only at bookstores. None appear to have found an audience of any size.

As the artists who attempted to create an oppositional culture out of the raw material of graphic narrative must realize, the form of the comic book is infinitely more fluid than the repetitive *historietas* produced in Mexico every week would make it seem. But if the form is malleable, it appears that the audience's relationship to the form is not. The comic book audience, for better or worse, has been fixed in place; it is not likely to change its demands on comic book producers. Although sales now appear to be gradually declining, there is still a strong demand for the modernist melodrama that has characterized *historietas* for the past forty years.

Comic books, and arguments about them, helped create postrevolutionary Mexico. But their success trapped them. Nothing about them—neither the way they look, nor the stories they tell, nor the ideologies they uphold, nor the uses that readers find for them, nor the criticisms they inspire— can be changed now by even the most talented, dedicated participant in the business. *Historietas*, which played their part in the stabilization of the Mexican state, can change only when Mexican society changes around them.

Conclusion

The Lessons of Cultural Conservatism

> "You must begin a reading program immediately so that you may
> understand the crises of our age," Ignatius said solemnly. . . . "You
> may skip the Renaissance and the Enlightenment. That is most
> dangerous propaganda. Now that I think of it, you had better
> skip the Romantics and the Victorians, too. For the contemporary
> period, you should study some selected comic books."
> —John Kennedy O'Toole, *A Confederacy of Dunces*

 Why bother studying Mexican comic books and the other
trashy periodicals that sit beside them on newsstands? There
are good reasons to think them trivial.

As chapters 3 and 4 showed, comic books and similar
publications were at the center of several political controversies between 1942 and 1976. But these campaigns against the use of
bad language and depictions of naked ladies had few direct results. They
did push the government into creating laws regulating the content of
illustrated periodicals and setting up a censorship bureaucracy. But since
the laws were unenforceable—indeed, they may have been designed to be
unenforceable—the promulgation of these new regulations and the hiring
of censors was hardly a triumph of popular activism. Furthermore, anti-
historieta and antipornography campaigns were only examples of the many
forms of antimedia protest that cropped up in Mexico after about 1930.
Trashy periodicals were nothing exceptional to the people who protested
against them and the protests came to nothing in any case.

Like the politics around *historietas*, the comic books themselves might
be described as dwindling into nothing. As chapter 5 demonstrated, the
present-day aesthetic potential of Mexican comic books is, to be polite,
strictly limited: they do not offer much visual or narrative pleasure any-
more. Other authors have begun to construct a canon of the great artists
and writers of the past, such as Carlos Vigil, José G. Cruz, Guillermo Marin,

and Yolanda Vargas Dulché. To describe and evaluate their work strikes me as a worthwhile task, but a sad one; unfortunately, their art is barely accessible to scholars and entirely inaccessible to the general public. And the majority of the serial pictorial narratives sold in Mexico since 1934 do not belong to this canon (after about 1955 to the present, the vast majority). At best, they are generic repetitions of stories that have long since grown tired; at worst, they are ugly, sloppy, and inept copies of those sleepy old tales. These *historietas* have been hugely popular, but that doesn't make them good or even interesting. There is not much point in applying the tools of art history or literary criticism to them.

Moreover, the enormous appeal of *historietas* and related genres does not necessarily mean that they had any influence over their millions of readers. As chapters 1 and 2 point out, comic book creators designed their stories only to sell more *historietas*, often in direct dialogue with their audiences: so who was influencing whom? Indeed, the patchy evidence on readership all indicates that audiences found their own, idiosyncratic meanings in the magazines they consumed. And the evidence suggests that these meanings may have been constructed at least as much from the broader cultural discourses in which audience members participated as they were from the details or the moralities of the *historieta* tales themselves. It is nearly impossible to speak of the influence of this most popular form of popular culture, except in the vaguest terms. So neither the politics around the comics, nor the comics themselves, nor their influence over their audience, in themselves caused anything else to happen.

Yet these stories, taken together, form an important part of the history of postrevolutionary Mexico. When we see how various Mexicans—producers, consumers, censors, critics—interacted around comic books, we see how the ultimate victors of the revolution transformed their faction into both a government and the idea of a nation. Through arguments like those that swirled around *historietas*, the state reproduced and legitimized itself. This was a circular—not to say labyrinthine—process. These interactions shaped Mexican *historietas'* contents; then these comic books helped define a national culture that, in turn, legitimized postrevolutionary political arrangements. And then the postrevolutionary state—both the government itself, as well as the giant media conglomerates that supported and helped shape it—helped to freeze the styles and stories of the comic books into their generic and usable forms. Meanwhile, the attacks on comic books added more directly to the power of the Mexican state: by mediating among all the other actors in the debate, the government strengthened its position as the unavoidable center of Mexico's economic, social, and cultural structures. Looking at comic books and the arguments against them, we see the subtle and complex process through which power in Mexico came to rest in the same hands that hold it today.

Comic books and related periodicals were not the only forms of mass media and popular culture that were part of this process in postrevolutionary Mexico. Similar stories could be told about many entertainments: shopping, television, recorded music, dance, cinema, cooking, fashion, and holidays, to name only a few. In one way or another, all these forms developed their own interpretive communities, which certainly would have included critics as fiercely conservative as any anti-comic-book protester. All of them engaged in a series of interactions among producers, consumers, and critics that more or less resembled the interactions within the interpretive community for comic books. All depended on government support and faced government regulations in some form. All shaped and were shaped by the urbanization and industrialization that transformed Mexico in this era. And, most likely, all of them will turn out to fit this essentially Gramscian model of the construction of hegemony in the postrevolutionary decades.

As promised at the beginning of this long story about the politics of comic books, however, there is a happy ending. And so, though it has become the worst cliché of cultural studies, I return to the shared insight (as clichés become clichés when they succinctly express truths) that culture can be politics-by-any-other-means. The interpretation—the use—of comic books enabled their most fervent critics to create a series of oppositional moments, if not an oppositional movement; to find a language in which to express dissent; to locate a political battle on relatively advantageous terrain; to keep their disagreements alive through the height of Mexico's political consensus around "revolution"; and most of all, to plant a counternarrative of tradition within the field of modernization stories.

These conservatives are not the dissenters that a left-leaning historian might hope or expect to find in the recent Mexican past. From some points of view, they only added to—at best, distracted from—the troubles that besiege Mexicans today. In particular, the manner in which they invented and insisted on an image of the ideal Mexican woman as self-sacrificing martyr troubles me far more than the state-sponsored counterstereotype of the ideal woman as modernist patriot. But what other strategy, what other opposition group, has done more (or could have done more) to shape the consciousness of Mexicans?

Conservative Mexicans created an ample space for their dissenting project by deciding, very early on, to treat mass media seriously. Even if we find their project despicable, there is much to be learned from the study of how they imposed it on the rhetoric of politics, gender, and amusement in the postrevolutionary period. Cultural conservatives in Mexico can teach us that students of culture who go looking for counterhegemonic discourses may not find transcendent moments of liberatory consciousness, but only a set of ideas, stories, and pictures that are more appealing than the state version only because they oppose it. But cultural conservatives can teach us, too, that no hegemony is perfect: the seamless surface of modernity could be broken through, in Mexico and elsewhere, with luck and a powerful story.

Notes

Introduction

1   "Gloria Trevi, contra el fallo de al Corte de Justicia de EU," *La Jornada*, 22 June 1992, p. 39. For a foreign overview of Trevi's career and the media response to her, see Enrique Fernandez, "Gloria Mexicana," *Village Voice* (New York), 30 March 1993, pp. 69–70.

2   Heriberto Arriaga Garza, "Comisión Calificadora de Publicaciones y Revistas Ilustradas," in *Analisis y proyección sectorial del plan nacional de desarrollo, 1989–1994* (Mexico City: Secretaría de Gobernación, 1990), p. 171. I will be using several terms—la Comisión Calificadora, the censorship commission, the classifying commission, the commission—to refer to this organization.

3   For laws governing la Comisión Calificadora, see *Diario Oficial*, 11 March 1944 and 12 June 1951.

4   I witnessed this event while doing research at the commission.

5   Raquel Peguero, "Si Reagan pudo, por que yo no? Trevi," *La Jornada*, 3 September 1993, p. 25.

6   Televisa exemplifies the vertical and horizontal integration of Mexican media. Trevi records for one of Televisa's subsidiaries, and her calendar and comic book are printed by another Televisa offshoot. The conglomerate now appears to own a controlling interest in all but one of the biggest businesses (the Vargas Dulché family periodical group) that produce comic books in Mexico. See Karen Fleishman, "Televisa before NAFTA" (paper delivered at the International Latin American Studies Student Conference, Austin, Tex., 6 March 1993). For the Televisa group's increasing domination of the

comic book industry, see Irene Herner, *Mitos y monitos* (Mexico City: Nueva Imagen, 1979), pp. 116–18; and Marta Alcocer and Alicia Molina, "Mexican Comics as Culture Industry," in *Comics and Visual Culture*, ed. Alphons Silbermann and H. D. Dyroff (Munich: K. G. Saur, 1986), pp. 196–97.

7   Gramsci, in Jackson Lears's helpful formulation, was trying to answer the question, "How does a ruling class rule?" See Jackson Lears, "The Concept of Cultural Hegemony: Problems and Possibilities," *American Historical Review* 90 (1985): 574. Gramsci wrote that mass culture tended to reinforce the existing relations of the production and distribution of power, and that no state could exist without benefit of this reinforcement, even if certain forms of media opposed themselves to particular regimes. He meant, by "hegemony," the willing consent of the governed to the government, by a small group of powerful and prestigious people, of every aspect of life—not just political arrangements, but also social and cultural forms. See Antonio Gramsci, *Selections from the Prison Notebooks*, ed. and trans. Quentin Hoare and Geoffrey Nowell Smith (New York: International, 1971), pp. 12, 326–33. As historians of U.S. culture have discovered, hegemony is a handy concept for justifying research into the history of soap operas or lunch boxes, but it is awfully hard to pin down. For a pioneering attempt at integrating Gramscian theory into the study of Latin American cultural politics, see Néstor García Canclini, "Culture and Power: The State of Research," *Media, Culture, and Society* 10 (1988).

8   This account of postrevolutionary Mexico is indebted to Alan Knight's pioneering work on the era. See Alan Knight, "The Peculiarities of Mexican History," *Journal of Latin American History* 24, suppl. (1992). Knight argues against historians of Mexico who depict the twentieth century as a story of possibilities lost, dreams betrayed, and promises broken. Instead, he sees the "peculiarities" of the Mexican past as adding up to a list of disasters averted: unlike other Latin American countries, Mexico since 1920 has suffered relatively little (or not at all) from military rule and other forms of dictatorship, from starvation, from failure to industrialize, from civil war. In part, Knight attributes this to the recalcitrance displayed by the subjects of the Revolutionary state's cultural project. While "recalcitrance" is arguably not the best way to describe the complicated interactions between the state, consumer culture, and the citizenry, Knight is right to see these interactions as central to the political history of the era.

9   Ilene O'Malley, *The Myth of the Revolution*, (Westport, Conn.: Greenwood Press, 1986) pp. 134–36; Elizabeth Salas, *Soldaderas in the Mexican Military: Myth and History* (Austin: University of Texas Press, 1990), pp. 82–119.

10 Notorious women like Frida Kahlo, Tina Modotti, Delores del Rio, Leonora Carrington, Maria Félix, La Tigresa, and Tongolele certainly were not numer-

ous enough to be a political bloc. Their importance lay in the manipulation of their image (by themselves most of all) as a counter to the trope that celebrated Mexican women as suffering, stoic, and silent. The argument over how to represent (or how to be) Mexican women went on in the cultural production of these extraordinary figures, of course, but the debate also raged in newspaper gossip columns, true-crime magazines, sermons, wrestling arenas (with the inclusion of *luchadoras* and the invention of personas for them), and in comic books.

11 See Marjorie Becker, *Setting the Virgin on Fire* (Berkeley and Los Angeles: University of California Press, 1995); Florencia Mallan, *Peasant and Nation* (Berkeley and Los Angeles: University of California Press, 1995).

12 See Alan Knight, "Revolutionary Project, Recalcitrant People: Mexico, 1910–1940," in *The Revolutionary Process in Mexico,* ed. Jaime Rodríguez O. (Berkeley and Los Angeles: University of California Press, 1990).

13 Comic books have been a popular target of protests against mass culture in this century. For anti-comic-book debates outside Latin America, see Fredric Wertham, *Seduction of the Innocent* (New York: Holt, Rinehart, and Winston, 1954); Martin Barker, *A Haunt of Fears: The Strange History of the British Horror Comics Campaign* (London: Verso, 1989); James Gilbert, *A Cycle of Outrage: America's Reaction to the Juvenile Delinquent in the 1950s* (New York: Oxford University Press, 1986); and Frederick Schodt, *Manga! Manga! The World of Japanese Comics* (Tokyo: Kodansha, 1983). Fredric Wertham led a crusade in the United States against comic books that resulted in congressional hearings and the institution of industry self-censorship.

In Latin America, with the exception of Mexico, movements against comic books are slightly less visible. For the general history of comic books and comic strips in Latin America, see Susana Contesti, "A batallas de humor, campos de risas," *Cambio 16,* no. 1055 (10 February 1992); Alvaro de Moya, "Comics in Brazil," *Studies in Latin American Popular Culture 7* (1988); and David William Foster, *From Malfalda to Los Supermachos: Latin American Graphic Humor as Popular Culture* (Boulder, Colo.: Lynne Bienner, 1989). Argentina, Brazil, and Chile developed comic book industries of their own after 1945, and in these nations, as in Mexico, people argued over the content of locally produced cartoons. See, for example, a critique of the Chilean comic *Mampato* in Ariel Dorfman, *The Empire's Old Clothes* (New York: Pantheon, 1983), pp. 177–96. In Uruguay, Venezuela, Colombia, and Peru, however, control of periodicals meant little more than control of imports. There, the key distinction was between comic books imported from the rest of Latin America—especially Mexico—and comic books imported from the United States.

The Mexican government was receiving official protests against exported Mexican *historietas* by 1955. See Comisión Calificadora de Publicaciones y Revistas Ilustradas (hereafter CCPRI), Javier Piña y Palacios to Bernardo Reyes, *Minutario 1955 20.*, 3 August 1955; *Actas 1955*, acta 15, 10 June 1955, acta 24, 12 August 1955, "Asuntos para tratar," 12 August 1955, and "Asuntos para tratar," 30 September 1955; "Asuntos para tratar," *Minutario 1955–1956*, 3 February 1956; *Minutario 1956 10.*, acta 5, 3 February 1956; *Minutario 1957*, acta 1, 18 January 1957; and Javier Cu Delgado to Jorge H. Flores, 17 March 1976, in *Minutario 1976 20.*, ofc. 504–234. Venezuela banned certain imported publications, but a beautifully produced, government-funded weekly comic book for children, replete with articles on history and geography, was intended to take the place of the forbidden Mexican periodicals. See Archivo General de la Nación (hereafter AGN), Propriedad artística y literaria file 949 S/reg. 4, file 985 S/reg. 5, and file 1333 S/reg. 10. Colombia refused to allow *Vodevil*, and other racy Mexican magazines like it, to cross its borders in 1956. It also banned the comic books *Adelita y las guerrillas*, *Misterios del Gato Negro*, *Canciones inovidables*, and *Paquín*, as well as the translated version of *Classics Illustrated*, which was produced in Mexico. See CCPRI, "Asuntos para tratar," *Minutario 1955–1956*, 3 February 1956. Colombian censors were hard on Mexican *historietas*, but they generally approved of comics from the United States, allowing the Mexican-made translations of many North American comic books — including *Dennis the Menace*, *Bugs Bunny*, and the cowboy-and-Indian comics *Hopalong* and *Durango Kid* — to enter the country. See CCPRI, "Asuntos para tratar," *Actas 1955*, 12 August 1955. Similarly, Peru did not judge North American comics harshly, although in 1976 it outlawed the importation of *Batman* and *Mighty Mouse* in their Spanish-language forms. At the same time, Peru made all horror comics illegal (most were Mexican products) while specifying that twenty other Mexican periodicals, including the comic books *Hermelinda linda*, *Dulce Amor*, *Cárcel de mujeres*, and *Enigmas*, were also forbidden. See CCPRI, Cu Delgado to Jorge H. Flores, 17 March 1976, in *Minutario 1976 20.*, ofc. 504–234. In other places, governments did not censor imported periodicals, but *historietas* faced sharp local criticism: newspapers in Havana, Cuba, for example, editorialized against *Paquín* and *Paquito Grande* in 1955. See CCPRI, *Minutario 1955*, acta 26, 9 September 1955, p. 1.

14 But see Fernando Curiel, *Mal de ojo, iniciación a la literatura iconica* (Mexico City: UNAM, 1990); and Scott McCloud, *Understanding Comics* (Northampton, Mass.: Kitchen Sink, 1993).

15 Among the exceptional cases of comic books that have traveled well are the Tintin series by the Belgian cartoonist Hergé, which has been overwhelmingly popular among western European children since about 1940; Disney's

children's comics, which have done well in parts of Asia and Central and South America (but not Mexico) since about 1950; and Mexican romance comics and photonovels, which have sold steadily throughout the Spanish-speaking world since the mid-1950s.

16 Few circulation figures are publicly available for Mexican periodicals. I am extremely grateful to Blanca de Lizaur for sharing her unpublished research on audited circulations with me; see her "Cuadro comparativo de tirajes en revistas no especializadas," Mexico City, 1992.

17 For an authoritative, and quite beautiful, multivolume overview of *las historietas* from their nineteenth-century roots to (so far) the 1950s, see Juan Manuel Aurrecoechea and Armando Bartra, *Puros Cuentos: La historieta en México* vols. 1, 2, 3 (Mexico: Grijalbo, 1988, 1992, 1994).

Chapter One   The Creation of Mexican Comic Books, 1934–1952

1 See Jeffrey Bortz, "Política salarial en México," in *Industria y trabajo en México*, eds. James Wilkie and Jesús Reyes Herzog (Mexico City: Universidad Autónama de México, 1990), pp. 315–32.

2 *Anuario estadístico de los Estados Unidos Mexicanos, 1958–1959* (Mexico City: Secretaría de Industria y Comercio, Dirección General de Estadística, 1960), p. 48. See also James Wilkie, *The Mexican Revolution: Federal Expenditure and Social Change since 1910*, 2d ed. rev. (Berkeley and Los Angeles: University of California Press, 1970), p. 208.

3 *Anuario estadístico de los Estados Unidos Mexicanos, 1968–1969* (Mexico City: Secretaría de Industria y Comercio, Dirección General de Estadística, 1971), p. 42. Fernando Peñalosa notes that in the 1950s many more people could follow the text of a comic book than a book without pictures. See *The Mexican Book Industry* (New York: Scarecrow Press, 1957), p. 32. And while Wilkie, *Mexican Revolution*, p. 214, writes that "by 1950 there were more people unable to read and write in Mexico than there were in 1910," that reflects a rapid increase in Mexico's population. More important, from the point of view of the periodical industry, the number of Mexicans capable of reading a comic book had also risen sharply over those decades.

4 This is a general description of a complex and fascinating subject. For nuanced analyses of the actual processes of negotiation, accommodation, resistance, and acceptance that took place in the aftermath of Article Three's promulgation in specific rural areas, see Marjorie Becker, *Setting the Virgin on Fire: Lazaro Cárdenas, Michoacan Peasants, and the Redemption of the Mexican Revolution* (Berkeley and Los Angeles: University of California Press, 1995); Elsie Rockwell, "Schools of the Revolution," in *Everyday Forms of State Formation: Revolution and the Negotiation of Rule in Modern Mexico*, ed. Gilbert

Joseph and Daniel Nugent (Durham, N.C.: Duke University Press, 1994); and Mary Kay Vaughan, "Women Schoolteachers in the Mexican Revolution: The Story of Reyna's Braids," *Journal of Women's History* 2, no. 1 (1990).

5 Yolanda Moreno Rivas, *Historia de la musica popular mexicana* (Mexico City: Alianza Editorial, 1979), p. 70.

6 Vaughan, "Women Schoolteachers," p. 296.

7 Advertisement for Cia. Mexicana de Luz y Fuerza Motriz, *Excelsior,* 3 January 1934.

8 Peñalosa, *Mexican Book Industry,* p. 118.

9 The complaints of regional papers, including the accusation that comic books were printed on government-subsidized newsprint, can be found in Archivo General de la Nación (hereafter AGN), Fondo presidenciales, Ruiz Cortines file 545.22/36. For book publishers' complaints, see AGN, Fondo presidenciales, Avila Camacho file 136.1/11.

10 Cited in Juan Manuel Aurrecoechea and Armando Bartra, *Puros Cuentos: La historieta en México, 1874–1934,* vol. 1 (Mexico City: Grijalbo, 1988), pp. 229–30.

11 Adelson, "Competition," p. 25, reports that the Mexico City daily "*Novedades* was founded out of ten million pesos profit from *Chamaco Chico.*" Peñalosa, *Mexican Book Industry,* p. 39, says that *Pepín*'s success provided the initial investment for the daily sports and celebrity tabloid *Esto.*

12 For an account of one group of young cartoonists' struggles (they eventually ended up working for *Chamaco*), see Dorothy Adelson, "Competition for Superman," *Inter-American* 2 (June 1943): 26.

13 Aurrecoechea and Bartra, *Puros Cuentos,* vol. 1, pp. 251–57.

14 I heard this on many occasions in 1990–92, sometimes used in a campy way by ordinary comic book consumers, sometimes used seriously by librarians and archivists.

15 In fact, *Chamaco* printed syndicated newspaper cartoons exclusively, barely surviving until it switched to *Pepín*'s tactic of adding local cartoonists and promoting them heavily.

16 Adelson, "Competition," p. 25.

17 Circulation figures have been hazy and scarce at best in the Mexican publishing industry. This figure, cited in "Primer Manifesto Monero" (in the fanzine *El Gallito Inglés,* July 1992), represents a commonly held belief among present-day Mexican comic professionals. Harold Hinds Jr. and Charles Tatum, in *Not Just for Children: The Mexican Comic Book in the Late 1960s and 1970s* (Westport, Conn.: Greenwood Press, 1992), p. 3, cite a figure for *Pepín* of "at least 320,000 daily."

18 Javier Piña y Palacios to Centro Social de Peluqueros del Distrito Federal,

12 April 1955, in Comisión Calificadora de Publicaciones y Revistas Ilustradas (hereafter CCPRI), *Actas 1955*, ofc. 274. For more general comments on
barbershops as lending libraries for *pepines*, see José Agustín, *Tragicomedia
mexicana 1* (Mexico: Editorial Planeta, 1990), p. 137; and Armando Bartra,
"The Seduction of the Innocents: The First Tumultuous Moments of Mass
Literacy in Postrevolutionary Mexico," in *Everyday Forms of State Formation:
Revolution and the Negotiation of Rule in Modern Mexico*, ed. Gilbert Joseph
and Daniel Nugent (Durham, N.C.: Duke University Press, 1994), p. 309.

19 These conservative figures are based on totals of the comic books registered
with la Comisión Calificadora and/or Derechos de Autor, and/or granted
second-class mailing privileges by the Oficina de Correos. CCPRI, *Minutario
1945, Actas 1952–1954*, and *Actas 1953–1954;* also AGN, Propriedad artística y
literaria, registers for 1945–52.

20 See Bartra, "Seduction," pp. 310–19.

21 Aurrecoechea and Bartra, *Puros Cuentos*, vol. 2, pp. 169–217.

22 I picked August because it is of no special significance—no major religious
holidays or patriotic anniversaries occur during the month. I chose 1941 because it is long enough after the magazine's founding for its formula to be
well established, but still before the first moral panic over comic books began
in 1942. Finally, I picked this particular issue from that particular month and
year by closing my eyes and pointing.

23 *Pepín*, no. 891, 21 August 1941, pp. 5, 27, 28, 63.

24 Within a year, the majority of these slogans would wax patriotic. For example, "In the current moment all Mexicans must forget factions to come
together as a single man of the Fatherland," and "The victims immolated
by Nazi barbarism did not die in vain, they unified the Mexican people in
defense of their *patria*," could be found underneath pages 21–22 of *Pepín*,
no. 1225, 21 July 1942.

25 Vargas eventually published his own long-running, popular, and hilarious
comic book, *La Familia Burrón*. See Hinds and Tatum, *Not Just for Children*,
pp. 159–86; and Charles Wick, "The Burrón Family: Class Warfare and the
Culture of Poverty," *Studies in Latin American Popular Culture* 2 (1983). Vargas
and many of his colleagues, it should be noted, were spectacularly productive
by current standards of comic book production in the United States. It takes
a whole team working full time for a month to sketch, ink, color, write, letter,
and edit a twenty-four-page comic book; European cartoonists find even this
production schedule alarmingly pressured (Elisabeth Vincentelli, personal
communication, 3 July 1996). In producing this serial, therefore, Vargas was
doing work every day that would now take at least three U.S. cartoonists at
least a week to complete, and even then, they would not turn out nearly so

visually pleasing a product. In *Pepín*, no. 891, at least three other cartoonists—A. Tirado, José Cruz, and Guillermo Marin—were working just as hard.

26 This serial ran for eleven years in *Pepín*, beginning in 1936. Its creator, José G. Cruz, had a long, lucrative, and controversial career in the comic book industry. He left *Pepín* in 1948 to found his own company, where he began to publish a series of comic books and photonovels that frequently inspired complaints to the censorship commission; conservatives saw them as racier than their competition. One of the comics he published in the 1950s was a continuation of the *Adelita* saga and another starred Adelita's boyfriend, Juan Sin Miedo (Fearless John). Cruz's most successful product, the photonovel *El Santo*, appeared from 1949 through 1976, when the wildly popular wrestler who was the model for the series sued the artist, who had never paid him for the use of his name and image. See Elena Poniatowska's 1977 interview with El Santo, "El Santo a dos que tres caidas," in her book, *Todo México* (Mexico City: Editorial Planeta, 1990), pp. 269, 277.

27 *Pepín*, no. 409, 24 March 1940, pp. 22–29.

28 Conversely, cartoonist Zea Salas reported that he was unable to kill off his hero Aguila Roja (a series in *Chamaco*) because as soon as the vaquero was threatened with death, his publisher would receive "a mountain of letters from all over the country" insisting that the story continue. Bartra, "Seduction," p. 33.

29 The analysis in this section is based on *Pepín* and *Chamaco* (both of which ran from 1936 to 1953), and *Paquito Grande* (a successor to *Paquito* that existed from 1949 to 1955), most of which are in the Fondo García Valseca of the Hemeroteca nacional, Mexico City. To the best of my knowledge, no archival collection of *Paquín* exists; also, the Hemeroteca has no complete runs of any comic book, so that all of *Pepín* for 1945 (for example) is missing. However, the complete contents of every issue of *Pepín*, *Paquín*, *Paquito*, and *Chamaco* for 1944–46 are carefully detailed in censors' reports in CCPRI, *Minutario 1945*.

30 Their exact size varied over the years, due to the changing availability of paper and types of presses in use, but *Pepín*, *Paquín*, and *Chamaco* were roughly the size of a small paperback. *Paquito* used the same format until 1948, when it renamed itself *Paquito Grande*, doubled in size, and cut its number of pages in half. Before that, Mexican comics were never as large as their North American competitors, but they were always thicker.

31 "1 precioso y variada lote de juguetes" appeared in every issue of *Pepín* in September and October 1938.

32 As a benchmark of what a working-class Mexican family might be expected to own a little later than this period, Oscar Lewis's *The Children of Sanchez*

(New York: Random House, 1961), p. xvi, reports that in one large Mexico City tenement in 1956, there were

> inside toilets . . . and piped water. . . . 79 percent of the tenants . . . had radios, 55 percent gas stoves, 54 percent wrist watches, 49 percent used knife and forks [rather than spoons and tortillas], 46 percent had sewing machines, 41 percent aluminum pots, 22 percent electric blenders, 21 percent television.

33 *Pepín*, no. 647, 1 January 1941, p. 14.

34 *Pepín*, no. 666, 15 January 1941, pp. 34–35.

35 "Recorta y guarda este cupon," *Tesoros*, no. 38, 30 May 1952, p. 9.

36 *Pepín*, no. 410, 25 March 1940, p. 39.

37 *Pepín*, no. 410, 25 March 1940, p. 39, *Pepín*, no. 399, 13 March 1940, p. 39; *Pepín*, no. 406, 20 March 1940, p. 39; and *Pepín*, no. 397, 11 March 1940, p. 39.

38 *Pepín*, no. 403, 18 March 1940, p. 40.

39 *Pepín*, no. 363, 31 January 1940, p. 33; and *Pepín*, no. 358, 25 January 1940, p. 33.

40 *Pepín*, no. 369, 7 February 1940, p. 33.

41 *Pepín*, no. 420, 6 April 1940, p. 19.

42 Ibid., p. 20.

43 Ibid., p. 23.

44 *Pepín*, no. 1164, 21 May 1942, p. 51.

45 For North American "true-life" romance comics, see Joe Simon and Jack Kirby, *Real Love* (Seattle, Wash.: Eclipse, 1990).

46 A photo of Marin appeared in *Pepín*, no. 861, 22 July 1941, p. 51, with the following caption: "We are delighted to publish his portrait, thus attending to the numerous requests of our readers who, since the extraordinary serial CUMBRES DE ENSUEÑO began, have not stopped asking us for it." Another photo of Marin ran in *Pepín*, no. 1210, 6 August 1942, p. 55.

47 *Confidencias*, no. 1, 12 May 1943, p. 1.

48 This advertisement first appeared in *Paquito Grande*, no. 2037, 22 January 1950, p. 3.

49 This subtitle first appeared on the cover of *Paquito Grande*, no. 2043, 4 February 1950.

50 The exceptions to this trend of "disappearing" artists and writers all were active in the industry well before 1952: Yolanda Vargas Dulché, "Avril" (Laura Bolanas, ex-editor of *Chamaco*), German Butze, and Carlos Vigil.

51 *Corazon*, no. 1, 13 January 1955, p. 2.

52 For example, *El Libro Policiaco de color*, no. 369, 9 August 1988. One critic claims that all contemporary Mexican comic books could be understood as

belonging to the genre of "true-life" story; see Kurt Hollander, "Historietas de la vida real," *Poliester* 2, no. 6 (summer 1993): 14–17.

53 Direct, unsolicited audience participation in the construction of narrative in Mexico is not limited to comic books. Blanca de Lizaur, who used to write for the television network Televisa, told me that readers' letters were so important that an assistant director would intercept them before they got to the screenwriters. He would sort them and *sell* the most interesting or original ones to the screenwriters (Personal communication, 8 June 1992).

Chapter Two Home-Loving and without Vices: "Modernity," "Tradition," and the Comic Book Audience

1 See Robert Redfield and Milton Singer, "The Cultural Role of Cities," *Economic Development and Social Change* 3 (1954), and *Tepotzlan* (Chicago: University of Chicago Press, 1930); Luis Gonzalez y Gonzalez, *Invitación a la microhistoria* (Mexico City: Secretaría de Educación Pública, 1973); Guillermo Bonfil Batalla, *Mexico profundo* (Mexico City: Secretaría de Educación Pública, 1987); Steve J. Stern, *The Secret History of Gender: Women, Men, and Power in Late Colonial Mexico* (Chapel Hill: University of North Carolina Press, 1995), p. 309; and Alan Knight, "The Peculiarities of Mexican History," *Journal of Latin American Studies*, suppl. (1992), and "Revolutionary Project, Recalcitrant People: Mexico, 1910–1940," in *The Revolutionary Process in Mexico*, ed. Jaime Rodríguez O. (Berkeley and Los Angeles: University of California Press, 1990).

For a sweeping critique of the essayists and anthropologists who have been most influential in constructing or deconstructing Mexican national culture, see Claudio Lomnitz-Adler, *Exits from the Labyrinth: Culture and Ideology in the Mexican National Space* (Berkeley and Los Angeles: University of California Press, 1992), pp. 1–19, 247–60. The regional history literature that followed Gonzalez's influential invitation is reviewed in Thomas Benjamin, "Regionalizing the Revolution," in *Provinces of the Revolution*, eds. Thomas Benjamin and Mark Wasserman (Albuquerque: University of New Mexico Press, 1990). Redfield's most important critic was Oscar Lewis; see his *Life in a Mexican Village: Tepotzlan Restudied* (Champaign-Urbana: University of Illinois Press, 1951), and *Tepotzlan, a Village in Mexico* (New York: Holt, Rinehart and Winston, 1961). On Redfield's influence, see Arturo España Caballero, "La practica social y el populismo nacionalista," in *La antropología en México, Panorama historico*, vol. 2, ed. Carlos García Mora (Mexico City: Instituto Nacional de Antropología e Historia, 1987). On the argument between Lewis and Redfield, see Lomnitz-Adler, *Exits*, p. 122.

2 Adriana Malvido and Teresa Martínez Arana, "La historieta en México: un mundo ancho y ajeno," *Casa del tiempo* 42 (July 1984): 19.

3 Oscar Lewis, *The Children of Sanchez* (New York: Random House, 1961), p. xxiii.

4 Ibid., p. 44.

5 Ibid., p. 133.

6 Quoted in Alan Riding, *Distant Neighbors* (New York: Knopf, 1984), pp. 354–55.

7 Larissa Adler Lomnitz, *Networks and Marginality: Life in a Mexican Shanty-town* (New York: Academic Press, 1977), p. 182.

8 Jonathan Kandell, *La Capital* (New York: Random House, 1988), p. 506.

9 Ariel Dorfman and Armand Mattelart, *How to Read Donald Duck: Imperialist Ideology in the Disney Comic*, trans. David Kunzle (New York: International General, 1975).

10 Dick Reavis, *Conversations with Moctezuma* (New York: William Morrow, 1990), p. 213. Thanks to Bill Beezley for the reference.

11 Irene Herner, *Mitos y monitos* (Mexico City: Editorial Nueva Imagen, 1979), p. xi.

12 These are the only statistical analyses of the audience that I could find, except for those published by Herner, *Mitos y monitos*, and Harold Hinds Jr. and Charles Tatum, *Not Just for Children: The Mexican Comic Book in the Late 1960s and 1970s* (Westport, Conn.: Greenwood Press, 1992). Unfortunately, these studies survive only in some notes sent by another UNAM professor, Alfonso Quiroz C. Rubrica, to la Comisión Calificadora in 1961. Dr. Alfonso Quiroz C. Rubrica to Javier Piña y Palacios, 5 July 1961, in Comisión Calificadora de Publicaciones y Revistas Ilustradas (hereafter CCPRI), *Minutario 1961 10.*

13 The broad conclusions of these surveys are worth reporting, if only because they agree, generally, with data collected a quarter century later (Herner, *Mitos y monitos*, pp. 111–33; Hinds and Tatum, *Not Just for Children*, pp. 16–20): roughly a third of the population admitted reading at least one comic book per week, and the audience was split more or less evenly between men and women.

14 "Que puede esperarse de una Juventud a la que se ha procurado prostituir?" *El Hombre Libre* 2053, 18 June 1944, p. 1. The sinarquistas were the extreme right wing of Mexican politics in this era, sympathetic to (and perhaps funded by) European fascist parties.

15 *Lágrimas, Risas y Amor,* and *Memín Pingüin* began publication in the 1950s and lasted until 1997, placing them among the most durable narratives in

Mexican media. Yolanda Vargas Dulché's first book of short stories (1944), two of her radio drama scripts (1943, 1946), and a film script (1944) can all be found in Archivo General de la Nación, Propriedad artística y literaria, files 731–420, 734–543, 646–14101, 703–15676, 1178–9. These florid early works already exhibit the author's gift for engaging audiences and building suspense through the use of working-class characters and sentimentality.

16 Hinds and Tatum, *Not Just for Children*, pp. 54, 66; Beth Miller and Alfonso Gonzalez, *26 autores de Mexico actual* (Mexico City: B. Costa-Amic Editor, 1978), pp. 375–84; and Angelina Camargo Brena, "De escritor a editor: entrevista con Guillermo de la Parra de Editorial Argumentos," *Libros de Mexico* 5 (1986): 17–20.

17 Hinds and Tatum, *Not Just for Children*, p. 59.

18 *Pepín*, no. 865, 26 July 1941, pp. 12–19.

19 *La Familia Burrón*, no. 16231, 11 July 1955, p. 21. Conflict between the mother and father of the Burrón family over their daughter's behavior has provided an infallible comic plot device for the four decades of the comic book's existence.

20 "Ocaso," *Pepín*, no. 1141, 28 April 1942, p. 12.

21 I picked this narrative as the subject for a close reading almost at random and, in part, for reasons unconnected to the purposes of this chapter: its cartoonist had a particularly clear and comprehensible style, its author used relatively few extraneous subplots in constructing the story (at least by *Pepín*'s standards), and the story itself was quite concise (again, by *Pepín*'s standards). Most important, the entire run of issues that included chapters of the story—numbers 3779 to 3928—were available in the Hemeroteca Nacional. None of this should obscure the fact that I am asking readers to trust me when I assert that this serial is typical, in most respects, of all the *novelas* and *historietas* under discussion here.

22 The episode in *Pepín*, no. 3849, 2 October 1949, contained the least amount of dialogue (eight lines), while the episode in *Pepín*, no. 3843, 26 September 1949, contained the most (twenty lines).

23 On the other hand, many secondary characters fill two or more functions in the narrative, such as Chato, who acts as both a small-town boxing promoter and big-city boxing trainer (as well as the hero's best friend) at different points in the plot. This strains credulity, but reduces the number of characters a reader must keep track of over a six-month span.

24 The installment in *Pepín*, no. 3843, which, as mentioned above, has more lines of dialogue than any other episode, contains 305 words. Still, it uses only twenty-four nouns, four adjectives, thirty-five verbs, and four adverbs (in various numbers, genders, and tenses), supplemented with pronouns and prepositions, and augmented by an enormous degree of repetition.

25 For an enthralling discussion of levels of complexity in cartooning, including questions of abstraction and iconography, see Scott McCloud, *Understanding Comics* (Northampton, Mass.: Kitchen Sink Press, 1993), pp. 24–137.

26 This radically simplified form of narrative has come to dominate comic book plot design in Mexico, but in the first decade of the industry's existence (1934–44), more complex modes of storytelling were common. The serial "Almas de niños" (which ran in *Pepín* from December 1943 through November 1946 and was scripted by Yolanda Vargas Dulché) exemplifies a more complicated style of plot construction. In a July–August 1946 segment, for instance, the central story of a few mischievous boys was interrupted by a six-week flashback told through the eyes of an old man whom the boys met in prison. This flashback, furthermore, contains flashbacks and dream sequences within itself. Vargas Dulché even intercuts this flashback not only with images of the children listening to the elderly prisoner, but also to the children's families in a distant city.

This baroque level of complexity reasserted itself in Mexican comic books only in the late 1950s, as they completed a shift from the lengthy episodic form described in this chapter to the single-issue *novela* form now taken by the vast majority of Mexican *historietas*. For example, the July 1971 issue of *Mini carcel de mujeres* (no. 275) took place largely within a flashback to the recent past inside the mind of a dying woman, but included one fantasy sequence and one flashback to the distant past, both embedded within the larger flashback. The majority of *historieta* plots, however, still follow the simple chronological order of *El Viejo Nido*.

See Maria Blanca de Lizaur Guerra, "Arte verbal 'dominante-no prestigiado'" (Lice. thesis, UNAM, 1993) for further discussion of plot structures in "subliteratura."

27 There is little evidence available on the people involved with the comic book industry during this period other than the descriptions they themselves sometimes included in their work and the testimony some of them gave before the Comisión Calificadora de Publicaciones y Revistas Ilustradas. For example, in 1952, *Tesoros* ran seven single-page features titled "Gente de Tesoros," which introduced some of its cartoonists: all of them lived in Mexico City, all joked about their poverty and how they hoped to escape it, and all but one were born in a small town well outside Mexico City (*Tesoros*, nos. 28–35, 7 March–2 May 1952).

As late as 1971–74, when the commission began keeping track of the birthplace and age of everyone who testified before it, precisely 50 percent of those called before the government body were born outside Mexico City. All but one (of thirteen) of those born in the capital were under forty years old and most were in the second generation of a family business (CCPRI, *Actas 1971–1972, Actas 1973–1974,* and *Minutario enero-abril 1972*).

28 *Pepín,* no. 3779, 24 July 1949, p. 2.

29 Ibid., p. 5.

30 Ibid., p. 6.

31 *Pepín,* no. 3780, 25 July 1949, p. 11.

32 *Pepín,* no. 3784, 29 July 1949, p. 36.

33 *Pepín,* no. 3790, 4 August 1949, pp. 34–35.

34 Ibid., p. 36.

35 *Pepín,* no. 3799, 12 August 1949, p. 21.

36 *Pepín,* no. 3802, 16 August 1949, p. 12.

37 *Pepín,* no. 3859, 12 October 1949, p. 43.

38 Ibid., pp. 49–50.

39 *Pepín,* no. 3902, 24 November 1949, p. 26.

40 *Pepín,* no. 3893, 15 November 1949, p. 16.

41 *Pepín,* no. 3911, 3 December 1949, p. 30.

42 *Pepín,* no. 3913, 5 December 1949, p. 7.

43 *Pepín,* no. 3916, 8 December 1949, p. 26.

44 *Pepín,* no. 3924, 16 December 1949, p. 32.

45 *Pepín,* no. 3926, 18 December 1949, p. 5.

46 *Pepín,* no. 3927, 19 December 1949, p. 8.

47 *Pepín,* no. 3928, 20 December 1949, p. 16.

48 Ibid., p. 17.

49 Ibid., p. 20.

50 *Pepín,* no. 3920, 12 December 1949, p. 8.

56 *Pepín,* no. 3803, 17 September 1949, pp. 16–17.

52 For the connection between "progressive society" and rapid transportation before the revolution, see William H. Beezley, *Judas at the Jockey Club* (Lincoln: University of Nebraska Press, 1987), pp. 41–52; on the same topic a few decades later, see Wendy Waters, "New Roads, Old Directions: Calles' Caminos and the Creation of a Capitalist Culture" (paper presented at the Rocky Mountain Conference on Latin American Studies, Fort Worth, Tex., February 1994).

53 I thank William H. Beezley for the suggestion that Mexican comics can be seen as "moral anchors" for their readers (Personal communication, 19 February 1994).

54 There is a single exception: Elena Poniatowska, in "Gabriel Vargas y su Familia Burrón," *El Gallo ilustrado: suplemento dominical de El Dia* 33 (10 February 1963): 2, refers to a collection of letters that Vargas received, mostly

containing suggestions for modifications of his long-running humor series. Cited in Hinds and Tatum, *Not Just for Children*, p. 31.

55 For example: In addition to "Cumbres de Ensueño," which as discussed earlier ran reader photographs from 1940 through 1944, comic books that printed readers' portraits included *Tesoros* (1951–52), *Historietas* (1952), and *Rolando el Rabioso* (1969). *Chamaco* ran four reader drawings daily in April 1944; *Tesoros* published five reader drawings in every weekly issue from 7 September 1951 to 27 July 1952; *Rolando el Rabioso* printed two or three per week between 23 April 1966 and 11 January 1969; and *Pepín* printed reader drawings once or twice a month throughout its existence.

56 Lewis, *Children of Sanchez*, pp. 44, 81.

57 *Paquito Grande*, no. 2034B, 5 July 1950, p. 2.

58 *Paquito Grande*, no. 2016, 7 June 1950, p. 2.

59 *Paquito Grande*, no. 2034, 11 January 1950, p. 2. The phrase "not looking for adventures" here means that the writer is emphatically denying an interest in sexual adventure, rather than rejecting the possibility of romantic excitement.

60 Some statistics can be extracted from the lonely hearts page; they contain few surprises. Although *Paquito Grande* appears to have been aimed at women, 53 percent of the advertisers were male. All advertisers used the magazine as a mail drop, so there was no requirement to locate themselves. But of the 54 percent who did give an address, only a quarter lived in Mexico City. Another 23 percent had addresses in four other major cities—Guadalajara, Tampico, Tijuana, and Veracruz—but the rest were scattered evenly across the country, in small towns and rural areas. Seven percent lived outside Mexico, mostly in Guatemala and Texas. (Two lonely Spaniards, members of the French Foreign Legion, wrote from Indochina.) The median age for male advertisers was twenty; for female advertisers, seventeen. Yet, since this was a group of readers looking for marriage partners, that statistic says little about the comic book audience as a whole. The range of ages represented in the advertisements may provide a better clue: the youngest advertiser was fourteen and the oldest was fifty.

61 Both the facts and the linguistic analysis here were extracted from a database that contains approximately 600 of the ads published in *Paquito Grande* between 1949 and 1952. *Paquito Grande* actually contained about 3,600 such advertisements, but I only entered the ads from one issue in every six into the database, because the process was so time-consuming and the advertisements seemed so consistent.

62 The importance of Catholicism to readers was perceived, too, by the creators of comic books. In the introduction to a serial with the provocative title "Blas-

phemy," writer Antonio Gutiérrez carefully explained to his audience that he was not advocating heresy: "do not judge [the story] until we get to the end. We believe it necessary to offer this warning, given the delicacy of the theme, taking into account that 90% of our readers are Catholic" (*Pepín*, no. 2752, 9 September 1946, p. 17).

Chapter Three   The Uses of Tradition: Conservative Opposition to Comic Books

1   William H. Beezley, *Judas at the Jockey Club* (Lincoln: University of Nebraska Press, 1987), pp. 16–17.

2   Margarita de Orellana, *La mirada circular* (Mexico City: Joaquín Mortiz, 1991), pp. 32–33.

3   Many historians have mentioned cultural aspects of the revolutionary reconstruction of the Mexican state, but they are most neatly summarized by Alan Knight, *The Mexican Revolution*, vol. 2 (London: Cambridge University Press, 1987), pp. 501–3.

4   See Marjorie Becker, *Setting the Virgin on Fire* (Berkeley and Los Angeles: University of California Press, 1995).

5   See, for example, the description of the state's successful effort to defang Spanish-language rock music in Eric Zolov, *Refried Elvis* (Berkeley and Los Angeles: University of California Press, 1998). See also, Roderic Camp, *Intellectuals and the State in Twentieth-Century Mexico* (Austin: University of Texas Press, 1985), pp. 13–25; Carlos G. Velez-Ibañez, *Rituals of Marginality* (Berkeley and Los Angeles: University of California Press, 1983), pp. 183–204; and Evelyn P. Stevens, *Protest and Response in Mexico* (Cambridge, Mass.: MIT Press, 1974).

6   Jean Meyer, *The Cristero Rebellion: The Mexican People between Church and State, 1926–1929*, trans. R. Southern (London: Cambridge University Press, 1976), pp. 210–12.

7   See Alex M. Saragoza, *The Monterrey Elite and the Mexican State* (Austin: University of Texas Press, 1988).

8   This description owes much to John W. Sherman, *The Mexican Right: The End of Revolutionary Reform, 1929–1940* (Westport, Conn.: Praeger, 1997).

9   For a painstaking description of an exemplary group of conservative but nonaligned upper-class Mexicans, see Larissa Adler Lomnitz and Marisol Perez-Lizaur, *A Mexican Elite Family, 1820–1980* (Princeton, N.J.: Princeton University Press, 1987), pp. 192–230.

10   Carlos Monsiváis, "La nación de unos cuantos y las esperanzas romanticas: Notas sobre la historia del termino 'cultura nacional' en México," in *En torno*

a la cultura nacional, eds. José Emilio Pacheco et al. (Mexico City: Fondo de cultura economica, 1976), p. 208.

11 José Agustín, more precisely, writes that the decisive moment was not Avila Camacho's 1940 announcement of his Catholic faith (in his notorious self-description as "a believer"), but his 1941 amendment of the constitution's Article Three. José Agustín, *Tragicomedia mexicana 1* (Mexico City: Editorial Planeta, 1990), pp. 25, 49.

12 Monsiváis, "La nación de unos cuantos," p. 211.

13 Rodney Alvarez, personal communication, 14 February 1997.

14 See Alan Knight, "Revolutionary Project, Recalcitrant People: Mexico 1910–1940," in *The Revolutionary Process in Mexico,* ed. Jaime Rodríguez O. (Berkeley and Los Angeles: University of California Press, 1990), pp. 256–58.

15 Alan Knight, "The Peculiarities of Mexican History," *Journal of Latin American Studies,* suppl. (1992): 136. See also Hector Aguilar Camín and Lorenzo Meyer, *In the Shadow of the Mexican Revolution,* trans. Luis Alberto Fierro (Austin: University of Texas Press, 1993), pp. 262–63.

16 Alan Knight, "The Politics of the Expropriation," in *The Mexican Petroleum Industry in the Twentieth Century,* eds. Alan Knight and Jonathan Brown (Austin: University of Texas Press, 1992); and Agustín, *Tragicomedia,* pp. 132–33.

17 See Camín and Meyer, *In the Shadow,* pp. 174–77.

18 Juan Manuel Aurrecoechea and Armando Bartra, *Puros Cuentos: La historieta en México,* vol. 2 (Mexico City: Grijalbo, 1994).

19 "Nuestro criterio," *Apreciaciones,* 11 March 1944, p. 2.

20 *Apreciaciones,* 10, no. 28, 10 July 1943, p. 1; and *Apreciaciones* 10, no. 25, 19 June 1943, p. 1.

21 Dr. E. Glennie B., "Revistas para niños," *Apreciaciones* 10, no. 36, 4 September 1943, p. 2.

22 Most important, the movie business—unlike the publishing industry—was already closely regulated by the state. See John King, *Magical Reels* (London: Verso, 1990), pp. 47–54, 129–40.

23 *Apreciaciones* 12, no. 22, 2 June 1945, p. 1.

24 Dr. E. Glennie B., "Hechos," *Apreciaciones* 10, no. 37, 11 September 1943, p. 2.

25 Luis G. Villalpando to President Manuel Avila Camacho, Mexico City, 24 September 1944, in Archivo General de la Nación (AGN hereafter), Fondo presidentes, Avila Camacho papers, file 704/582. The fine mentioned was levied on *Pepín* (see "Mil pesos de Multa Para una Revista Infantil Inmoral," *La Prensa,* 24 September 1944, p. 4), but never collected.

26 On the mythology of the *soldadera,* see Elizabeth Salas, *Soldaderas in the Mexican Military: Myth and History* (Austin: University of Texas Press, 1990), pp. 83–118.

27 Juana Armanda Alegría, *Psicología de las mexicanas* (Mexico City: Editorial Samo, 1974), pp. 144–45. Thanks to Lana Wong for the reference.

28 Ana Montes de Oca de Lira, "Los Tiempos en que vivimos," *Acción femínina* VI, no. 144 (January 1945): 4.

29 "Puntos de Vista," *El Universal*, 16 February 1943, p. 3.

30 Gonzalo de la Parra, *El Universal*, 19 February 1943, p. 3.

31 *El Universal*, 26 February 1943, p. 3.

32 Agustín, *Tragicomedia mexicana 1*, pp. 54–56.

33 Editorial Pro-Cultura, "Carta a los Srs. Gobernadores de Estado," 6 November 1937, in AGN, Fondo presidencial, Cárdenas papers, file 704/12.

34 *Periquillo*, no. 1, 27 October 1937, in AGN, Fondo presidencial, Cárdenas papers, File 704/12.

35 Editorial Pro-Cultura, "Memorandum para el Sr. Lic. Ignacio García Tellez," 10 December 1937, in AGN, Fondo presidencial, Cárdenas papers, file 704/12.

36 Advertisement for *La Cruzada* in *Apreciaciones* 9, no. 38, 12 September 1942, p. 2.

37 Fernando Peñalosa, *The Mexican Book Industry* (New York: Scarecrow Press, 1957), pp. 39–40; and "Vida de la Organización," *Acción feminina* 150 (July 1945): 4. *Piloto* also was sold through advertisements aimed at "mothers! catechists!" in every issue of *Acción feminina* between 1940 and 1946; a decade later, *Tesoros* occasionally printed pictures of its editors meeting with priests and bishops.

38 Less frequently, conservative groups attempted to publish "clean" adult entertainment that would provide the same melodramatic satisfaction as the *historietas*. The *sinarquista* newspaper *Omega*, for example, advertised books such as *40 Noches con Maria Magdalena*, "a sad book, not scandalous or immoral, that paints a somber picture of the sinful and miserable underworld" (*Omega*, 11 February 1943, p. 4).

39 Dorothy Adelson, "Competition for Superman," *Inter-American* (June 1943): 29.

40 "Novelas y historietas quedaran proscritas," *El Universal*, 22 February 1942, p. 11.

41 Some of these letters are preserved, along with a memorandum listing them, in AGN, Fondo presidencial, Avila Camacho papers, file 708/582.

42 For example, la Unión Nacional de Padres de Familia (National Parents' Syndicate) barely participated at all. As late as January 1944, in their presentation to a nationwide education conference, they stuck to their old issues—such as the revision of textbooks and deregulation of parochial schools—making no mention of popular culture in any form (see *El Universal*, 10–15 January 1944). It was not until mid-1944 that self-identified members of the Unión

Nacional began writing anti-*historieta* letters to the government, and there never were many of them (see AGN, Fondo presidencial, Avila Camacho papers, file 704/582).

43 "¡Padres de Familia!" in AGN, Fondo presidencial, Avila Camacho papers, file 704/582.

44 Mario Rauche Garciadiego, "Los Pasquines y la Juventud," *El Hombre Libre*, 1961, 17 December 1943, p. 1.

45 "Los vendadores de periodicos son perseguidos tenazamente por un cacique de la Villa de Guadalupe," *El Universal*, 4 October 1944, p. 5.

46 "Tubercolosis, Masoneria, Comunismo y Paquines en la Escuela Nacional para Varones," *El Hombre Libre*, no. 2120, 22 December 1944, p. 1. As the headline implies, the article used a medical metaphor to characterize all four problems equally as "plagues."

47 Luis Morel Suarez to President Avila Camacho, 24 October 1943, in AGN, Fondo presidencial, Avila Camacho papers, file 704/582. See also, *El Universal*, 4 November 1943.

48 Guillermo Asantos to President Avila Camacho, 10 April 1944, in AGN, Fondo presidencial, Avila Camacho papers, File 704/582.

49 Maria Elena Sodi de Pallares, "Genialidad de Walt Disney Desvirtuada por extraños," *El Universal*, 8 October 1944, p. 1.

50 Crispín Villanueva Rivera, "Películas de Penetracación Yanqui," *El Hombre Libre*, no. 2081, 22 September 1944, p. 1.

51 *Apreciaciones*, 11 October 1947, p. 1.

52 Peñalosa, *Mexican Book Industry*, pp. 39–40.

53 "Se Prohibe la Publicación de Pueriles Revistas Amorales" and "Lecturas Infantiles," *Acción femenina*, no. 136, 5 May 1944, pp. 13, 19; and "Supongamos . . . ," *Acción femenina*, no. 137, 4 June 1944, p. 19. Articles and advertisements in other conservative periodicals also continued to suggest parental vigilance, and offer alternative reading for children throughout 1944 and 1945. For instance, "La Buena y la Mala Lectura para los Niños" (*El Hombre Libre*, no. 2120, 22 December 1944, p. 1) advised replacing "dangerous trash" with translations of Virgil.

54 Pedro Crespo, "El Congreso contra el Vicio, los Pasquines y el Desastre de la Educación en México," *El Hombre Libre*, no. 1996, 8 March 1944, p. 1.

55 Journalist Magdelena Mondragon described a typical pattern of Mexican press censorship while complaining of pressure on her humor magazine, *Chist:*

There appeared two military gentlemen who refused to identify themselves, claiming that "they had come to see me on behalf of the government" . . . asking me, in effect, to completely change the nature of the

magazine, beginning with its editorial cartoons, as otherwise "the government" would . . . refuse paper to Editorial Serna, which is where the magazine is printed. . . . It seemed that the officers . . . would be very unlikely to
appear in my house without specific orders, and I asked them to show me
the orders they carried to allow them to speak to me that way, to which they
replied that "they did not have to give me explanations." I have witnesses
to these acts. . . . I had no option but to stop, that instant, the presses.

Magdelena Mondragon to Avila Camacho, 11 December 1944, in AGN, Fondo
presidencial, Avila Camacho papers, file 704/239. For other descriptions
of mechanisms of media control, see Camp, *Intellectuals and the State*, pp.
177–207; Daniel Levy and Gabriel Székely, *Mexico: Paradoxes of Stability and
Change* (Boulder, Colo.: Westview Press, 1983), pp. 86–99; Alan Riding, *Distant Neighbors* (New York: Vintage, 1984), pp. 117–19; and Stevens, *Protest and
Response*, pp. 29–46.

56 "Caciques y Autoridades Imposicionistas Hostilizan a los Agentes de *Omega
y El Hombre Libre*," *El Hombre Libre*, no. 2248, 17 October 1945, p. 1; and
"Los Atentados contra los Periódicos Reclaman una Vigorosa Solidaridad,"
Omega, no. 2008, 8 January 1944, p. 1. For the government's justifications
for closing the paper *El Sinarquista*, see "Libertad y libertinaje," *El Universal*,
7 June 1944, p. 3.

57 Adelson, "Competition for Superman," p. 29.

58 Compare the U.S. comic books targeted by Fredric Wertham and his followers in the 1950s: part of their response was to print cartoon stories
addressing the censorship crusade directly, either by lampooning Wertham
or calling him a communist.

59 For issues of freedom and constraint in the news media, see David LaFrance,
"A Survey of Mexico City Newspapers," *Studies in Latin American Popular
Culture* 4 (1985).

60 Ibid., p. 105.

61 *El Universal*, 3–7 April 1942.

62 Letters and telegrams in AGN, Fondo presidencial, Avila Camacho papers,
file 704/698.

Most anti-comic-book crusaders elided the question of adult readers by
referring to *pepines* as "magazines for children." One editorialist even claimed
that their advertisements, "like the advertisements for doctors who might
be very efficient but their propaganda should be made some other way and
somewhere else," merely demonstrated that the *historietas* were sneakily attempting to disguise themselves as publications for adults ("Los padres de
familia," *Apreciaciones*, 8 January 1943, p. 2). A Family Action Section leaflet answered the question of adult male readership differently: it admitted

that, "true, these types of comic books are read by many grown people," but some adult readers were "individuals with retarded mentalities, uncultured," and most were "looking for unhealthy entertainment." Yet the leaflet conceded, "we want to occupy ourselves only with children and youth." Their response, in short, was that the potential damage to youth from comic books outweighed the potential (and sinful) pleasure for adult males ("¡Padres de Familia!" in AGN, Fondo presidencial, Avila Camacho papers, file 704/582).

63 Adrian Blanco C. et al to Avila Camacho, 17 March 1944, in AGN, Fondo presidencial, Avila Camacho papers, file 704/582.

64 "Proyecto para depurar la literatura infantil," *El Universal*, 6 January 1944, p. 1.

65 "Informe que, sobre sus labores durante el primer año de su ejercicio, rinde la comisión calificadora de revistas ilustradas al C. Secretario de Educación Publica," in Comisión Calificadora de Publicaciones y Revistas Ilustradas (hereafter CCPRI), *Minutario 1945*.

The committee that was to become the new commission, chosen by the secretary of public education (SEP) and the attorney general's offices, did not even meet until February 28—at which point they gathered in the offices of the Department of Public Education's lawyers to read the new regulations that would govern their activities. The principal authors of the law probably were SEP lawyers Heraclio Rodriguez Portugal and Gonzalo Hernandez Zanabria, who advised the commission on the interpretation of the law in subsequent years and sat on the commission (representing, at different points, the ministries of the Interior, the Federal district, and the attorney general's office) for most of the period between 1953 and 1958 (in Rodriguez's case) or 1976 (Hernandez).

66 Crespo, "El Congreso," p. 3.

67 *Diario Oficial*, 11 March 1944, p. 1.

68 CCPRI: Pedro Muro Asunsolo/Dep. de Información para el Extranjero/Sec. de Relaciones Exteriores to Rafael Muñoz/Dep. de Publicidad y Propaganda/Sec. de Educación Publica, 22 June 1944, in *Minutario 1945*; Acta 5, *Minutario 1956 10.*, 3 February 1956; and Javier Cu Delgado/CCPRI to Jorge Flores/Camera Nacional de la Industria Editorial, 17 March 1976, in *Minutario 1976 20*. Dr. E. Glennie B., "La Legión Mexicana de la Decencia en America del Sur," *Apreciaciones*, 17 February 1945, p. 3.

Fredric Wertham, the notorious U.S. anti-comic-book crusader, also cited Mexican efforts as a catalyst to his work in the late 1940s (*Seduction of the Innocent*, p. 293).

69 "Sesión de la Legión Mexicana de la Decencia," *El Universal*, 13 November 1953, p. 6.

70 José M. Martinez Reyes to Ruiz Cortines, 16 November 1953, in AGN, Fondo presidencial, Ruiz Cortines papers, file 704/208.

71 CCPRI: *Actas Marzo 1953–Diciembre 1954*, acta, 27 August 1954, p. 6; *Actas Marzo 1953–Diciembre 1954*, acta, 29 October 1954, p. 6; *Actas 1956–1958*, acta 11, 2 August 1957; and *Minutario 1958 20.*, acta, 24 March 1958.

72 Antonio Lomali to CCPRI, in CCPRI, *Minutario 1960*, 3 October 1960.

73 CCPRI, *Minutario 1960*, acta 11, 24 November 1960; *Minutario 1961 10.*, acta 5, 2 February 1961.

74 "Aclaración de la Comisión Calificadora de Revistas," *El Universal*, 10 November 1953, p. 24.

75 Ruiz Cortines, like Avila Camacho before him, received two to four telegrams and letters a week on this subject from all over Mexico. AGN, Fondo Gobernación file 38-2000(29)/258; and AGN, Fondo presidencial, Ruiz Cortines papers, files 704/208 and 704.12/1.

76 Antonio E. Izaguirre et al., Confederación de Cameras Nacionales de Comercio, to Ruiz Cortines, 25 March 1955, in AGN, Fondo Gobernación file 38/2000(29)/258.

77 There was already a precedent for, if not a tradition of, male high school and college students staging public demonstrations against mass media and in defense of the purity of female classmates: similar actions had occurred in Mexico City in 1934, at the height of the controversy over sexual education in the public schools. See Anne Rubenstein, "Raised Voices at the Cine Montecarlo," *Journal of Family History* (1998).

78 Agustín, *Tragicomedia mexicana 1*, pp. 150–51.

79 Agustín, *Tragicomedia mexicana 1*, p. 137.

80 The classic account of these events is Elena Poniatowska, *La noche de Tlatelolco* (Mexico City: Ediciones Era, 1971).

81 For the cultural politics of the 1968–76 period, see Zolov, *Refried Elvis;* José Agustín, *Tragicomedia mexicana 2* (Mexico City: Editorial Planeta, 1993), pp. 17–129; and Judith Adler Hellman, *Mexico in Crisis* (New York: Holmes and Meier, 1978).

82 Agustín, *Tragicomedia mexicana 2*, pp. 51, 61, 105.

83 Monsiváis, "La nación de unos cuantos," p. 11; and "Senelan que hay infiltración de Comunistas en Educación Pública," *El Universal*, 21 June 1976, p. 7.

84 Telegrams collected in CCPRI: *Minutario junio–julio 1972; Telegrams junio 1972 20.; Telegrams junio 1972 30.; Telegrams junio 1972 40.; Telegrams junio 1972 50.; Telegrams julio 1972 20.;* and *Minutario marzo–diciembre 1973*.

  I believe that some volumes—perhaps the majority—have been lost and that the government may have received several thousand more telegrams than are recorded here. Of the existing telegrams, it should be noted that relatively few (125) originated in Mexico City; the plurality (1,285) came from the famously conservative and Catholic state of Jalisco, with 714 coming from its capital, Guadalajara. Typically, though, telegrams arrived from small towns, suburbs, and villages that rarely sent more than two each. The telegrams came from 122 locations altogether.

85 CCPRI: *Minutario 1971–1972*, ofc. 1293, 30 November 1972; *Minutario enero–marzo 1971 10.*, ofc. 105, 1971; *Minutario enero–abril 1972*, ofc. 356, 20 April 1972; *Actas marzo–julio 1972*, ofc. 583, 1 June 1972; *Minutario agosto–septiembre 1972*, ofc. 928, 17 August 1972; *Minutario agosto–septiembre 1972*, ofc. 1017, 5 September 1972; *Minutario agosto–septiembre 1972*, ofc. 1094, 29 September 1972; *Actas 1972–1973*, ofc. 1298, 26 October 1973; *Minutario julio–septiembre 1975*, ofcs. 674 and 675, 9 July 1975; *Minutario enero–junio 1976 20.*, ofc. 504–149, 20 February 1976; *Minutario enero–junio 1976 20.*, ofc. 504–159, 3 March 1976; *Minutario julio–diciembre 1976 10.*, ofc. 929, 3 September 1976; and *Minutario julio–diciembre 1976 10.*, ofc. 1171, 21 September 1976.

86 CCPRI: *Actas agosto–diciembre 1962*, acta, 9 August 1962; and *Minutario agosto–septiembre 1972*, ofcs. 928, 1017, see above.

87 Between November 1971 and October 1976, the classifying commission received at least one letter or telegram every month from each of three groups: the Aguascalientes Committee for Social Improvement, the Committee for Mental Health and Social Orientation, and the Group for Moral, Civic, and Material Improvement (the last two, both of Guadalajara), sometimes with examples of offensive periodicals attached.

88 Javier Cu Delgado to Jesus Medina Ascencio and José Luis Lazcano Espinosa, 29 September 1972, in CCPRI, *Minutario agosto–septiembre 1972*, Ofc. 1094; Javier Cu Delgado to Roberto Rendon Serrano, 3 May 1972, in CCPRI, *Actas marzo–junio 1972*; and Javier Cu Delgado to Prof. J. Ignacio Rubio, 29 September 1972, in CCPRI, *Minutario agosto–septiembre 1972*, ofc. 1095.

89 Javier Cu Delgado to Jesus de Luna R. et al., 17 December 1971, in CCPRI, *Minutario 1971–1972*.

90 "Senalan que hay infiltración de Comunistas en Educación Pública," *El Universal*, 21 June 1976, p. 9.

91 "How Brazen Can You Get? In Mexico, Not Quite as Far as This," *New York Times*, 31 July 1996, p. A4.

Chapter Four   The Uses of Failure: La Comisión Calificadora, 1944–1976

1 There are no documents in the commission's archive from those years, and I found no outside references to any commission activities in that period in any other sources. Nobody associated with the commission in 1991–92 knew

anything about that era in the commission's history. Commission documents from late in 1952 and 1953 refer to the process of reestablishing the commission after its regulations were rewritten and republished in June 1951. On the other hand, no document exists that records any decision to close down or reestablish the commission. So the four-year gap in its activities remains slightly mysterious. I believe it to be simply the most extreme case of a general trend: the commission was most active during periods when public outcry against comic books and other magazines was loudest.

2   The law, as paraphrased here, is "Reglamento de revistas ilustradas en lo tocante a la educación," *Diario Oficial,* 11 March 1944. It went into effect on 19 March 1944. A slight revision of the law is "Reglamento de los articulos 4o y 6o, fracción VII, de la Ley orgánica de la educación pública, sobre publicaciones y revistas ilustradas en lo tocante a la cultura y a la educación," *Diario Oficial,* 12 June 1951. The most significant change was in the title of the commission, with the words "publicaciones y" being added.

3   From 1944 through 1946, much of the work of censorship was done by people who were not officially members of the classifying commission. Most documents emanating from the commission were signed by Fernando Ortega, the secretary of the office, who did not have any official decision-making power. Every page of every comic book was carefully checked, but not by the commissioners; they hired two men to provide weekly written reports on the content of each daily issue of *Chamaco, Paquín, Paquito,* and *Pepín.* Comisión Calificadora de Publicaciones y Revistas Ilustradas (hereafter CCPRI), *Minutario 1945,* contains 272 pages of reports from these censors.

4   "Entusiasmo Feminíl," *El Universal,* 4 September 1944, p. 1; "La Mujer de México," *El Universal,* 7 September 1944, p. 1; Roderic Ai Camp, *Mexican Political Biographies, 1953–1981,* 2nd ed. (Tucson: University of Arizona Press, 1982), p. 58; and "A.C.L.," *Mujeres* 24B, 30 July 1971, pp. 18–35.

5   One new representative of the Federal District in 1958 never appeared at the commission's office at all, not even to collect his paycheck.

6   Pay receipts in CCPRI, *Actas marzo–diciembre 1954, Minutario 1956, Minutario 1957, Minutario 1962 1o., Minutario 1963, Minutario 1964, Minutario 1965 2o., Minutario 1966 2o., Minutario 1967 2o., Minutario 1968 2o., Minutario 1969 2o., Minutario 1970, Minutario 1971–72, Actas 1972–73, Actas 1975–76;* CCPRI, "Informe que, sobre sus labores . . . rinde la comisión calificadora," *Minutario 1945;* CCPRI, "Nomina de la Comisión Revisora de Publicaciones y Revistas Ilustradas," *Minutario 1971–72,* 1958; and CCPRI, *Actas 1956,* acta 23, 5 August 1955.

7   Salary receipts as cited above; and CCPRI, "Puntos para un memorandum," *Minutario 1965 2o.,* n.d.

8   Censors' primary employment usually came from the ministries they repre-
    sented on the commission. Javier Piña y Palacios earned 46,200 pesos in
    1966 from a job with the Department of Public Education as the director
    general de asuntos juridicos y revalidación de estudios. The following year,
    Piña y Palacios's successor as president of the commission, Benito Palomina
    Dena, would also inherit his primary job with the SEP. In 1971, the next
    president of the commission, Javier Cu Delgado, received no salary at all
    because he earned so much in other SEP roles that he had reached the limit
    of a civil servant's potential legal earnings at his rank. Similarly, Professor
    Melchor Sanchez Jímenez, who represented Gobernación on the commis-
    sion from 1965 through 1970, added to his meager 7,200 peso commission
    salary a more comfortable 39,600 pesos a year as the private secretary to the
    secretary of state, another Gobernación job; but he seems to have spent most
    of his time writing biographies and poetry. Some of the commissioners with
    other employment were energetic and enthusiastic censors, including José
    Guadalupe Nájera (president of the Consejo Nacional Técnica de Educación
    Pública, a government-sponsored advisory board) and María Lavalle Urbina
    (Mexican delegate to UNESCO in 1957 and director of the Department of
    Social Welfare, Secretariat of Government, 1954–63). See the salary receipts
    as above; also CCPRI, "Asuntos de tratar," *Minutario 1957*, 13 March 1957, and
    Minutario 1964, ofc. 1887; and Camp, *Political Biographies*, p. 166.

9   Only two commissioners—Amalia Castillo de Ledon and María Lavalle
    Urbina—appear in Roderic Ai Camp's biographical dictionary of Mexican
    politicians (*Political Biographies*, pp. 58, 166). Castillo de Ledon went on to a
    career as a diplomat, serving on the Mexican delegation to the organizing
    conference of the United Nations, heading the Mexican delegation to the
    International Organization of Atomic Energy, and representing Mexico as
    ambassador to Finland, Sweden, and Austria. Lavalle Urbina's subsequent
    positions included senator from Campeche, judge of the Tribunal Superior
    in Mexico City, and Subsecretary of Public Education. Why should service
    on this commission have been less of a backwater for female than male
    politicians? It is tempting to speculate, in the absence of evidence, that
    men who concerned themselves professionally with issues of public morality
    risked seeming too prissy or Catholic to function successfully within the
    PRI, whereas a certain concern with public morality was acceptable, even
    expected, from female politicians.

10 At least once, the commissioners' habit of holding outside employment led
    to a direct conflict of interest. Octavio Colmenares was both the publisher
    of Editorial Meridiano and a former commission member when he defended
    his magazine, *Mujeres Inmortales*, which had been declared illicit, in a 1975

hearing. Colmenares's former colleagues did not levy a fine or further punishment on his periodical (CCPRI, *Minutario 1967* and *Minutario 1968 10.,* certificaciones de licitud; and *Actas 1975–76,* acta 196, 5 August 1975). Colmenares also published the left-wing comic book *Los Supermachos,* which never was declared illicit; he appears to have pressured Rius, the periodical's creator, into toning down (and eventually leaving) the comic, but at the same time, he avoided a direct confrontation with the commission over this particular magazine.

11 CCPRI, *Minutario 1953,* acta, 19 June 1953. This comic was reluctantly approved after a six-month delay, but the publisher abandoned it after six issues in the face of continuing complaints from the commission.

The general complaints against cowboy-and-Indian comics from the United States was that they were racist and provided a strongly North American point of view on Mexican history. Besides their structural reliance on the image of the bloodthirsty savage (already a problem for the commission, given the state's sporadic rhetorical commitment to *indigenismo*), they also frequently used the lazy (*mestizo*) and treacherous ("Spanish") Mexican stock figures as villains. Many of their plots were set in Texas during or immediately before or after the Mexican-American War, which they inevitably depicted as a heroic liberation.

Many other translations of cowboy-and-Indian comics from the United States, such as *El Durango Kid, El Vaquero Escarlata, Red Ryder, Audacias del Oeste, El Pequeño Sherif, Kid Montana, Indomitos del Oeste, Valores del Oeste, El Sheriff del Tomstone, Aguila Roja,* and *Juan Pistolas,* occasioned similar battles in the classifying commission. CCPRI: *Actas marzo 1953–diciembre 1954,* actas, 11 June 1954, 16 July 1954, 1 October 1954, 22 October 1954, 29 October 1954; *Minutario 1958 20.,* acta 7, 4 July 1958; *Minutario 1959,* ofc. 860, n.d.; *Minutario 1961 10.,* acta 4, 26 January 1961; *Minutario 1961 20.,* ofcs. 52, 753, n.d.; and *Minutario 1962 10.,* ofc. 697, n.d.

12 These very specific questions were most commonly raised about images of *semidesnudas,* half-dressed women. But some censors worried about the effects of smeared or small print on children's eyesight, and to 3-D special effects on the same grounds.

13 CCPRI, *Minutario 1959,* ofc. 88, 16 February 1957.

14 CCPRI, *Actas 1956–1958,* acta 23, 23 November 1956.

15 For example, see CCPRI, María Lavalle Urbina, "Dictamen sobre *Scene,*" *Minutario 1961 10.,* 24 February 1961.

16 These fines were neither so small as to be meaningless nor so large as to be crippling to the publishers: as a point of comparison, in 1944, 5,000 pesos could buy 50,000 comic books.

17 CCPRI, "Informe que, sobre sus labores durante el primer año de su ejercicio, rinde la comisión calficadora de revistas ilustradas al C. Secretario de Educación Pública," *Minutario 1945.*

18 CCPRI, Javier Piña y Palacios, "Informe a la comisión," *Actas marzo 1953–diciembre 1954*, 10 July 1953. Interestingly, none of the publications in question were comic books: the court cases involved soft-core pornography—*Vea, Solo para Hombres*, and *Chiquita*—and true-crime tabloids—*Nota Roja, Policia, Alarma*, and *Crimen.*

19 Javier Piña y Palacios to Director General de Correos, 9 October 1954, in CCPRI, *Actas 1952–1954*, ofc. 553.

20 CCPRI, *Actas 1952–1954*, acta, 18 June 1954. In the same report, Piña y Palacios showed that he could deploy similar tactics:

> It has been suggested that we acquire . . . the office of the Pensions representative who only shows up occasionally in the afternoons. . . . Our furniture could be moved [there] . . . now that it has been recovered from the office of the Semanario de Cultura Mexicana.

21 Javier Piña y Palacios, the president of the commission, said of *Marinos en Acción*, a translated version of the U.S. war comic *Marines in Action*, "the entire magazine is designed to foment hate against communist countries . . . a mentality sufficient to set some nations against others, a tendency opposed to the position Mexico has always adopted" (CCPRI, *Actas marzo 1953–diciembre 1954*, acta, 10 December 1954). *Marinos en Acción* survives in the collection of the Hemeroteca Nacional, Ciudad Universitaria, Mexico City; it is difficult to disagree with Piña y Palacios's opinion of it. For an aesthetic appreciation of the Korean War comic genre, however, see Michael Barrier and Martin Williams, *A Smithsonian Book of Comic-Book Comics* (New York: Smithsonian/Abrams, 1981), pp. 295–310.

22 CCPRI, *Actas marzo 1953–diciembre 1954*, acta, 19 June 1953.

23 CCPRI, *Actas marzo 1953–diciembre 1954*, acta, 10 July 1953.

24 CCPRI, *Actas marzo 1953–diciembre 1954*, acta, 11 September 1953.

25 Eduardo Trueba Urbina to Ruiz Cortines, 5 October 1953, in Archivo General de la Nación (hereafter AGN), Fondo presidencial, Ruiz Cortines papers, file 704/201. Beginning with this telegram, Ruiz Cortines's assistant, Luís García Larranaga, followed the case—sending notes to the secretary of public education and requesting information from judges—until it was eventually thrown out of court a year later.

26 *El Universal*, 13 October 1953, p. 9, and 14 October 1953, p. 6.

27 CCPRI, *Actas marzo 1953–diciembre 1954*, acta, 13 November 1953, p. 5.

28 Ibid., pp. 6–7.

29 Ibid.

30 Both comic books remained on the list of proscribed magazines in July 1954 (CCPRI, "Revistas y publicaciones negado licitud," *Actas 1952–54*, n.d.).

31 Casiano Castellanos to Luís García Larranaga, 8 April 1954, in AGN, Fondo presidencial, Ruiz Cortines papers, file 704/201.

32 A few copies of each of these comics, dated 1953–54, exists in the collection of the Hemeroteca Nacional. It is possible, however, that they lasted past that date without being collected by the Hemeroteca. On the other hand, the masthead of *Desfile de Historietas* claims a circulation of only 20,000 per monthly issue. (Compare this to *Pepín*, which five years earlier printed up to 300,000 copies every day and twice on Sundays.) Neither comic book appears to have found an enthusiastic audience.

33 Arturo Pueblita, representative of the publishing industry, wrote the report to the commission on Trueba Urbina's horror comic, *¡Miedo, Terror, Espanto!*:
> [It] can do little harm to . . . anglo-saxon youth, but in dealing with our children and our adolescents, the project takes on a more serious and dangerous nature, since . . . the national character has a propensity for cowardice and terror . . . that ought to be fought . . . since in Mexico already there breathes a new philosophy which simply and profoundly tries to combat the fear . . . sown in us by old women and our own parents.

Pueblita inverted the national pride that was Nájera's most frequent topic, but maintained the careful distinction between local and foreign popular culture that Nájera and Rodríguez agreed on. The commission sent Trueba Urbina a copy of Pueblita's report. One wonders what he made of it. CCPRI, *Actas marzo 1953–diciembre 1954*, acta, 27 August 1954.

34 CCPRI, "Acta de la sesión extraordinario," *Actas marzo 1953–diciembre 1954*, 16 February 1954.

35 For an analysis of the political content of Mexican comic books and photo-novels, see Irene Herner, *Mitos y monitos* (Mexico City: Editorial Nueva Imagen, 1979), pp. 278–91. For a description of some of the mechanisms of collaboration between media and government in Mexico, and their effect on the content of print, television, and radio, see Evelyn Stevens, *Protest and Response in Mexico* (Cambridge, Mass.: MIT Press, 1974), pp. 29–58.

36 CCPRI, *Actas marzo 1953–diciembre 1954*, acta, 13 January 1954.

37 The commission occasionally received queries from customs inspectors at the Texas border asking what should be done with illicit shipments of Spanish-language pornography headed into Mexico, implying that at least some of the magazines were being printed in the United States. See, for example, CCPRI, *Actas 1971–72*, acta 6, 30 March 1971.

38 CCPRI, *Actas marzo 1953–diciembre 1954*, acta, 4 December 1953, and acta, 29 January 1954. The complaint against *Eva* and *Can-Can* by the Legion of

Decency was echoed in a February 1954 letter from Antonio de Ibarrola, director of a group called the National Commission to Moralize Society. He, too, was sent a copy of the classifying commission's files on the offending publications (CCPRI, *Actas marzo 1953–diciembre 1954*, acta, 12 March 1954).

39 CCPRI, *Actas marzo 1953–diciembre 1954*, Acta, 12 March 1954.

40 CCPRI, *Actas 1955*, acta 5, 11 February 1955.

41 The newspapers were in Guanajuato, Cuatla, and Tapachula, Chiapas (CCPRI, *Actas 1956–1958*, acta 19, 28 September 1956).

42 Javier Cu Delgado to Celerio García Sosa and others, 2 March 1972, in CCPRI, *Minutario enero–abril 1972*.

43 CCPRI, *Minutario enero-abril 1972*, ofcs. 321, 326, 328, 345, 353, 355–57, 443–45, 448, 452–54, and 456–62, 13–27 April 1972.

44 Javier Cu Delgado to Jesus de Luna R. and Antonio Esparza Lopez, Comité Pro-Mejoramiento del Ambiente, 17 December 1971, in CCPRI, *Minutario 1971–72*.

45 CCPRI, *Minutario enero–marzo 1971 10.*, ofc. 62, 29 October 1971; and CCPRI, *Minutario 1971–72*, ofc. 1115, 11 October 1972, and ofc. 1293, 30 November 1972.

46 CCPRI, "Dictamen sobre *Idilio*," *Minutario marzo–mayo 1971 20.*, n.d.

47 CCPRI, "Dictamen sobre *Dos*," *Minutario marzo–mayo 1971 20.*, 20 April 1971.

48 CCPRI, *Actas 1955*, acta 15, 10 June 1955; and CCPRI, *Actas marzo 1953–diciembre 1954*, acta, 12 November 1954.

49 They objected, for example, to *Cosmopolitan* (Jorge Rios Gonzalez to Javier Cu Delgado, 15 July 1976, in CCPRI, *Minutario 1976 10.*).

50 CCPRI, *Minutario 1976 10.*, ofc. 832, 6 August 1976.

51 CCPRI, *Actas 1955*, acta 10, 25 March 1955.

52 Javier Piña y Palacios to Oscar Esquina Rodríguez, 11 May 1955, in CCPRI, *Minutario 1955–1956*.

53 CCPRI, "Asuntos para tratar," *Actas 1955*, 15 April 1955.

Chapter Five   Comic Books Respond to Their Critics, 1944–1976

1 Irene Herner, *Mitos y monitos* (Mexico City: Editorial Nueva Imagen, 1979), p. 24.

2 This chapter discusses not only comic books, but periodicals from related genres, such as Sunday supplements, gossip magazines, and true-crime tabloids. Such magazines were often produced by the same people who produced comic books. Photonovels—comic books' more daring sibling—were even more likely to be made and distributed by people from the comic book industry. Some entrepreneurs moved away from producing comics and toward photonovels, as José G. Cruz did. On the other hand, the de la Parra

family began their rise in the industry with a women's magazine, *Confesiones*, featuring photonovel stories, but their best-sellers were all comic books, like *Lágrimas, Risas y Amor*. Increasingly, after the 1942–44 campaign (which was directed specifically against comics), people complaining about print media tended to lump all the publications they wanted suppressed under the rubric of "pornography" or "trash." The only way to know whether they were referring to tabloid newspapers, girlie magazines, photography manuals, photonovels, comic books, or something else was to know precisely which publications they loathed.

3 "Una invasión peligrosa," *Jueves de Excelsior*, 24 July 1952, p. 5; see also Rogelio Rivera, "La prensa de Mexico podrá ser controlado por extranjeros," *El popular*, 30 July 1952 p. 1. Both are cited in Fernando Peñalosa, *The Mexican Book Industry* (New York: Scarecrow Press, 1957), p. 38.

4 Roderic Ai Camp, *Entrepreneurs and Politics in Twentieth-Century Mexico* (New York: Oxford University Press, 1989), p. 5; see also pp. 116–22.

5 Modesto Vázquez González, *La Historietica* (Mexico City: Promotora K, 1981), p. 21. Vázquez was the production director of the comic book company Promotora K when he wrote his book; his creation, *Kalimán*, is one of the best-selling Mexican comics of all time.

6 *Biographias Selectas* was published from 1959 through at least 1962. This slogan appeared every issue, usually on the inside back cover.

7 The comic book was *Tesoros*, whose title was registered in 1951: Archivo General de la Nación (hereafter AGN), Propriedad artística y literaria 981/12715. The slogan appears on the masthead in, for example, *Tesoros*, no. 35, 13 June 1950, p. 26.

8 *(Paquito Presenta a) Sombras*, no. 17014, 7 November 1953, p. 32.

9 The slogan appeared on the cover of every issue of *Dulce Amor* in 1974 and 1975, alongside a box quoting the magazine's price in the currencies of Bolivia, Costa Rica, Ecuador, El Salvador, the United States, Guatemala, Honduras, Nicaragua, Panama, Peru, Venezuela, and various Caribbean islands. The editor, Elia D'Erzell, is quoted in Comisión Calificadora de Publicaciones y Revistas Ilustradas (hereafter CCPRI), *Actas 1972–1973*, acta 100, 10 July 1973.

10 *Joyas de la Mitologia*, no. 237, 26 September 1973, p. 28. Rafael Rentería, then the editor of all Novaro comic books, must have been considering such a *historieta* since the last great wave of public protest against print media in the mid-1950s. In 1955, when he was editor at Ediciones Recreativas, he registered a copyright for the title *Leyendas de America*, a "title for an illustrated magazine of comic-book stories, monthly" (AGN, Propriedad artística y literaria 1191/25700).

11 *Tesoros*, no. 30, 12 March 1952.

12 *Joyas de la Mitología*, no. 242, 30 October 1973, back cover.

13 Representations of the nineteenth century were more common. Many serials, such as *Charros del Bajío* (*Pepín*, 1940–41), took place in the independence era. Also in 1940, *Pepín* put a series of color portraits of Mexican victors of nineteenth-century battles against the Spanish and French on its covers. Maurice Horn, in *Comics of the American West* (New York: Winchester Press, 1978), pp. 167–68, writes that in the 1940s, *Paquín* made a specialty of "Mexican westerns," many of which were set in the late-nineteenth or early-twentieth centuries.

14 Advertisement from *La Vida y los Amores de Pedro Infante*, no. 1, 29 April 1957, inside back cover.

15 Javier Piña y Palacios to Rafael Junquera Maldonado, 7 October 1965, in CCPRI, *Minutario 20.*, ofc. 842.

16 Ortega to Dirección General de Investigaciones de la Procuraduría de Justicia del Distrito Federal, 5 December 1955, in CCPRI, *Minutario 1955 20.*

17 *Fray Escoba, San Martin de Porres* was a weekly that began publication in 1958 and lasted at least until 1963. *La Sagrada Familia*, a weekly that also included a risque romantic serial called *Born to Be Bad*, ran from 1971 through at least 1973. *Milagros de Cristo* is mentioned in CCPRI, *Minutario 1963 10.*, ofc. 194, 2 April 1963, as belonging to a group of periodicals that the classifying commission had refused to characterize as "cultural or educational" to Hacienda (the taxation bureaucracy), thus denying them tax-exempt status.

Sometimes a cover that verged on blasphemy wrapped a disappointingly tame tale. One photonovel bannered "the SON of the PRIEST, A TRUE STORY" over an image of a handsome young curate embracing a pretty young woman; inside, the comic chastely described a young man's decision to enter a seminary and his ex-girlfriend's unsuccessful attempt to change his mind by spreading a rumor (*Dulce Amor*, no. 282, 27 February 1975).

18 The collection of the Hemeroteca Nacional holds *El Santo* up to 1974. Santo's adventures in the photonovel typically had little to do with sports—tending rather toward werewolves and miraculous visitations from the Virgin—but Cruz usually balanced this with a page or two of some more factual feature on wrestling.

19 The Felíx and Negrete comics are advertised in *La vida y los amores de Pedro Infante*, no. 7, 10 June 1957, inside back cover. The Tin-Tan comic is described in Fernando Ortega to Roberto S. Benjamin, 3 August 1955, in CCPRI, *Minutario 1955 20.*, ofc. 574.

20 *Figuras presenta a Pedro Infante* is described in Fernando Ortega to Jorge Ledesma, 4 July 1955, in CCPRI, *Minutario 1955 20.* The other two comics,

Pedro Infante el Muchacho Travieso del Cine and *La vida y amores de Pedro Infante* are in the collection of the Hemeroteca Nacional.

21 *Los Supersabios*, nos. 29–31, 7–28 July 1955.

22 *Fotomisterio*, no. 129, 2 January 1974, p. 1. Faced with a complaint from the classifying commission, *Fotomisterio's* editor argued that the "characters presented are fictional" even though the reality of the locations was an important feature of the photonovel (Jorge Torelli B., quoted in CCPRI, *Actas 1975–1976*, acta 184, 10 June 1975.)

23 *Pepín*, no. 200, 1938, n.d., p. 7.

24 *Dick Tracy*, no. 14, September 1952, p. 7.

25 The slogan sounds better in Spanish: "SEA . . . SI ES una revista SANA." It appeared at the bottom of every page of *Aventura* (no. 54, 15 February 1957, for example).

26 Advertisement for the products of Libreria Amenidades in *Aventuras*, no. 14, 1956?, p. 32.

27 *Domingos Alegres, La Pantera Rosa*, no. 1118, 3 December 1975, advertisement, inside front cover.

28 Advertisement in *Dick Tracy*, no. 72, February 1958, p. 32.

29 *Dick Tracy*, no. 62, April 1957, p. 30.

30 Occasionally, comic books that had been refused classifying commission licenses, or that had never troubled to apply for them, claimed that they also had this government certification, as on the cover of the José G. Cruz comic book *Munequita*. Fernando Ortega to José G. Cruz, 6 June 1955, in CCPRI, *Minutario 1955 20*.

31 "He aqui 10 razones por las que conviene subscribirse a Tesoros," *Tesoros*, no. 30, 21 March 1952, p. 35.

32 One character, who had slaughtered her family, told her tale to a cellmate and expired before receiving the sacraments: the author apparently felt that her deeds were so dreadful that the audience might not accept the notion of God forgiving her (*Minicarcel de Mujeres*, no. 275, 1968?).

33 *Pepín*, no. 4062, 3 May 1950, p. 1.

34 Adding such a label to a magazine cover did not make a periodical's licensing process any smoother, either. Commissioner Pueblita wrote of *Chamaco*, "Even though its cover says that it is for adults, children can read it too" (CCPRI, *Actas marzo 1953–diciembre 1954*, acta, 26 June 1953). In declaring *Santo* illicit, Commissioner Lavalle described "the expression SUITABLE FOR ADULTS" as a confession that "even the editors of this publication consider it totally inadequate for minors" (CCPRI, *Minutario 1957*, acta 14, 18 October 1957).

35 *Pepín*, no. 516, 21 August 1940. The photos were printed at intervals through-out 1941.

36 *Tesoros*, no. 5, 28 September 1951, p. 35; *Tesoros*, no. 17, 21 December 1951, p. 60; *Tesoros*, no. 18, 28 December 1951, p. 19; *Tesoros*, no. 19, 4 January 1952, p. 48; *Tesoros*, no. 30, 21 March 1952, p. 15; and *Tesoros*, no. 39, 6 June 1952, p. 34.

37 Javier Cu Delgado to Francisco Cabral Flores, 13 April 1972, in CCPRI, *Minutario enero–abril 1972*, ofc. 325; and Javier Cu Delgado to Fernando Cabral Flores, 12 April 1965, in CCPRI, *Minutario enero–abril 1972*, ofc. 329.

38 Herner, *Mitos y monitos*, pp. 160–62.

39 AGN, Fondo Presidencial, Avila Camacho papers, file 705.2/445.

40 Unsigned letter on *Don Timorato* letterhead, 6 April 1945, in CCPRI, *Minutario 1945*.

41 CCPRI, *Actas marzo 1953–diciembre 1954*, acta, 13 January 1954.

42 See, for example, the commission's refusal to examine a sketch for a new magazine, *Don*, in the minutes of CCPRI, *Minutario 1967 20.*, 9 November 1967.

43 CCPRI, "Versión taquigrafica," *Actas marzo 1953–diciembre 1954*, acta, 20 March 1953. A similar incident, involving the comic book *Marcelino*, is described in CCPRI, "Dictamin sobre *Marcelino*," *Minutario 1963 10.*, 15 April 1963.

44 CCPRI, *Actas 1973–74*, acta 153, 4 October 1974.

45 CCPRI, *Actas 1973–74*, acta 137, 9 July 1974.

46 Pan-American International Agency to Luis Wagner Z., Gerente Administrativo, Libros y Revistas S.A., 19 July 1955, quoted in CCPRI, *Actas 1955*, acta 22, 29 July 1955.

47 Ortega to Victor Fernandez MacGregor, 5 August 1955, in CCPRI, *Minutario 1955 20.*

48 CCPRI, *Actas 1955*, acta 16, 17 June 1955.

49 CCPRI, *Actas marzo 1953–diciembre 1954*, acta, 13 January 1954.

50 CCPRI, *Actas 1973–74*, acta 129, 13 May 1974.

51 Marcos Trejo Puentes to Secretaría de Hacienda, Direción General de Impuestos, 23 November 1967, in CCPRI, *Minutario 1967 20.*

52 CCPRI, *Actas 1956–1958*, acta 14, 18 October 1957. The rest of the commission stuck to more precise complaints about the use of slang and "morbid" photographs in *Prensa Roja*. When Rubio promised to suppress these, the commission let him go with a warning.

53 CCPRI, *Actas 1975–76*, acta 193-B, 22 July 1975.

54 CCPRI, "Versión taquigrafica," *Minutario 1967 20.*, acta, 8 September 1967.

55 CCPRI, *Actas marzo 1953–diciembre 1954*, acta, 27 August 1954.

56 For an appreciation of *La Familia Burrón*'s artistic merit, see Charles Tatum, "*La Familia Burrón:* Inside a Lower-Middle Class Family," *Studies in Latin American Popular Culture* 4 (1985).

57 Javier Piña y Palacios to Ricardo Garcia Villalobos, 15 June 1955, in CCPRI, *Minutario 1955 20.*

58 CCPRI, *Minutario 1956 10.*, acta 3, 20 January 1956.

59 CCPRI, *Minutario 1956 10.*, acta 4, 27 January 1956.

60 Ibid.; and CCPRI, *Minutario 1956 10.*, acta 6, 17 February 1956.

61 Javier Cu Delgado to Ruben Ramirez Garza, 17 December 1971, in CCPRI, *Minutario 1971–1972*, ofc. 1088.

62 The phrase is Jonathan Kandall's, from *La Capital* (New York: Random House, 1988), p. 516.

63 For example, Commissioner Hernandez wrote in 1962 about *Los 4 Fantastic,* "This comic book . . . could traumatize infant minds . . . [but] nothing in the Regulations . . . allows us to refuse [licitude] to this type of publication" (CCPRI, *Minutario 1966 20.*, acta, 12 September 1962).

64 When the Aguascalientes Committee for Social Improvement sent the commission thirteen pornographic magazines purchased at local newsstands, it turned out that the commissioners had never seen any of them before. Javier Cu Delgado to Jesus de Luna R., 17 December 1971, in CCPRI, *Minutario 1971–1972.*

65 CCPRI, *Minutario 1961 10.*, acta, 23 November 1961.

66 Benito Palomina to HRH Publishing, 18 January 1968, in CCPRI, *Minutario 1968 20.*, ofc. 15; and Benito Palomina to Ministerio Pública Federal de Cuernavaca, n.d., in CCPRI, *Minutario 1968 20.*, ofc. 67.

67 CCPRI, *Minutario 1970*, ofc. 1066, 1969, n.d.

68 Memorandum, CCPRI to the Dirección General de Asuntos Jurídicos, SEP, 25 November 1970, in CCPRI, *Minutario 1970.*

69 For *Esquire*, see the 3 July 1963 letter from the office of Relaciones Exteriores, Dirección General de Prensa y Publicidad to CCPRI (CCPRI, *Minutario 1963 10.*). This letter notes the complaint received by the Mexican consul in Chicago that *Esquire,* which had given up the project of a Spanish-language edition, could not even offer subscriptions to the English-language version in Mexico as postal workers would not let it through the mails. For *National Lampoon,* which faced problems much like *Esquire*'s but appears never to have attempted a Spanish-language edition, see Javier Cu Delgado to Joaquín Carrio Solano, 21 April 1976, in CCPRI, *Minutario 1976 20. enero–junio*, ofc. 504/328/504-E-483. For *Rolling Stone,* see Javier Cu Delgado to Juan Manuel López Sanabria, 29 March 1972, in CCPRI, *Minutario enero–abril 1972*, ofc. 287.

70 Outside of the records of their dealings with la Comisión Calificadora and other government agencies, I found no written record of the Lombardinis. Few of their publications remain in the Hemeroteca Nacional; I could not locate the Lombardinis themselves. The only other personal details about them came from a woman who, as a child, lived next door to Hector Lombardini's family in a middle-class Mexico City neighborhood through the 1960s. She recalls that he worked out of his home and that even some aspects of the printing process took place there. Her parents believed him to be involved in some sort of shady business (Gabriela Cano, personal communication, 23 October 1995).

71 Their name suggests that they were, like many of the publishers who ran into trouble with the commission, immigrants; this would have added to the Lombardinis' marginal status. A number of editors of marginal or soft-core photonovels, in particular, came from the region of Milan, Italy (see, for example, the testimony of Jorge Torelli B., in CCPRI, *Actas 1975–76*, acta 170, 14 January 1975). Italy had its own thriving photonovel industry, portrayed by Fellini in his film *The White Sheik*.

72 CCPRI, "Versión taquigrafica," *Actas marzo 1953–diciembre 1954*, acta, 20 March 1953.

73 CCPRI, *Actas 1952–54*, acta, 4 July 1954. Even this small step toward an actual arrest was not taken unanimously: Commissioner Pueblita, who represented the "press sector" on the commission, voted against it.

74 Piña y Palacios quotes him as saying "that he leaves the Commission in complete liberty to proceed on those terms which they may find appropriate" (CCPRI, *Actas 1952–54*, acta, 19 August 1953).

75 CCPRI, *Actas marzo 1953–diciembre 1954*, acta, 10 July 1953. That same year, his comic books *Yolanda* and *Charro Negro* were conceded provisional licitude: they were legal so long as the commission found no new problems in subsequent issues. The ostensible trouble with *Yolanda* was its illegible typography, but the commission also found it distastefully frivolous. Hector's comic book *Rojinegro* made the same list in 1954 (CCPRI, "Sujetas a revisión," *Actas 1952–54*, n.d., and CCPRI, *Actas 1955*, acta 14, 3 June 1955).

76 CCPRI, *Actas 1955*, acta 16, 17 June 1955.

77 CCPRI, *Actas 1956–58*, acta 8, 7 June 1957.

78 Hector, too, had used the plagiarism defense; he once told the commission that *Vodevil* "only printed artistic nudes taken from other magazines, like those in the last issue which were taken from the [French] magazine *Nus*" (CCPRI, *Actas 1952–54*, acta, 20 March 1953).

79 CCPRI, "Versión taquigrafica," *Actas 1956–58*, acta 13, 4 October 1957.

80 CCPRI, *Minutario 1958*, acta, 31 March 1958.

81 Javier Piña y Palacios to José Alvarez Garduño, 11 July 1955, in CCPRI, *Minutario 1955 20.*, and Javier Piña y Palacios to Jefe de Departmento del Distrito Federal, 14 July 1955, in CCPRI, *Minutario 1955 20.*

82 CCPRI, *Actas 1955*, acta 19, 15 July 1955. The censors' remarks at this meeting following Lombardini's departure make it clear that, in fact, the periodical was available already at newsstands; the issue for the Lombardinis, more likely, was not how widely the magazine was distributed but how openly it was displayed.

83 The licenses for these titles were recorded in CCPRI, *Minutario 1967 10.*, *Minutario 1968 enero–septiembre 10.* A few copies of all these publications are in the García Valseca collection of the Hemeroteca Nacional.

84 Title license in CCPRI, *Minutario 1971.*

85 Cu Delgado to S. Lombardini, 17 April 1971, in CCPRI, *Minutario marzo–mayo 1971*, ofc. 312.

86 CCPRI, *Minutario agosto–octobre 1971*, acta, 21 September 1971.

87 Javier Cu Delgado, "Dictamen re *Vida en Broma*," 22 March 1972, in CCPRI, *Minutario enero–abril 1972.* This new look at the magazine, along with ten others including Sergio's *Pico Pico*, was prompted by a letter of complaint from the head of the post office. Javier Cu Delgado to Delgado Chavez, n.d. (September 1971?), in CCPRI, *Minutario agosto–octobre 1971 20.*

88 Javier Cu Delgado to Oficina Federal de Hacienda no. 19, 10 July 1972, in CCPRI, *Actas marzo–julio 1972*, ofc. 758.

89 CCPRI, *Minutario marzo 1953–diciembre 1954*, acta, 8 January 1954. A decade later, a similar case—involving a high school principal in Atoyac de Aluvarer, Guerrero, who wanted one of her teachers and his pupils punished for printing an anti-U.S. newspaper ("they insist on saying that Mexico will recover the lands that the yankees stole")—met with equal sympathy and an equally reluctant refusal to censor political speech (Geneva Resendiz de Serafin to Serafin Nuñez Ramos, 8 February 1965, in CCPRI, *Minutario 1965A*).

90 CCPRI, *Minutario 1957*, acta 1, 18 January 1957.

91 Unless otherwise noted, the biographical information that follows was taken from Harold Hinds Jr. and Charles Tatum, "Eduardo del Río (Rius): An Interview and Introductory Essay," *Chasqui* 9, no. 1 (1984).

92 *Los Agachados*, no. 60 (n.d.), p. 32.

93 Rius (Eduardo del Rio), *Rius para principantes* (Mexico City: Grijalbo, 1995), pp. 15–17. Rius sometimes fudges the extent of his education. In his introduction to *Marx for Beginners*, he writes that he is "aware of my limits (5th grade elementary!)" and is "just a poor guy" compared to the "illustrious Marxist theoreticians" who, he says, advised him against undertaking the

project (Rius, *Marx for Beginners*, trans. R. Appignasi [New York: Pantheon, 1976], pp. 8–9).

94 Rius, *La vida de cuadritos* (Mexico City: Grijalbo, 1984), back cover.

95 AGN, Fondo presidencial, López Mateos papers, file 704/486.

96 Circulation figures cited in Harold Hinds Jr. and Charles Tatum, *Not Just for Children: The Mexican Comic Book in the Late 1960s and 1970s* (Westport, Conn.: Greenwood Press, 1992), p. 70; it seems inflated. By comparison, in 1962, three weekly comics printed circulation figures of 10,000 (for *Tawa*, an adventure comic), 65,000 (for the romance *Lágrimas, Risas y Amor*), and 90,000 (for the romance *Libro Semanal*). By the end of the decade, the most popular comic books—*Kalimán* above all—were probably selling considerably more. Still, it seems unlikely that, even at the peak of its popularity, *Los Supermachos* was selling much more than 100,000 copies per week.

97 Despite the cartoonist's protestations, it does not appear that the political stance of *Los Supermachos* changed significantly after Rius's departure. See Hinds and Tatum, *Not Just for Children*, pp. 90–106.

98 He did, however, return to *Los Agachados* from 1978 to 1980, when he folded the comic for good (Hinds and Tatum, *Not Just for Children*, p. 72).

99 Hinds and Tatum, "Interview," p. 12.

100 Hinds and Tatum, "Interview," p. 5.

101 Rius, *La vida de cuadritos*, p. 98.

102 Hinds and Tatum, "Interview," p. 14.

103 See Hinds and Tatum, *Not Just for Children*, p. 78.

104 *Los Agachados*, no. 60, 1968.

105 *Los Agachados*, no. 279, 1972.

106 Hinds and Tatum, "Interview," p. 14.

107 In 1990, a used copy of one of the *Para principantes* books for sale on the streets of Mexico City cost about fifteen times the price of a new, full-color comic book; even though Rius's books were cheaper used than new, they were still far out of reach of the vast majority of readers who could afford comic books.

108 Rius, *La vida de cuadritos*, p. 73.

109 Rius, *La vida de cuadritos*, p. 111.

110 Ibid.

111 For example, his *tropicales, barroquerias y más turbaciones* (Mexico City: Grijalbo, 1990).

112 See his 1991–93 series *Cuadernos de vida y ecologia*, financed by SEDUE and the Consejo Nacional para la Cultura y las Artes.

113 I refer here to *Esporádica, Golem, Bronca,* and *El Gallito Inglés*, all of which appeared between 1988 and 1993.

Index

Anne Rubenstein is Assistant Professor in the Department of
History at Allegheny College.

Library of Congress Cataloging-in-Publication Data
Rubenstein, Anne.
Bad language, naked ladies, and other threats to the nation :
a political history of comic books in Mexico / Anne Rubenstein.
p.   cm.
Includes index.
ISBN 0-8223-2108-4 (cloth : alk. paper). —
ISBN 0-8223-2141-6 (paper : alk. paper)
1. Comic books, strips, etc. — Mexico — History and criticism.
2. Mexico — Politics and government — 20th century.   I. Title.
PN6790.M48R83   1998
741.5'972 — dc21   98-7517   CIP